Divorcing a Narcissist:
One Mom's Battle

Written by Tina Swithin

Foreword by Kristine Danback, Ph.D.

The Fine Print

This work is a memoir that is based, in part, on actual events. However, numerous characters, locations, incidents, and companies portrayed, and the names used herein, are fictitious. Any resemblance to real people, living or dead, or to any actual event or existing company, is entirely unintentional and coincidental, as none of the persons mentioned in this book are real.

The author and contributors are offering their own personal perspective on the subject matter of narcissism and how it relates to the family court system during divorce. This book is not intended to offer legal, psychological, or therapeutic advice nor should it be used for that purpose. The author and contributors are not responsible for personal decisions based on the subject matter contained in this memoir. You are advised to seek professional assistance in your area of residence with individuals who are qualified in the subject matter contained in this memoir.

All rights reserved. No part of this book may be reproduced in any manner without written permission by the author.

Credits:

Cover Design: Bill Stansfield

Editing: Kelsey Haugen

Contact Information:

Tina Swithin

PO Box 123, San Luis Obispo, California 93406

tina@tinaswithin.com

ISBN-13: 978-0615720555

ISBN-10: 0615720552

First Published: 2012. Revised Publication: 2018

Divorcing a Narcissist: One Mom's Battle © 2018 Tina Swithin

TABLE OF CONTENTS

Foreword by Kristine Danback, Ph.D.	5
Note from Author	11
Part 1: The Beginning	15
Part 2: The Marriage	55
Part 3: Category Five Divorce Hurricane	103
Part 4: No Calm After the Storm	233
Part 5: Open Letter to Family Court Professionals	253
Part 6: To the Warriors on the Battlefield	257
Love and Gratitude	261
References	263

Abuse Only Thrives in Silence by Kristine Danback, Ph.D.

Tina Swithin's battle is one story, yet it mirrors all our stories. It depicts a woman's strength and empowerment as it does hundreds of women who battle an individual with narcissistic personality disorder (NPD). From the onset of Tina's struggles to arriving at a place of thriving, she brings awareness to women who are embarking on their escape. Tina is a victim and a survivor of narcissistic abuse.

Domestic abuse is a global issue. It is a problem affecting men and women both as aggressors and victims. This book discusses the harm of NPD from a woman's perspective because domestic abuse is the most common form of violence against women. Statistically, men tend to suffer from NPD more frequently than women; 50-75% of those with NPD are male (American Psychiatric Association, 2013). As you will see, Tina makes it evident that survivors of narcissistic abuse are among the most empathic, intelligent, and intuitive individuals. These traits make her, myself, as well as other women … targets.

It is incredible empathy, kindness, and the ability to nurture, which initially cause victims to avoid consciously knowing we have a partner who is incredibly dangerous and toxic. Often minimizing and concealing his repeated psychological and emotional harassment, and deprivation of financial, physical and personal resources, because we think he is merely angry, and our compassion and devotion will ameliorate his maladaptive personality traits. Economic dependence, the shame of divorce due to religion or culture, the fear of not being believed, and not having family support or any positive solutions to the abuse, all make leaving feel terrifyingly unsafe and unpredictable. Tina sees Seth's blame, belittling, and selfishness and inescapably realizes…abuse only thrives in silence. As a result, Tina created the One Mom's Battle (OMB) organization, as well as multiple books depicting her experience bringing awareness to others in similar circumstances. Tina's disclosure promotes women to have more insight, leading them to constructive solutions and greater well-being. Her story clarifies reality. Her efforts afford women freedom, awareness, and a means to empathize with themselves.

Tina steps toward freedom by exercising strength and independence through fighting an arduous, insurmountable court battle. Due to the significant disability in personality functioning manifesting through impairments in empathy, grandiosity, deceitfulness, and hostility, the individual with NPD is intrinsically impaired with understanding their own needs, their children's needs, as well as having a general insight and interest in others and the greater good. Therefore, it is customary for high conflict court battles to endure for years; judges laboriously examine intimate details of families attempting to reach reasonable decisions. The ruling directly affects the future care and psychological well-being of children. Court orders may leave victims feeling controlled and more abused, or sometimes…they actually "get it right." Either way, Tina's survival is an accomplishment.

As a clinical psychologist and survivor of narcissistic abuse, I specialize in developing resilience and adjusting to life's difficulties. I dedicate a part of my psychotherapy practice to treating narcissistically abused men and women and coaching them through their high-conflict divorces. I also participate in One Mom's Battle and write and speak on this topic. Specifically, the women I treat are accused of dramatizing and second-guessing reality due to the narcissist's gaslighting, and feel terrified because this journey of abuse is unique and very hard to explain without it looking as if the victim is disordered. I work with women at all stages of their awareness—some beginning to question their maltreatment, and others involved with financially crippling legal wars. Others have firm boundaries against the individual with NPD, yet they continue to try to insulate themselves from his enticing participation in toxic games of manipulation and deception despite his remarriage, new children, or career responsibility. During the continued harassment, One Mom's Battle is a refuge to thousands of women, as it was during my battle.

In my work, I also support women assailed persistently by the individual with NPD, or his family or girlfriend. My patients regularly ask why the abuser's family or new love interest continue to encourage him. The answer is, these collaterals are colluding. Collusion is lying to protect a false feeling of emotional safety and connection due to their inability to have a healthy reliant relationship with one another. Upon having the requisite knowledge, the family of the individual with narcissism decides to ignore their depraved secrets. Colluding is supporting an unethical, unhealthy, destructive person for all their players to feel emotionally safe, and to avoid a personal defeat. Some examples of loss are reputation, friendship, prestige, money, a home, or avoidance of jail. As it specifically pertains to a new girlfriend, she may collude to ensure his company, marriage, handy work around the house, or having a child. The process consists of deceiving others, reinforcing the delusion by conditioning others to believe his perspective of reality, and punishment if they resist. If the family or girlfriend keep up his warped standards, then they become a part of his corrupt world and are rewarded…and the cycle continues. His family and those he has infiltrated either have no notion of the continued harassment and ways the individual with NPD continues to disrupt a victim trying to survive, or they contribute to the attempted demise adding years to a court battle. The more she thrives, the more potent his energy to sabotage; a fact that judges need to understand.

Tina's in-law's unethical collusion entails denying her brother in-law's alleged volatile and violent behavior. Tina reports witnessing her brother-in-law harming animals during a family event and overhearing his threats to rape and murder past girlfriends. Upon asking the court to keep Tina's brother-in-law away from her children, the family ganged up on Tina to feel a false sense of connection and camaraderie at her children's expense. Seth and his family declared to the court that the brother-in-law did not present any risk. Their collusion was designed with threads of damaging information about Seth's brother. They withheld testimony for fear of risking their reputation in the community or compromising their positions as mandated reporters.

The individual with NPD has a pathology fastidiously covered up by an inauthentic competent persona that he is an expert at demonstrating. Seth's generosity, and ability to be a gentleman as their courtship began, depicts this notion. Initially, the narcissist's goal is to gain attention, money, acceptance, and status from another; swayed by whomever they believe can fill up their emptiness. Tina discusses there is no ethnic, racial, educational, or socioeconomic status which protects against their seduction of captivation and manipulation of the victim's empathy. Charm, misrepresentation, embellishment, and fabrication are vehicles used in their submissions to the courts, friends, family and the victim. During a divorce, the individual with NPD persists with deceitful hyper-focus toward the ex-spouse—expending energy continuing the insidious abuse lasting years. This behavior is not easily seen or believed by others, including court officials, friends, and their next victim; the narcissist has an impeccable ability to blame others and has no capacity for self-reflection. They control others to camouflage their private feelings of powerlessness, weakness, and worthlessness, which are never entirely disavowed, hence their continued abuse and fantastic talent for acting. Tina stands on her convictions, not defiantly, contumaciously, or out of retaliation, but because the situation calls for it to protect her children. Women in court battles must face the individual with NPD by voicing that his indignity is wrong. Tina has the right to criticize Seth because she is not unacceptable, undesirable, unsuitable, or deficient in any way that he has tried to make her and others believe. The individual with NPD is the bully because, unconsciously, he feels weak and vacuous. He is disordered.

Judges, attorneys, evaluators, and women fighting a battle will become more acquainted and familiar with NPD and its destructive effects on families because of the founder Tina Swithin's book, *Divorcing a Narcissist: One Mom's Battle*. She writes this book with courageous humility facing a problematic situation with awareness as her goal. Tina wrote the first edition of this book while in the dimness and obscurity of battle, trying to record her crisis for others. In this version, you bear witness to her formidable character as she faces stalking, inundation of menacing text messages, interaction with Child Welfare Services, and most notably, her belly bulge being simply … "unacceptable." This book revises her story, coming from a place of transparency. Currently, Tina has the freedom and courage to heal and thrive because she looks at the past with awareness and compassion by processing what she experienced. She has no choice but to move ahead and push on to something better … sharp intuition, understanding, and insight. She is sagacious enough to avoid maltreatment in the future and to help others identify it in their lives.

There comes a time when the trauma is past, and it is time to go to the next step of healing and thriving. The perspective a survivor maintains is most important … from the love bombing courtship through the battle to the court's ruling … from cheating and lying to filing for divorce … from arriving early to drop off the children and telling them Mommy is not home because she would rather be with her new boyfriend (when in fact she is actually grocery shopping), to your children having a way to protect themselves from the lack of empathy their father demonstrates. Some women give up, due to an emotional collapse or lack of finances. Others comply with court orders that feel wrong, resenting the court and others who have not supported them, and they rebel in a harmful way. These women do not thrive.

Some withstand the tragic situation and process the experience through hours of contemplation and psychotherapy—handling the horrific experience of encountering the disease of NPD. However, it can be enriching and strengthening as women use it as a road to self-knowledge to acquire health and integration. Being free is the power to shape and create ourselves, thus achieving freedom incrementally with awareness and forgiving ourselves as the starting line. When we are aware, we can choose to live, and our responsibility for ourselves takes on new meaning. Our insight is allowing aliveness and decisiveness, as it once felt saddled with a despairing burden forced upon us. We accept responsibility for this battle and sublimate our experience for the greater good of our family.

Having new experiences grounded in new relationships is what leads us to change. Development includes the help of a psychotherapist, friends, and a new love interest. Archaic patterns inevitably repeat to a degree. However, a therapist, a support group such as One Mom's Battle, and reading everything about this mental disorder can help you move beyond the pain and find new ways to relate and have resilience. People are often afraid to continue beyond the prestige of survivorship; however, once the threat is past, there is a potential trap in calling ourselves by names taken on during the most terrible time of our lives. Tina thrives because she is aware and advocates for herself, her children, and others through court actions, her online presence, and this book. Tina understands thriving means the bad times are behind us, and, despite the verdict, we won.

Kristine Danback, Ph.D., is a licensed clinical psychologist in New York and Connecticut who has devoted over 25 years of clinical experience working with individuals with abandonment trauma, relationship struggles, and anxiety/depression. She is an interpersonal-relational psychotherapist with psychoanalytic training and values a collaborative approach to treatment. Strengthening resilience is her specialty by helping others discover their awareness. She conducts face-to-face psychotherapy sessions and tele-therapy sessions, helping people with various presenting problems, with a specialty in narcissistic abuse. She also provides divorce coaching and has been an OMB advocate since its inception. Dr. Danback's articles include Courtroom Insights: Narcissistic Personality Disorder Affects Parenting and Child Development; Assessing Progress in Analysis Interminable; and The Therapeutic Interaction and How It Effects Mentalization. As of November 2018, she offers divorce mediation services as part of her practice. She is a mother, a psychologist, and a warrior of a ten-year court battle. Contact her at www.kristinedanbackphd.com.

Note from Author

I grew up yearning for the "happily ever after" that I had read about in storybooks and fairytales. As a young girl, I grew up being told that if a boy is mean to you, it means that he likes you. I dated the bad boys who were mean to me through my teens and early 20's and I learned my lesson with each heartbreak. After a handful of bad-boy types, I took a year off from the dating roller coaster to dive in and work on myself with a very skilled and respected therapist.

At the age of 26, I was swept off my feet by my modern-day Prince Charming. He was sweet, attentive, kind, and seemed too good to be true. He was night-and-day different from anyone I had dated in the past. We married within 18 months of meeting, and I soon discovered that something was amiss with my fairytale. Behind the public facade of being the "golden couple," our marriage was fraught with lies, deception, gaslighting, tears, and heartbreak. Our marriage lacked intimacy, love, respect, and companionship. I was left in a constant state of confusion and felt more alone than I had ever felt in my life. This wasn't the man that I married ... or was it?

Seven years into my marriage, I heard the term, "Narcissistic Personality Disorder" from a therapist. At the time, I didn't want to believe that my husband's issues were beyond repair nor did I want to accept the harsh reality that the therapist had presented to me. It was more than two years after my marriage ended that I began to throw myself into research about Narcissistic Personality Disorder and other Cluster B personality disorders. It was there that I began to make the connection between my logic-defying, high-conflict divorce and personality disorders. On one particularly difficult night when I was feeling beaten down, the light bulbs began going off when I stumbled upon an online article written by Dr. Karyl McBride, Ph.D., titled, "Help! I'm Divorcing a Narcissist." As I clung to Dr. McBride's words, I found myself in complete shock but managed to absorb every single word that she wrote. The reality of my 10-year relationship with Seth was becoming crystal clear. It was as if God had heard my cries of desperation and delivered the answers that I needed. I felt as though the article had been written about my own divorce and custody battle.

I became a sponge for knowledge and education while digging deeper and reading everything that I could find on the topic. As I was eagerly but painfully absorbing information, I was learning that the only thing more difficult than being married to a narcissist is divorcing a narcissist. It isn't for the weak. This battle isolates its warriors because few can understand the gut wrenching, soul baring battle cries. This battle leaves people so beaten down and drained that they question whether they can make it another day.

Every issue, no matter how seemingly insignificant, is a battle when you are divorcing a narcissist or forced into a co-parenting situation with a narcissist. It is a battle to hold your ground with a narcissist, and it's a battle if you give in to their relentless demands. More daunting is being faced with a family court system that sorely lacks education on personality disorders. Essentially, the healthy parent's hands are tied by a very broken, archaic, and uneducated court system that claims to act in the best interest of the child but fails miserably at every turn. It is a battle to maintain composure when you know and understand the dark reality of the person that you are facing yet the court sees a doting parent because the mask has yet to fall off.

My face is just one of many faces in this battle. If you are relating to my plight to protect my children, our stories are likely entwined and intermingled. The stories that I've heard over the years are so similar to mine, I have often questioned if many of us were married to the same person. Once I realized that I was not alone and I became empowered through education, things began to shift and I slowly began to find my inner strength. I firmly believe that beyond the madness of this battle lies a purpose. Every day, I am connecting people who share similar experiences and together we are educating ourselves on the harsh realities of divorcing a narcissist. Together, we are learning coping mechanisms and equipping ourselves with knowledge and solidarity.

Since my battle first began in 2009, my ultimate goal and my driving force was to protect my daughters from a Cluster B personality disordered individual. My daughters have fueled my mission and my advocacy in the family court system over the years and, now, my daughters and I have complete peace. I have been a voice for my own children, and I hope to do the same for yours. Like others, I find it disheartening that the fate of a child can be determined in less time than it takes to adopt a puppy from an animal shelter. The family court system is ill equipped to handle high-conflict divorces with the time and precision that is demanded. The family court system puts a greater emphasis on parental rights than they do on children's rights. A healthy parent fights for custody of their children for the right reasons but a personality-disordered individual will fight for custody just to hurt and control the healthy parent.

There were so many times that I shook my fist at the sky and questioned why all of this was happening. Now, I can look back and understand every single victory and every single heartbreak. I know in my heart that it all happened the way it was supposed to. My life calling is to educate the public, the media, and family court professionals through my story and my work. I accomplished my initial goal of protecting my children and, now, my energy and life is dedicated to bringing change and awareness to a system that is need of an educational overhaul when it comes to high-conflict divorces and custody battles.

For those in a similar situation, no matter how dark it may seem right now, there is a light at the end of the tunnel. There were many times that I had to dig deep to find the strength to stay afloat. Divorcing a narcissist and fighting to protect my daughters in the very broken family court system is the single most difficult thing that I've ever done. If you take nothing else from this story, I hope you realize, as I have, that being a victim doesn't have to be your way of life. You can choose to be a survivor. You can choose to be a thriver. You are strong. You are reading this book, which means you are still in the fight. You have what it takes to survive this battle, learn from it, heal from it, and move forward with your life—the life that only you can define. I originally wrote *Divorcing a Narcissist: One Mom's Battle* in 2012 while my plight was still ongoing. I was silenced from speaking the full truth by the potential repercussions on my custody case, but my case is now in my rearview mirror, so I plan to share my full story. I plan to "tell the truth, the whole truth, and nothing but the truth." My goal is to encourage and inspire you regardless of where you are on your journey. I am an optimist, but I am also a realist. I want you to know that divorcing a narcissist may be the most difficult thing you've ever done but you will look back and be thankful that you did it.

My second reason for writing this book is to help educate those on the outside: the family court professionals and the mental health professionals who are also in the trenches but on a professional level. It is one thing to read about the clinical definition of NPD but quite another to have a front-row seat into the day-to-day life of a personality disordered individual. When we hear the term "narcissistic," images come forth of someone with an inflated ego; but, NPD is so much more than that. This is a disorder that will have lifelong effects on myself, my children, and thousands of others who have suffered at the hands of someone with a personality disorder. As a family court or mental health professional, you may not have personally walked this path, but I ask you to take my hand and walk beside me to learn—and so that my daughters' suffering was not in vain.

Part 1: The Beginning

I remember sitting on my therapist's couch as a 24-year old girl feeling that something was incredibly wrong with my "man picker." I knew that I did *not* want to be sitting on my therapist's couch talking about how messed up my life was at the age of 35. I wanted to fix myself so that I no longer felt the need to fix others. I knew that I had a lot of work to do when it came to facing childhood issues, which seemed to have carried into my adulthood. I had to do some major soul searching and self-reflection.

In one of the first sessions, I remember my therapist, Pam, standing in front of a dry-erase board with a marker in hand asking me to describe traits that I liked about myself. I told her that I liked my toes. My cute, bubbly toes! That was the only thing that I liked about myself. One could gain from that statement a bit of insight into my self-esteem. At the end of the session, the therapist looked straight into my eyes and into my soul. She said she would work with me if I promised not to date for one year. Without a degree of hesitation, I agreed.

Over the next year, I attended frequent counseling sessions and began working on myself. I started my own business, and I made new friends. I enrolled in classes at a local community college and had major dental surgery and orthodontia to correct problems with my teeth that had haunted me for years.

I discovered that I liked walking on the beach alone, and going to lunch without a companion was not the end of the world. I found joy in the quiet moments and, for the first time in my adult life, went to sleep in my own bed without a man. My 25th birthday soon rolled around, and I decided to take a vacation. Alone. I boarded a ferry and sailed to Santa Catalina Island for a week of solitude. I convinced myself that it was just like going to lunch alone. I knew I was kidding myself, but also, I knew that I could do this! I was excited and this trip was a celebration of how far I had come.

As I boarded the ferry, I quickly realized everyone on the boat looked like they were embarking on a honeymoon. Every couple was hugging, kissing, and acting giddy. I had a slight twinge of regret and questioned my purpose in taking this trip. For a split second, I wanted to jump from the boat and swim to shore. I was convinced that everyone was staring at me because when you are 25 years old, you believe the world revolves around you.

Before I knew it, we had arrived on the island, and I was whisked away to my hotel by shuttle bus. I was going to my hotel and I was going alone. I ate breakfast in bed every morning and stayed up late watching Lifetime movies. I embarked on daily adventures in my little golf cart, went to dinner alone every night and drank tropical drinks while mingling with the locals. I began to enjoy the reaction that I got from people when I told them I was traveling solo.

I was 25 years old, and I had my entire life ahead of me. I wrote in my journal a lot that week, and I pondered many of the things that my counselor had said to me over the past few months. I had several light-bulb moments, and I went back home feeling empowered and ready to take on the world.

Getting Back into Dating

The following spring, I was wrapping up one year of working with my therapist. I had not been on a date in 12 months and felt better than I ever had in my life. I'm almost positive the Chinese calendar that year said, "The Year of the Tina."

Not long after, Pam gave me the green light to start dating. I went out on a few dates, and I watched for red flags, orange flags, and even the light-yellow flags. This was a whole new world to me. I felt confident and happy. I knew that I didn't need a man in my life. I was searching for a friend who would complement my life, not someone who would consume me.

I looked forward to counseling sessions to share with my therapist the funny stories and moments in which I listened to my inner voice. I had dated a gorgeous body builder prison guard who told me on the third date that he wanted me to wear less makeup. I showed him to the door. I dated a cute surfer whose phone rang at all hours of the day and night. If it was truly his sister calling on all those occasions, as he explained to me, they had a very bizarre and questionable relationship. I sent him packing, as well. At this point, Pam and I had moved our sessions to monthly appointments versus bimonthly, as we both felt I was on the right track. I was enjoying my newfound independence and was becoming highly skilled at directing people to the nearest exit sign.

I went out on a few dates with a man named Chris who had just ended a three-year relationship. Our dates began to turn into therapy sessions where he would confess his devastation over his recent break up. It was not romantic to receive a late-night phone call from someone crying about his ex-girlfriend. Secondly, I saw the warning signs and did not want to be someone's rebound relationship. Instead of trying to fix him, I let him know that we could be great friends but that was the extent of our relationship. We continued to enjoy each other's company, but our relationship never entered a physical realm. I was proud of myself, as was my therapist.

Chris and I ended up going to the lake together one Sunday afternoon at the end of May. On the one-hour drive to the lake, we discussed his ex-girlfriend, and I jokingly talked about my hopes of meeting a new guy at the lake that day. We ended up at the lake's infamous party zone, which involved equal doses of alcohol, sun, music, and dancing. It was there that I met Seth.

Seth: Greek form of Egyptian Set, possibly meaning "one who dazzles." In mythology, this is the name of the ancient evil god of chaos, storms, and the desert.

The portion of the lake where we set up camp for the day was known to get a little bit wild and isn't necessarily the place to meet one's future husband. Thankfully, finding a husband wasn't even on my radar. The boat that had anchored next to us was occupied by two brothers, Seth and Robert, who were accompanied by several of their friends.

After some conversation, loud music and lots of laughter, the two brothers ended up on our boat. I spent a considerable amount of time that afternoon dancing with Seth, who repeatedly apologized to my friend Chris for "taking over" his date. Seth was quickly assured that we were just friends and that he had nothing to worry about. If I had only known, in that moment, what the next chapters of my life entailed, I would have surely fled for the hills.

I found Seth to be quite charming, yet I had no physical attraction to him. He was a horrible dancer and, while he had an air of confidence about him, there was something a bit off and he seemed socially awkward. Seth had reddish-blond hair and a receding hairline paired with a pale but slightly ruddy complexion. He was athletic and clearly worked out but was not my type at all. My type was the storybook tall, dark, and masculine. I made a conscious decision not to dismiss Seth based on looks alone.

I was the fun, outgoing one in the group, and I could tell that Seth was drawn to those qualities. I was young, single, and carefree. I was a bit on the wild side, yet I held the small-town naivety that seemed to capture Seth's attention. At the end of the afternoon, Seth asked for my phone number and email address. He also invited me to spend Memorial Day weekend with him and his brother at the lake. Seth told me that it would be his personal mission to ensure that my weekend was amazing from start to finish. How could anyone say no to an offer like that?

Dating Seth

Enter stage left: Prince Charming. I woke up Monday morning to an email from Seth, which instructed me to take the day off from work and enjoy a spa experience on him. He had called and placed his credit card with the nicest day spa in the county and paid for me to be pampered from head to toe. His email said that I deserved a day of relaxation. I was in complete shock.

> Red Flag Reflection: At the time, I remember questioning whether this was all too good to be true. I had never been treated this kindly and I wanted to believe that *this* was what adult dating felt like. In hindsight, if things seem too good to be true, they probably are.

I did not hear back from Seth that night or the next day. While I wondered why, I did not allow my brain to go into overdrive. On Wednesday night, Seth called me and asked me out to dinner the very next night. In that phone conversation, he casually mentioned that there was something fundamentally wrong with any man who would allow a woman to pay for dinner. I had met very few men who had paid my way on dates, so I found this to be chivalrous and intriguing.

Prior to our first date, Seth instructed me to dress up but to only worry about bringing my driver's license so that we could go for drinks afterwards. I hung up the phone after hours of conversation and felt completely giddy. Maybe there were still men in the world who believed in chivalry and maybe I had found such a man. I went to sleep that night anticipating a date with a true gentleman.

I arrived at work on the morning of our date and discovered a huge bouquet of flowers waiting for me. I could not believe it. We hadn't even been on a date yet, but Seth was pampering me at every turn. The card attached read, "I look forward to our date tonight." I opened my email that morning to another message that said, "I hope your day is as beautiful as you are." By this point, I could barely wait to head home and start getting ready for our first date. It felt surreal.

> Red Flag Reflection: I was caught up in the euphoria of this newfound dating experience. I had never been treated this way by anyone. In hindsight, this type of behavior is known as "love bombing" and is a true red flag. Love bombing is common with Cluster B personality disordered individuals. The recipient is bombarded with attention, which leaves little time for true contemplation and reflection. Quite literally, the attention is so overwhelming that you don't have time to think.

I reminded myself that I didn't know Seth and that I still needed to be smart. I could hear my therapist's voice reminding me to reel myself in and not get too carried away. I could hear her telling me to pay attention to the red flags.

I got into Seth's sports car for our first date and we sped away. Seth would not tell me where we were going but he gave me a hint that it was an hour away.

> Red Flag Reflection: I remember feeling uneasy about jumping into a car and driving an hour away from my home with a virtual stranger. Despite my intuition, which is incredibly powerful when I choose to tap into it, I pushed those feelings aside and replaced them with the excitement of the adventure. In hindsight, this was controlling behavior and a normal, healthy person would never put someone in this situation. Surprises are great once trust has been established between two adults, but this man was not a person who had earned my trust nor did I know him at all.

As we started driving, Seth pulled out a photo album of his dogs: two enormous, beautiful Malamutes. He knew that I owned a pet-sitting business and wanted to show me how much his dogs meant to him. His photo album showed every stage of his dogs' lives, and I could feel his excitement as he talked about his pets. These were not just any dogs, based on Seth's descriptions. Seth and his father had driven almost one thousand miles to personally select one of the dogs, and Seth bragged about her lineage being the best that money could buy. The other dog had been Seth's dog in college, and he talked about how much attention he received while walking the dog around the college. Seth told me that he owned another vehicle, a Jeep, solely to transport his dogs. I found it sweet to see how much he loved his animals.

> Red Flag Reflection: While it was touching that Seth loved his dogs, I now see it as odd behavior for a grown man. It also made for a socially awkward situation because there were only so many times I

could comment about how great his dogs were. Seth was trying to prove how much he loved his dogs by bombarding me with photos. With a photograph, he "captured" proof of his love. He was also mirroring what I wanted to hear which is common with Cluster B disordered individuals. I owned a pet-sitting business; therefore, he was reflecting back to me something that he suspected I wanted to hear.

We arrived at a fancy Cajun restaurant. Seth proceeded to tell me that he carefully chose this particular restaurant that was an hour away because he did not want to risk taking me somewhere that I had already been on a date. I quickly assured him that I had not been on the dating scene very long. I told him about my two long-term relationships and my one-year hiatus from the dating world. Seth was intrigued by this and went on to say that the problem with most of the women that he meets is they have been around the block; he told me that he was actively looking for a wholesome girl that liked to have fun but that didn't sleep around. I remember going into the bathroom during dinner and feeling like I wanted to pinch myself.

> Red Flag Reflection: Seth was already trying to "claim me" as his. He had been "actively hunting" and I was his prey. It wasn't about what I wanted or was looking for; it was about what Seth wanted. Seth was beginning to place me up on a pedestal by eluding that I was wholesome and everything he ever wanted. Placing the victim on a pedestal is a common tactic and, while that sounds like an amazing place to be, the reality is that the pedestal is a façade. The narcissist places his victim on a pedestal to thoroughly examine them, and then the pedestal crumbles and the victim comes crashing down.

During dinner, Seth told me about a blind woman that he befriended while in college. He went to her house each day and helped with her bills and mail, he took her trash out, and he cared for her yard. He explained that his family was Catholic and that he had been raised to be of service to those less fortunate. Seth then told me that he was friends with all his ex-girlfriends and still mailed them birthday cards each year. I was in awe of this person sitting across from me who was so selfless and was mature enough to stay on good terms with his past girlfriends.

> Red Flag Reflection: This is known as a preemptive defense in the world of narcissists and other personality disordered individuals. It is a glaring red flag when someone is trying to sell you on the fact that

they are a good or honorable person without any provocation from you. Seth was attempting to paint a picture of a trustworthy individual in what equated to a highly skilled sales pitch. Genuine, decent individuals do not have the desire to force their positive qualities and traits down your throat. Their actions will prove who they are over time and they do not feel the need to force feed you because they are confident in who they are. Actions speak louder than words but narcissists do not seem to comprehend this.

We left the restaurant and Seth wanted to show me a few of the local bars that he frequented while in college. As we walked to the first club, I realized that I made a huge error. I had forgotten my driver's license and had no form of identification. It was the one thing that Seth told me to bring, and I forgot it. I meekly informed Seth of the problem, and he made a joke about me being a true blonde and gave me a hug. He walked straight up to the doorman and let him know that his girlfriend forgot her ID. As Seth said this, I watched him slip the man a one-hundred-dollar bill.

The man slapped Seth on the back and opened the door to the club. I was mortified that I had just cost him so much money and asked that I be allowed to pay him back when we returned home. He laughed and said it was only pocket change. I had never been around someone who threw money away like Seth did. He had ordered the most expensive bottle of wine on the menu during dinner, and now he was spending this kind of money just to get us in the door to a bar.

> Red Flag Reflection: Seth was flashy. He flaunted his money and bragged about his cars, his dogs, his career, his college degree and his family. He knew that I had come from humble beginnings and that I was not accustomed to his lifestyle. In a short period of time, I had become very intimidated by Seth's lifestyle because it was all so new to me. I was enamored not because I was a gold digger but because I was honored that Seth, being so sophisticated and worldly, could even be remotely interested in someone like me who lacked the education background, social status, and financial resources that he seemed to take for granted. Seth knew all of this and was playing on it heavily.

As we stood in the club sipping our drinks, I immediately became concerned. I was naive about dating. I wondered if Seth expected me to have sex with him. As if he could read my mind, he leaned in and told me he never kissed on the first date. Seth was so charming and seemed completely sincere. I only accepted one drink after dinner that night because I wanted to retain my composure and be in control. Despite his reassurance, I still felt slightly uneasy.

After we left the club, we started the drive back home. I warned Seth that I was known to fall asleep easily on car rides. I held true to my word and dozed off fairly quickly. About 15 minutes later, I awoke to the sounds of the car tires hitting gravel as we came to a stop and Seth turned the car off. I opened my eyes, and it was pitch black outside. There were no streetlights and I had no idea where we were. I panicked. I was terrified that I had made a grave error by going on a date with Seth, and I had a sinking feeling in the pit of my stomach.

I slowly asked Seth why he stopped and demanded he tell me where he had taken me. Seth quietly responded that we were on top of the city in which he lived throughout college, and he simply wanted to show me the beautiful view. He said he loved mountains and watching the world from high above. I believe he could sense my nerves as I reminded him that I had to work early the next day and needed to get home. Seth apologized under his breath, turned on the car and started driving again.

> <u>Red Flag Reflection</u>: A considerate, adult male would have mentioned this planned stop in advance and would have considered the feelings of his date. By taking me out of my element and making me feel vulnerable, it was Seth's way of exhibiting control. My heart was pounding in my chest and I felt a sense of relief as Seth turned the key in the ignition and began to drive toward our town.

I remained wide-awake for the rest of the drive home. I tried to make small talk with Seth, but in the back of my mind, I was questioning my reaction. Why would I doubt him? Was I so damaged by my past relationships that I would doubt every honorable man that ever crossed my path? I told myself that I should be excited, not doubting Seth. Seth had told me over dinner that he was excited to finally meet someone who had strong values and a good work ethic. Seth liked the fact that I was independent and had spent a week's vacation alone on an island. He liked the fact that I owned my own business and wasn't financially dependent on anyone. Now Seth seemed quiet, and I hoped that I had not scared him off by my reaction.

When I woke up the next morning for work, I found a note on my car window that said, "I hope that you enjoyed the night as much as I did. I look forward to spending the weekend with you at the lake." I was thrilled. Maybe I didn't blow it after all. Maybe I needed to take a deep breath and relax. I was thinking too much into things. I made an appointment to see my therapist the very next week, as I needed her insight and advice.

In the meantime, I started packing for the lake adventure with Seth and his brother, Robert. When Seth and I were speaking on the phone, I mentioned that I needed to grab a new beach towel and that I didn't even own a sleeping bag. He told me not to worry about it because we needed to stop for supplies on the way to the lake.

We first stopped at a grocery store, where Seth and his brother spent hundreds of dollars on food and alcohol before proceeding to a department store, where they bought nearly everything under the sun. They seemed to be highly entertained by making rude comments about the customers in the store. While their comments and behavior bothered me greatly, I pushed it aside.

> Red Flag Reflection: The fine art of ridiculing and belittling others is usually left on the elementary school playground. It is highly disturbing when grown men seem to take such pleasure in it. I made excuses in my mind for their behavior, but in hindsight, there is no excuse for this type of behavior. Over time, this topic became a highly contentious issue in our relationship.

Seth continued to turn up the charm and I had a blast that weekend. He catered to my every need and made sure that my margarita glass was always full. Seth assured me that I was safe to sleep in the same tent with him and that he would not take advantage of me in any way. He held true to this and was a complete gentleman.

After the first night, we ended up being invited into a home at the lake which was owned by Robert's friend and tent camping was pushed aside, much to my delight. In the morning, Seth cooked us breakfast and listened intently as I talked about my life, my world, and my thoughts. He seemed to hang on my every word. He introduced me to his college friends, and we had a great time that weekend.

> Red Flag Reflection: While having someone listening so earnestly to my background was refreshing, the narcissist hunts and gathers information for deceptive reasons. Initially, the victim feels that the narcissist cares about them and is sincere in their desire to become

their personal historian. The narcissist is gathering information that initially, he will use to win you over. Down the line, he will use these things against you when the relationship hits rocky ground or ends completely. The narcissist becomes your Band-Aid for past wrongs and then pulls the Band-Aid off and leaves you bleeding and in agony.

During the weekend, I had learned more about Seth's family and their lives. According to Seth, his father and mother, Leonard and Cleo, lived in a very affluent neighborhood and seemed to enjoy a lifestyle that I could only dream of. Seth told me how much his parents valued education and they had recently accepted jobs overseas. In a matter of six weeks, they would be going abroad for an entire year. Seth said that he would only introduce me to his parents if things became serious between us. I understood and respected his position.

Seth went on to describe brother, Robert. Seth explained that Robert was the Senior Class ASB President at the local Catholic School and was wildly popular but that he had really sold himself short by not pursuing a college degree and, instead, going into finish carpentry. He painted a picture of a popular guy who grew up fairly privileged and then, during high school, turned into a "cowboy redneck" seemingly overnight. Seth struggled to understand where this change originated from but described a fairly tumultuous and competitive relationship with his brother growing up. He told me that they were finally in a good place, which made his mom ecstatic.

The next week, I sat on my therapist's familiar couch, my safe place, and I told her everything that had recently transpired. I confided in her that I was worried about sabotaging this opportunity because I was desperately searching for flags of every color. In my head, I was trying to prove that Seth was bad without giving him a chance. I was second-guessing everything and felt unsure of how to proceed.

Meanwhile, I was hoping with every ounce of my being that Seth was who he claimed to be. I wanted to believe that there were men who were really this wonderful. I wanted so badly to have faith in chivalry and the "happily ever after" that I had grown up reading about as a child. I also confided in my therapist that I wasn't attracted to Seth, which continued to nag at me. I did not want to dismiss this potential relationship based on physical attraction alone but Seth was not my type at all. In fact, I felt turned off by him physically and found myself avoiding intimacy because of how unattracted I was.

My therapist spoke to me as if I was her daughter, and I trusted her advice. She told me that perhaps I wasn't attracted to Seth because this felt different than anything I had experienced in the past but that different wasn't necessarily bad. She worried that I was not attracted to normalcy and that I needed to relax a bit about this situation. Those words hit me to my core. She was correct. I had never experienced normalcy in a relationship, and maybe I was unconsciously sabotaging the first healthy, normal relationship that I encountered.

My therapist asked me some tough, soul-searching type of questions that day. She questioned whether I was holding Seth accountable for the wrongs in my past relationships. She said that maybe I needed to accept that good men do exist and that Seth was one of these men. That was what I wanted to hear. That was what I needed to hear.

> Red Flag Reflection: This may very well be the biggest lesson of all – I overrode my gut feelings and intuition in my therapist's office that day. My inner voice told me that some things were off and concerning. Even my body was revolting at intimacy. My therapist called Seth's behavior "sophomoric" when I expressed concern about him belittling people, but she believed I was overreacting and sabotaging. Many mental health professionals are often charmed by narcissists. The moral of the story is that your intuition is never wrong.

That first six weeks of our relationship was a whirlwind of flowers, cards, poems, and thoughtfulness. In hindsight, I was being love-bombed for the first time in my life. If I casually mentioned that I love Hollywood, Seth would whisk me away to southern California the very next weekend. If I made a comment about Las Vegas, I would find plane tickets on my pillow within a week. There were shopping sprees and if I so much as glanced at a pair of shoes, Seth would buy them right in front of me or surprise me with them later.

I couldn't believe this was my life. When I looked bewildered or uncomfortable about the purchases or trips, my concerns were met with laughter. Seth reminded me that I had never been with a real man—a gallant man with values. While it was uncomfortable in the beginning, I started to enjoy this newfound world.

In the weeks prior to meeting Seth, I had been invited to participate in a bikini fashion show. Once the show started and tequila shots were being passed around, I realized that, in fact, it was a bikini *contest* and not a fashion show as I had been told. I was originally mortified until the cheers began. For someone with miniscule amounts of self-esteem, I felt alive on that stage amidst the cheering crowd. I ended up taking second place in the bikini contest and agreed to come back the following month for another contest. I invited Seth to come; however, his new job didn't allow him to be there.

Seth expressed concern for my safety leading up to the second bikini contest and insisted on sending his brother, Robert. Robert's job was to ensure that I got to my car safely after the event. I found Seth's vigilance to be very sweet—he trusted me to do the contest, yet he wanted to make sure I got home safely. He didn't seem threatened by the fact that I was doing a bikini contest and, in fact, he shared the photos with anyone who would look at them. Robert attended the event with me and spent the evening drinking and taking photographs of the contestants. He kept his distance but assumed the role of my big brother during the event and after.

> Red Flag Reflection: At the time, I found it to be a huge compliment that Seth wanted to show my pictures off. I also found it refreshing that Seth didn't seem threatened by what I was doing. I was young, carefree, and in the best shape of my life. After feeling awkward and unattractive growing up, I was relishing this newfound confidence. Looking back and knowing how the narcissist's mind works, I was nothing more than a trophy girl who Seth used to impress clients, co-workers, and the men in his family. In reflection, the thought of this makes my skin crawl.

After about a month into dating, Seth took me to meet his mother, Cleo. I was honored that Seth wanted to introduce me to his mom so soon, especially given his speech about not introducing me to his parents until things were serious. At the time of our meeting, I could sense that Cleo was overwhelmed by her impending move overseas. I offered to help her pack and she took me up on that. I spent the following days assisting Cleo and Leonard as they packed their 4,200-square-foot home. One the third day, I left to get lunch for the family and, as I drove back to the house, I felt an overwhelming sense of gratitude. Cleo and Leonard seemed to be the family that I longed to have. They had been married for 25 years, had four sons, and, by all accounts, seemed worldly and genuinely happy. Coming from such a broken childhood, I was smitten with Seth's entire family.

> Red Flag Reflection: There was a complete switch on Seth's part, which left me in a state of confusion. Initially, Seth was adamant that I wouldn't meet his mother until he knew that I was "the one" and, now, I was being paraded through the family compound. I now see this as Seth's closing sales pitch—he had me hooked, and the family worked together to finalize the deal. This reminds me of being on a car lot where the salesman brings in the manager of the dealership who is skilled in the art of closing the potential buyer.

The next week, I accompanied Seth, his mom, and his two younger brothers, Carter and Kyle, to the airport as they departed for their adventure overseas. Being a sensitive person by nature, I hate goodbyes. As I hugged Seth's family, I began to tear up. I felt so sad that they were leaving when I was just getting to know them. Kyle looked at me and said, "You don't even know us. Why are you crying?" I felt so silly in that moment and self-doubt began to creep in.

> Red Flag Reflection: In hindsight, I realize emotions weren't common in Seth's family. Emotions made them uncomfortable. On that day, I was given a nickname that stuck for years, "The Fountain." What originally began as a term of endearment later became a nickname that was used to taunt and ridicule me over the years. Over time, the taunts escalated to the point that I was called, "bipolar" if I cried or showed any type of emotion during our marriage.

With Seth's family now gone, I was left with stories of how remarkable they were. I was hearing so much about these people that I felt as though I knew them. Stories were relayed that made me even more eager to be a part of their world. I heard about their huge, festive Thanksgiving celebrations and family vacations. Seth bragged about their influence and standing in our tight-knit community and all they had accomplished over the years. This was the stability and the life that I had craved down to my very core. Seth's family was the picture of strength, love, and togetherness and they were the exact opposite of what I was exposed to as a child and as a young adult.

Seth began calling me each evening, and I looked forward to the hours spent talking to him. He was working in southern California and driving home several hours each Friday night to see me. At that point, I explained to him that I did not want to have sex unless I was in a serious and committed relationship. While I still did not feel a physical attraction to Seth, my therapist's words rang loudly in my mind. I made a conscious decision to focus on Seth's positive attributes and overlook what I had labeled as superficial issues. About six weeks into dating and a night of drinking, I gave in and we slept together.

Once the alcohol wore off and reality set in, I began to cry. I was so disappointed in myself. I did not want to get hurt, and I was afraid of being emotionally involved with Seth because this meant that I was once again vulnerable. I had been strong for so long and independent for over a year. I didn't want to be exposed to heartbreak ever again in my life. I felt like my mind was a yo-yo when envisioning my life with Seth and then becoming fearful and pulling away. I was beginning to find comfort in my autonomy and, now, I felt like it was being ripped away from me. I was scared that this line had been crossed. Seth took my face in his hands and promised that I didn't have to worry. He said that he would never hurt me.

Seth went on to assure me that while he had dated many women, I was different. He explained that I was exactly what he had been searching for. Seth said that my joyfulness reminded him of qualities that he admired in his mother and that my innocence was a turn on to him. Most women that he had encountered were into partying or were so involved in their demanding careers that they were stuffy. Seth said that I was the free spirit that he needed in his life and that that I possessed a healthy balance of both worlds. According to Seth, I was everything that he wanted in a partner.

After hours of pillow talk, Seth said something that caused me to recoil. He explained that his parents valued education and my lack of a college degree could potentially pose a problem. He assured me that we would worry about that when the time came. I felt taken aback by his comments because I didn't know how to process Seth's words. I felt insecurity knocking loudly. My takeaway that day was that the very family I admired and looked up to may not find me to be worthy of their son.

> Red Flag Reflection: This was the beginning of a cycle that I would come to know very well. Seth would set me high up on a pedestal, and then he would pull me down. He would build me up, and then, in a subtle but passive-aggressive way, he would remind me that I did not meet his or his family's standards. As our relationship progressed, Seth became my worthiness barometer.

A couple of months into our relationship, Seth explained to me that his job was transferring him to San Diego. In the same breath, Seth told me that he loved me. Those were the three words that I longed to hear but that I was equally afraid of. Seth then said that he wanted me to go with him to San Diego. I was in shock. A million thoughts ran through my mind that night. We spent hours talking and, by the time the sun rose the next morning, I was planning my move.

> Red Flag Reflection: Seth told me that he loved me two months into our relationship; in reflection, it wasn't romantic. The words themselves may sound romantic but it *felt* like a business deal. Over time, I came to realize that his idea of love meant that he slowly owned more and more of me with each passing day. I wish someone had said, "You just met this man eight weeks ago! You can't give up your life and move away with him!" The truth is, I wouldn't have listened. I prided myself on my spontaneity, and the mere idea of this new start and commitment felt exhilarating.

Moving in with Seth

Before I could get too carried away in my moving plans, I needed to tell my family. I prepared my statement and delivered it the very next day. As crazy as it sounded, I had already made up my mind and there was no stopping me—I was moving. I'm sure that came across to everyone who knew me and loved me.

My family didn't try to stop me nor did they talk me out of my decision. In fact, they were also taken in by Seth's charm. My dad came to town on a visit shortly after I made my decision to move, and Seth was so concerned about impressing my dad that he went home to change into a dress shirt prior to their meeting. Seth's dedication to making a good impression on my dad was endearing to me and I thought it spoke volumes about who he was as a person.

Within a few minutes, I overheard Seth ask my dad to join him outside on the porch. My heart dropped as my sister and I ran to the window to eavesdrop. My dad is very protective, and I was concerned about the direction of their conversation. When you picture the overprotective father cleaning his shotgun at the kitchen table when teenage boys came over, that was my dad.

My dad and Seth ended their conversation after about thirty minutes. They seemed jovial, and I could tell that Seth had passed the test. That night on the porch, Seth won my dad over when he looked him in the eyes, shook his hand and promised to take care of me forever—financially and in every other way. I could tell that I had my father's blessing and I was further at peace with my decision to move.

> <u>Red Flag Reflection</u>: Seth promised my father that he would be my honorable and dependable life partner. While I wasn't seeking someone to take care of me monetarily, it was much more than the promise of financial security that Seth delivered that day. Seth knew that I craved stability in my life, so he molded himself into the pillar of stability. Once again, he became my Band-Aid. Seth made the closing sales pitch and set the wheels in motion to move me away from the stability I had worked hard to obtain. It was years later that I discovered that isolation is one of the first stages of domestic violence. The goal was to take me away from my trusted network and isolate me to the point where I became dependent on Seth.

I felt a huge sense of relief. Over the years, I had felt like I repeatedly disappointed those closest to me with my bad relationship choices. I had finally stumbled upon what I viewed as a healthy, quality person to spend my life with. With each passing day, I felt increasingly excited about the impending move. I gave notice at my job, hired employees to help me run my business, and notified my landlord that I was moving. Everyone appeared genuinely happy for me, which only heightened the eager anticipation that I felt while envisioning this next chapter of my life.

One Sunday afternoon while at brunch, Seth casually mentioned that I should sell my furniture before we moved. I didn't know how to respond to this request. I had worked so hard to purchase everything in my little apartment. I loved my couch, my shabby chic kitchen table, and my new bedroom set. The silence in the room was deafening as I struggled to find words to answer Seth. Seth went onto explain that he wanted us to buy all new things to start our life together. He suggested that I sell my belongings and put the money into a savings account.

Seth promised that he would take care of the financial end of things and pay for all new furniture and household items. My only job was to get rid of everything that I owned down to the silverware in my kitchen drawer. He became animated and excited while talking about how fun this was going to be and that we would save money on moving everything. I was trying to be happy about the thought of a fun shopping spree to kick off our next adventure, but I felt equally panged while thinking of how hard I had worked to build a life of my own. Was I being ungrateful? I was desperately trying to channel my spontaneity, but I couldn't shake the fear of being left with nothing of my own.

> <u>Red Flag Reflection</u>: I equate this to boot camp in many ways. Seth wanted to rid me of any portion of my past life and mold me into what he wanted. It was his way of controlling me and making me dependent on him. It was also his way of spinning the fact that my possessions did not measure up to his standards and that he needed to dispose of these things before his friends or colleagues knew he was mingling with someone of a lesser rank.

Seth took both of my hands in his and, within the hour, he had me feeling like a small child anticipating Christmas. I had never purchased new furniture. I had always looked for bargains, and the thought of furnishing an entire house from top to bottom was beyond my financial comprehension. It scared me but was exhilarating at the same time. I often felt like pinching myself—could this all be happening to me?

By this point, I was becoming emotionally invested in the relationship. Seth worked several hours away and drove to my home every weekend without fail. Every week, he would make the long trek on Friday night and stay until the last possible minute, which, many times, would be 4:00 a.m. on Monday morning, allowing him to be at his desk by 8:00 a.m. Seeing this type of commitment from him gave me confidence in our relationship and reassured me that he was dedicated to me.

In my mind, our relationship seemed perfect from every angle. My therapist agreed with me wholeheartedly and applauded my personal accomplishments of growth over the past year and a half. We agreed that my life was moving in the right direction and, due to my impending move, we ended our sessions together.

I spent the next few weeks selling my furniture and looking for a rental property for us in San Diego. We made a few trips down there to view properties and found the experience to be much more stressful than expected. The rental market was very competitive and houses were being rented before we could even complete our application.

On one trip to look at rentals, Seth became very agitated and implied that I wasn't doing enough to secure a home. He raised his voice and explained that his job was stressful and he couldn't be bothered by these things. He was doing everything to hold his end of the financial deal, and all he needed me to do was find the house. I was taken aback and felt as though I was failing him.

I began struggling with the inner voices that made me question myself. Was I really not living up to my portion of the workload? I was exhausting myself in this housing search and continued to hit roadblocks due to Seth's two, very large Malamutes, combined with the general state of the rental market. I didn't know how to process Seth's new behavior. It concerned me and he could tell. Seth immediately apologized and said that he wasn't used to seeing this side of me. I was confused. This side of me?

> Red Flag Reflection: I was beginning to doubt myself more and more. Seth could take any concern that I had about him and repackage it, which left me questioning everything that I knew to be true about myself. If I was concerned about Seth's attitude or temper, it became my fault for not working hard enough or for not being everything that he needed me to be. I had always felt like I had a gift of reading people, but when it came to Seth, I struggled. I once told him that I was not the mind reader that he was expecting me to be.

Seth said that he had fallen in love with the happy, fun spirit that I embodied, and now he was seeing signs of stress and tension. Seth said that the one thing that he admired so much about his mother was the fact that she was always happy no matter what was happening in life. He had so many responsibilities at work and with the move—he just needed me to be the same positive person that he had met.

> Red Flag Reflection: Seth wanted me to be just like his mother, Cleo. It is abnormal for a person to be happy all the time. Over the years, I learned that Cleo lives in denial by choice and has for as long as I've known her. She sees the severe dysfunction in her family, yet she enables her family members and goes to great lengths to cover their problems up while maintaining a smile on her face. Sadly, it took me several years to see the writing on the wall. For the first few years, I wanted to be just like Cleo. Once I saw behind the curtain, I wanted to be the exact opposite of who Cleo was.

I spent a lot of time thinking about that conversation in the car and Seth's elevated tone. I thought about the angry look in his eyes as he spoke to me. I replayed it all in my mind and defended his actions. He was under a great deal of pressure at his new job, after all. I made a conscious decision not to share this incident with my family because I knew this wasn't who Seth really was. I believed that once we were settled and things were less stressful, Seth would return to normal.

I began hearing stories for weeks about Seth's colleagues from his new job, and it sounded like they were being very difficult. He was forced to take orders from someone in the office with "half a brain who didn't even have a college degree." He often expressed that he couldn't wait to move and be done with these people. I remembered how sincere he had been while apologizing to me. Things had been perfect for all of these months; I wasn't going to let one incident during a moment of stress concern me.

> <u>Red Flag Reflection</u>: Seth constantly made jabs about people not having college degrees. He was always quick to say, "I'm not talking about you; I hope you don't take it personally." By doing that, he was passive aggressively shoving a dagger into my heart but then pulling it out just enough to ease the pain. In a warped and twisted way, he would make me feel special at the same time he was putting me down. Essentially, Seth was saying that people who didn't obtain college degrees were pathetic but that I was special enough in other areas for him to give me a chance. Lucky me. In my mind, Seth believed in me, and I didn't want to fail him.

I did take what Seth said to heart and stepped up my efforts to find us a place. I tried to take care of the property search without involving him in the process. I became clever by calling each property management company daily to check in on new listings and one such call paid off. It turned out they had just received notice from a tenant, hours before, and the house had not yet been advertised. They knew how persistent that I had been and offered to email me photos.

Seth and I toured the house the very next weekend and signed the lease for a year. He was thrilled with my accomplishment and praised me repeatedly that weekend. I had proven to him that I could handle a task with a smile on my face. I was ecstatic that I had secured our new home, which, in turn, relieved some of the stress from Seth. I brushed my concerns aside and justified Seth's behavior in my head—we all have stressful moments in which we act out or say something that we shouldn't.

During the week, Seth's job kept him four hours away, so he often arranged for me to hang out with Robert in his absence. Many nights after work, Robert and I would grab dinner together before I headed home, sometimes with mutual friends and, every once in a while, on our own. On one particular evening, we went to a local bar and grill, leaving my car at Robert's house and driving together in his truck. On the way home, Robert mentioned that he was going to take the back way to his house, which took us into a very rural area.

His truck left the road at one point, coming to a stop in a dirt driveway. "This is where Tex Allen Brebbs lived and murdered those two college girls," Robert said very matter-of-factly. I didn't even know how to respond. The Tex Allen Brebbs case had riveted our community two years prior. He had stalked, horrifically tortured, brutally raped, and murdered two blonde college students in our area. Until he was caught, I lived in fear of this serial murderer, as did many in my small community. I was so fearful of this monster on the loose that my dad had purchased me a shotgun for protection as I lived alone during his murder spree.

Robert went on to say that he knew Tex through the local lumber yard, and Tex had made Robert's ex-girlfriend incredibly uncomfortable several times at her job as a bartender. In fact, she had asked Robert on several occasions to come to the bar when she was working because Tex was there. At the time, Robert's ex-girlfriend had no idea that Tex was the man murdering women in our town. Robert said he wasn't shocked when Tex was arrested and charged with the crimes. As I listened to his story, my heart hurt for the college girls. I felt so uncomfortable being in such close proximity to the site of the murders that I felt a huge sigh of relief when Robert started his truck back up and continued back to my car.

> Red Flag Reflection: While the sales pitch about Robert being my fierce protector in Seth's absence sounded sweet, it was incredibly bizarre in several arenas. For one, I had my own friends and didn't really need protected. In my naïve mind, I saw this as hope for the future because, to me, it signified acceptance into the family. It was concerning that Robert was willing to take on this role. Taking me to the home of a serial murderer without even talking to me about it in advance is extremely troublesome behavior. What I originally saw as genuine concern about the crimes, I later discovered was a morbid fascination. By this point, Robert and Seth had each taken me out of my comfort zone in the black of night—Seth on our first date and now Robert, to the site of a well-known murder.

Preparing for the Move

One week before our official move, we drove to southern California to purchase a truck for Robert. Seth had agreed to co-sign for his brother's new truck because Robert had very poor credit. As it turns out, we didn't just go to any car dealership; we went to one that was so large, it encompassed over six blocks of vehicles.

In total, we spent six hours at the dealership, while Seth negotiated on the price of a truck, even insisted on seeing the invoices for each. We left to get a hotel with the idea that we would go back in the morning, so he could talk them down even further.

That night, we ended up club hopping in Hollywood, and Seth seemed to be on a high from the car dealership experience. He was taking extreme pleasure in giving the sales crew a run for their money. The alcohol was flowing, and Seth's behavior began to shift from fun and lively to withdrawn, oddly feminine, and socially awkward.

I was becoming increasingly concerned with the amount of alcohol Seth was drinking. We were in a big city, and I didn't feel safe with him being so intoxicated. He continued to drink and ended up vomiting on the floor in the middle of a club. I was thankful Robert was there to help us back to the hotel.

> Red Flag Reflection: This wasn't the first time that I became concerned about Seth's drinking and behavior. If there was one bright, glaring red flag in our dating life, it was the one that involved alcohol. Again, I justified his behavior, reminding myself that we were in our twenties; he held a lucrative but stressful job and deserved to cut loose on his days off. "Work hard, play hard" was a common saying for Seth.

Upon waking and eating breakfast, we discussed what had happened the night before and my concerns were quickly turned around by the humor that was generated between the two brothers. We were in Hollywood, being young and carefree. I felt silly for wasting my time and energy worrying about such things. I reminded myself that just because I grew up around alcohol abuse didn't mean that everyone was an alcoholic. Around that time, we received a text message from the car salesman and headed back to the dealership.

Spending six hours at the dealership the day prior was nothing short of excruciating for me. I watched the clock tick by on the second day and, before I knew it, we were up to two more hours. It was more than I could handle, so I left for a shopping mall. Hours went by and, after a total of seven hours, they had completed their transaction, and I was on my way back to the lot.

I arrived to hugs, excitement, and a set of keys that were placed in my hand. Seth bought me a car. I was in shock and utter disbelief. I had never owned a new car in my life. A man that I had known for less than six months just handed me keys to my very own car. Seth bought two cars that day—one for Robert and one for me. He explained that he didn't feel comfortable with me moving to a big city and driving a used car.

I drove off the lot in my brand-new car and promptly called everyone that I knew. They shared my feelings of shock but were genuinely happy for me. The concern about the previous night was quickly dismissed as the excitement about my new car took over. I couldn't believe that men like this existed.

> Red Flag Reflection: Things like this may happen in the world of millionaires but normal, healthy men do not buy brand-new cars for women that they've only known for five months. The reality was, after recently landing his first job out of college, Seth was in no place to be purchasing a brand-new car for himself, let alone for me. The reality, which I didn't know at the time, was that my used car didn't meet Seth's standards and would tarnish his image.

I made the trip back home while talking on my new cell phone the entire way. In addition to the new car, Seth had also gifted me with my very first cell phone. He hated that he could only talk to me in the evenings, which I thought was sweet. My new fairytale was magical, and I didn't want to stop believing. Seth was such a caring, loving person and true to what he said; he only wanted the very best for me.

Everything in our lives was rushed and grandiose. Seth's favorite saying was, "Go big or go home." In the beginning, this seemed to fit nicely with my spontaneous spark. We were trying to cram in fun adventures while balancing the stresses of life, work, and the move. Seth bought tickets to a huge VIP adult costume party in San Diego on the very night that we were scheduled to move into our new house. He joked about starting our San Diego adventure with a big bang and that is exactly what it was.

We arrived at the new house with a small U-Haul truck after a four-hour drive. It was dark and we only had thirty minutes to spare before the party started. I went into the house to get into my costume and do my hair and makeup while Seth was parking the truck. I was in the restroom for fifteen minutes when I heard the front door slam and Seth yelling loudly at me.

I looked into Seth's eyes and immediately knew that he was irate. I was frightened. How could I not have known that he needed my help backing the truck in, he demanded? Seth was livid and physically shaking. He said that I had no appreciation for everything that he was doing for me. He stammered that the very least I could have done was to help him get the truck in, but I was selfishly worried about my hair and makeup. I was crushed by his words. I had never been called selfish and it went against everything I knew about myself. I would have dropped everything had I known that he needed my assistance.

> Red Flag Reflection: Instead of tuning into the fact that real men should not act this way, I took responsibility for the situation. I accepted his insinuation that I was being selfish and inconsiderate. Obviously, Seth could have opened the door and said, "Hey, I need help pulling the truck in!" Instead, I was expected to read his mind and know that he needed help even when we weren't in the same room.

We finally got the truck parked and headed out for the city. We had a fun night drinking, and we partied until the wee hours of the night. There was no mention of the earlier explosion, and I was happy that Seth could quickly let go of his frustration with me and enjoy our first night in the city. He was charming and delightful all evening, and I was relieved. I looked forward to getting settled into our new lives, which I knew would alleviate so much of our stress.

We woke up in our new home and unloaded the small load of things from the truck that had been approved by Seth to bring with us. We then made our way to a furniture store, where Seth applied for credit. This was a foreign concept to me at the time. I still had my community college credit card with a five-hundred-dollar limit. I didn't use credit and felt very naïve to the concept.

The thought of putting things on credit made me nervous, but the idea of a man making a lot of money was also foreign to me. I rationalized in my head that five hundred dollars to me was the equivalent of five thousand dollars to him. I needed to stop worrying and accept that this was my new life. Within a two-hour time frame, we spent over five thousand dollars in one store.

We then went to our local Bed Bath & Beyond store to purchase all our household supplies. After two trips to his Jeep to unload the new items, we had successfully bought new dishes, pots, pans, rugs, linens, kitchen items, bathroom items, and other odds and ends that made their way into our cart. The vehicle was packed from top to bottom, and we couldn't have added another towel if we tried. I joked at the time that Seth looked high, and we laughed about it.

Seth appeared invincible, and he didn't have a care in the world. This was the man that I was accustomed to. I knew that things would get better after the move. We spent the night decorating the house with new art, new curtains, and organizing our new place.

> Red Flag Reflection: The red flags here are obvious. Seth *was* high when he was spending. He was high when he was buying new and expensive items that set him apart from the rest of the world. Seth did not have the financial backing to support these extravagant purchases, but I did not know that at the time.

We talked about Seth's new position at work and discussed the types of jobs that I would be applying for. Seth reassured me that I should take a break for a few weeks before diving into the job search so that I could get acclimated to the area. I was really looking forward to this idea of down time. I helped him get his office area set up, and we enjoyed exploring restaurants and the sites of the new area.

Learning How to Live with Seth

The calls home to my family were filled with excitement. More than anything, I wanted them to be proud of me. I wanted them to stop worrying about me as they had about my past relationships. I wanted to be seen as a capable adult, which was how I finally viewed myself. I spoke of the highlights of my life, and I could sense how happy they were. I focused on all the positives, which I am notorious for—the new crepe café that I found and my new running shoes, which would allow me to hit the beautiful trail by our house. I was happy. They were happy.

I felt inferior and somewhat ignorant when I heard Seth talk about credit and his credit scores. His credit reports and score seemed like his Bible. It was a world that was very new but intriguing to me. He often spoke about the corruption in the credit industry and that he could beat them at their own game.

I remember lying on the couch one evening as Seth discussed ways around the system. Seth told me that his conscience wouldn't let him mislead people, but creditors and banks were another story. He said that banks misled people every day but most people weren't smart enough to turn the tables. Seth boasted that he was smart enough.

> <u>Red Flag Reflection</u>: Regardless of how the story is spun, when someone boasts about misleading creditors, banks, the system or people, this is an obvious and glaring red flag.

One Saturday morning, Seth announced that he wanted to buy another new car. Some people go for pancakes and coffee on Saturday mornings. What I didn't realize was that Seth bought cars just for the thrill of it. At that time, he already had a Jeep and his ever-prized sports car. We also had my brand-new car. Each of these vehicles carried a balance and a car payment. Not to mention the fact that he was carrying the loan for his brother's truck. I was trying to understand why two people needed more than three cars, but I justified his actions like I always did. This world was unfamiliar to me. Seth knew what he was doing, and I needed to trust in that.

We went down to a car dealership and, within an hour, Seth drove off the lot with a brand-new Subaru. He said it was perfect for zipping around the city and seeing clients. This was exactly what he had been looking for. Seth claimed that his other cars weren't good for business—the Jeep was used to transport his dogs and the sports car was too flashy for clients.

On the way home, Seth called me from his new car. He was pulling into a Toyota dealership because he wanted to buy a truck. A brand-new truck made complete sense to him because he was planning to sell the Jeep, which had too many miles on it. He told me that a truck would be much better for hauling his dogs around the city. Seth went on to educate me on the way the system worked. If he were to purchase two cars on the same day, the credit bureaus wouldn't harass him because it wouldn't even register in their system until Monday morning. When I questioned the legalities of what he was doing, he sounded irritated, which was my signal to step back. I let it go. Seth was so happy that he looked euphoric. How could I not be happy about his new job, our new life, and finally having financial stability in my life?

> Red Flag Reflection: Within a few months, I started to see signs that concerned me. Before moving with Seth, our relationship was limited to weekends and usually involved alcohol. I did not see Seth in day-to-day life. Once real life set in, I began to notice the stress-induced insomnia. Seth would pace back and forth in the middle of the night and mumble to himself.

On morning, I overheard Seth make a phone call to Robert. Seth was requesting a money transfer to his bank account until his next paycheck came. I asked him about it and got the message loud and clear once again: an uneducated girl without a college degree was not allowed to question him about finances. Seth had a million excuses and began talking down to me while explaining how the real world worked. Transferring money between family members is simply what family is for. The excuses started coming more frequently—he was waiting for a work bonus, or he just needed to sell that one car that sat in the driveway.

I learned that to have faith in Seth was easier than upsetting him. Upsetting Seth resulted in him shutting down—void of emotions and void of love. Upsetting Seth caused him to withdraw from me. Withdrawing from me triggered my deep abandonment issues. Seth told me many times that my job was to have faith in him and be positive, which was all he needed from me. I was supposed to act like his mother, Cleo.

> Red Flag Reflection: By this point, Seth grew fond of telling me that I made mountains out of molehills. This was a statement that would carry through to my divorce and custody battle. Having "faith" in Seth and remaining positive meant that I was forced to trust whatever he said with a smile on my face or there would be hell to pay. Having faith in Seth meant that I was expected to swallow his twisted reality and ignore actual reality.

Some days I felt like royalty, and other days I felt so beneath him. Talks that focused on my lack of a college education seemed to become more frequent as time went on. Seth introduced me to his work colleagues as his fiancé, which made me feel special and gave me a sense of stability in our relationship.

At one particular work event, I overheard Seth telling his boss that I was going to attend the local state college in the fall, which left me confused and upset. I pressed him on the way home, and he admitted that in professional settings, it was embarrassing when conversations about college came up. I was crushed. No one had ever told me that I embarrassed them. Almost instantaneously, I could feel the self-esteem that I worked so hard to regain slipping from my fingers.

The next day, I woke up and put on a smile. The last thing that I wanted was to be accused of being a Debbie Downer *and* an embarrassment. I walked into the kitchen to make coffee and found flowers waiting for me on the kitchen table. Seth bought flowers after his morning run. The card expressed how sorry he was for hurting me. Seth claimed that I was the furthest thing in the world from an embarrassment. I accepted his apology.

> <u>Red Flag Reflection</u>: The ups and downs were leaving my head spinning. Almost as quickly as Seth could crush me, he could build me back up with amazing, heartfelt words. Not only could I not make sense of the new world I was living in, I found it difficult to articulate to my friends or family what was happening. At one point, I started to write an email to my aunt but quickly deleted it. I didn't even know how to describe what I was feeling and experiencing. I couldn't even process it in my brain let alone explain it to someone.

One thing that was really starting to bother me was that Seth constantly spoke poorly of other people. Any public setting was an open opportunity to judge or critique those around us. Seth constantly pointed out knock-off purses and fake designer jeans. His opinion was clear: if you can't afford the real thing, don't pretend to own it. Seth spoke poorly of overweight people, those who were uneducated or without college degrees, and those who were homosexual. As always, he would catch himself and point out that I was the exception when it came to people without college degrees.

Robert spoke in an equally derogatory fashion about people but was much more vulgar and crass in his delivery. His definition of obese was disturbing and included anyone who weighed more than 115 pounds, regardless of their height. While drinking, he would embark on homophobic rants and even allude to his violent views when it came to gay men. His fuse was short, and I learned to avoid him whenever I picked up on the slightest hint of anger. Seth often seemed perplexed by Robert and continually commented that Robert was raised in an affluent family but had developed "redneck views" and mentalities sometime after high school.

I was sitting in a restaurant late one night while Seth made fun of an overweight woman and her meal choice. I had reached my limit and was physically shaking. I explained to Seth that my aunt was overweight, and she was the most important person in my life. I asked him to stop saying mean things about people because it really bothered me. Seth explained, "That is what I love about you, Tina. You are golden-hearted and it's genuine. You have things to learn from me, and I have things to learn from you. I am so sorry if I offended you."

He always knew what to say to me. He genuinely wanted to be a kind, loving person, and he admired me for having those qualities. Seth gave me hope that he truly wanted to be a better person.

"Let's find nice things to say about people from now on. That would make me happy," I told Seth. He hugged me and agreed. By this point, I was convinced that I needed him. I felt like the child who got picked first on the sports team. I was in the elite group and I felt safe. In a strange way, I felt fortunate to be accepted into his inner circle.

The next six months were uneventful. We were both working and really enjoyed where we were living. As we were driving around the city one afternoon, Seth asked me if I would consider going back to school. Nothing major, "just a few classes at the local community college," he explained.

I told Seth that I would explore the options available and met with a college counselor that same week. I could see the excitement in his eyes when I told him that I was considering it. Seth then made me a proposal that I couldn't refuse. He asked me to quit my job, and he would help me financially if I wasn't able to qualify for financial aid.

I did as Seth asked. I gave two weeks' notice and enrolled in school full time. I threw myself into my studies and things were very good between us. I often overheard Seth telling people that I was taking a full load and planned to transfer to a state university or state college within the next two years.

Seth began complimenting me constantly in cards, letters, and in person. I found that I loved school and was intent on getting perfect grades. I wanted Seth to believe in me and realize that I was someone that he could be proud of. I wanted him to know that he could have a future with me and that he wasn't settling. For the first time in my life, I was holding a 4.0.

For quite some time, things were smooth sailing. Seth worked a lot, and I kept busy with school. The primary concern that bothered me on a regular basis about our relationship had to do with drinking. I didn't like who Seth became while he was drinking alcohol. He acted completely different and, oddly, he acted feminine. It was something I didn't understand about him. On other occasions, he acted unstable and angry. I was learning when to be quiet and when to give him space.

Seth also liked to brag a lot while drinking, and I dreaded that side of him. I didn't feel safe while we were out in bars because he would drink to the point of not being able to take control of situations, and I felt vulnerable. I could tell that people around us in bars were annoyed with his behavior, yet he was oblivious or didn't seem to care. The more Seth drank, the less I drank because I didn't feel safe or protected while with him.

One night we were leaving a club to make the drive back to our house. Seth was very agitated about an encounter with someone in the bar. I told him that he was not pleasant to be around while drinking; it was embarrassing to me that he was bumping into people while dancing and his mood was dark. I delivered it in a very meek voice and regretted my critique before the words even left my mouth.

"You are a stupid bitch!" Seth screamed at me as he slammed his open hands onto the dashboard with a great deal of force. I couldn't catch my breath and became hysterical while begging him to stop. I had never seen this side of him and he was in a rage. This was the first time that I was physically fearful of Seth.

I pulled the car over and laid my head against the steering wheel and sobbed. I wanted to go home—not back to our house but back to my family. I didn't understand who this person was. I was incredibly confused. How could he send me flowers with the most beautiful words scrawled on a piece of paper and then call me a "stupid bitch" just five hours later? Under his breath, Seth told me to stop crying or he was going to get out and walk home. I stopped my tears and drove back to our house in silence.

> Red Flag Reflection: Seth was always able to blame his behavior on his alcohol consumption. Many times, he claimed not to remember his actions from the night before when confronted about his behavior. Seth got angry when I cried and often stated that he had never been with someone so emotional. I felt the opposite. No one had ever mentioned that I was dramatic or cried too easily. I didn't cry often but, when I did, I always felt that my tears were warranted. I began to dread any situation that could potentially cause me to cry.

I got up the next day and left an hour early for school. I wanted to sit in a peaceful spot on campus and process my thoughts. I felt so alone. I couldn't call my family to explain what had happened. They would never believe it after all of the stories I had told them about my fairytale life. I didn't even understand it, so how could I possibly articulate this bizarre reality, and how could I expect my family to understand?

Seth began calling my cell phone within thirty minutes of my departure from the house. I ignored call after call. He left messages. He was sorry. There was no excuse. He has never lived with a girlfriend before and he was under a lot of pressure financially. He didn't like being criticized but should have handled it better. He wanted to talk in person. He said that he was willing to take responsibility for his actions and promised that it would never happen again.

We met that afternoon in a coffee shop to discuss everything. Seth confessed that finances were strained, and he had a lot of pressure with upcoming deadlines due to the end of his quarter at work. He told me that he offered to help me financially without being prepared to really do that and that he had overextended himself. He was under an extreme amount of stress and knew better than to drink when he was feeling this way. By the end of the conversation, it was me who was apologizing. I did not want to be a financial burden and hadn't realized the pressures that I had placed on him when I started school.

The very next week, I took out a school loan to ease the strain. I was normally very intuitive when it came to reading people, but I had been so wrapped up in my own world that I didn't notice Seth was struggling to keep us both afloat. I felt a lot of guilt over everything that had transpired. I made a mental note to be more observant and be more aware of the stressors in his world.

> Red Flag Reflection: Seth was beginning to twist reality, and I was buying every bit of it. He could manipulate any situation to the point that I would find myself apologizing to him even if he was the one at fault.

Once again, Seth showered me with cute notes and flowers over the next few weeks. It was apparent that my student loan was a wise choice. The last thing that I wanted was to add to the pressure that he was already feeling. Things were feeling normal again, which allowed me to further justify his behavior; it was financial stress and not who Seth really was.

After dating for almost a year, Seth began dropping hints that he wanted to marry me. He would make statements that led me to believe that it was going to happen sooner rather than later. I asked him how his parents would feel about it, and he replied that they would approve if they knew I was working toward a degree. It didn't matter that I was still in school, as long as I finished. He assured me that they loved me, and it would all be fine.

Leading up to our one-year anniversary, Seth hinted several times to a possible proposal on our anniversary weekend. I couldn't believe that he wanted to marry me. My life leading up to this had been riddled with trials and tribulations. My childhood was dysfunctional, and the past twenty-four years of my life had been fairly unstable. I had made huge strides during my year in counseling and things were heading in the right direction. I knew that I was a good person, an honorable person, and that I deserved this new life.

I called my closest friends and family to share in my joys about this suspected proposal. I knew that Seth was planning a weekend getaway to Santa Barbara, California, and I also had a feeling that he was planning to pop the question. I craved the forever-kind-of-love that he pledged to me. I desired the stability that I'd yearned for my entire life.

Our big getaway weekend didn't turn out the way that I had suspected. Instead of ending the weekend with a diamond engagement ring on my finger as Seth had hinted, I left the weekend with a beautiful set of diamond earrings. Opening a jewelry box to find earrings was nice, but it wasn't what I expected based on the clues Seth had been dropping. Going into the weekend, I had mixed feelings that fluctuated between thinking it was too soon to become engaged and being excited about the idea of happily ever after.

I am known to wear my heart on my sleeve. If something is bothering me, it shows. There was a noticeable awkwardness between us for days, neither one wanting to discuss the obvious elephant in the room. Seth finally confided in me that he was horribly embarrassed. His credit had been denied everywhere he went to buy an engagement ring. He had been to five different stores and was denied at every one of them. I felt incredibly sad that I had put pressure on him. I hugged him and felt like crawling in a hole.

About four weeks later as I was cleaning up the kitchen, I found mail hidden deep inside of a drawer. There were several pieces of mail that were approved credit applications for jewelry stores. These were brand-new credit cards with thousands and thousands of dollars' worth of available credit. The accounts had been opened and approved several months prior to my birthday weekend.

Seth had lied to me. My head was spinning. After all of those talks that he gave me about the importance of honesty. This wasn't just a little lie. He had fabricated entire stories with intricate details about each jewelry store encounter. I later learned this was his forte—to make up elaborate exaggerations that overshadowed his lies.

I tried to catch my breath as I threw clothing in a bag and headed for the door. I wanted to get out of the house before he came home. I can handle quite a bit, but dishonesty of any kind will push me over the edge. I left the credit cards and applications sitting on the middle of the kitchen table. I was in a state of confusion and couldn't even think as I attempted to find a hotel for the night. Who was this person I had given up my life for?

Seth began calling me within an hour of my departure. I shut my phone off. I didn't even want to see his name on my phone screen. I didn't want to talk to him or anyone else for that matter. I climbed into my big hotel bed and cried for hours. I was more confused than I had ever been. The person who promised that he would never hurt me had hurt me. Again.

The self-doubt took over. My insecurities were flowing as fast as my tears. Seth didn't see me as marriage material. He was embarrassed to commit to me because his family wouldn't approve, and he was stringing me along. I had so many emotions but, most of all, I was humiliated. How was I going to explain this to my family? They thought that he was the greatest thing that had ever happened to me. Now, I needed to tell them that I wasn't good enough for him. I was too embarrassed to talk to my family, so I didn't.

The universe works in mysterious ways, and I had ironically offered to pet sit for a family in Carlsbad who happened to be leaving for a month-long vacation the very next day. I called the family and asked permission to stay at their house while they were away, and they seemed relieved that someone would be there full time. I was thankful for the breathing room and the time away from Seth. A full day went by and I still hadn't accepted his calls or listened to his voicemails. I was emotionally crushed to my core and didn't even want to hear his voice.

I spent another night crying myself to sleep and woke up drained with what could only be described as a severe emotional hangover. I knew that I had to face Seth and the reality of the situation sooner or later. I communicated with him by text message only for the next couple of weeks and threw myself into school and my job. He was relentless in his attempts to meet with me. I took a different route to school and went early for fear of running into him. I avoided Seth for as long as I could.

One morning, the phone rang promptly at 8 a.m., and I finally took his call. "I need to talk to you. Where are you?" Seth stammered. I was silent. I was frozen. "Will you go to dinner with me?" he asked. "Yes," I answered reluctantly.

Seth picked me up and we drove to dinner in silence. I didn't have a script ready. I was drained by every sense of the word. We arrived at a very nice restaurant complete with dim lighting and koi ponds. Those were blessings as the lights hid my teary eyes and the running ponds would drown out our conversation for anyone around us. Once we were seated, I realized that I couldn't even look him in the eyes. I stared at my clasped hands and waited for him to begin.

Instead of speaking, Seth handed me a card. The card read: "Tina, I'm sorry 1 million times over for lying to you. I have no excuse. It will now go down as one of my biggest errors or lapses in judgment. I've spent the past few weeks thinking about why I felt comfortable lying to you. I've come up with no explanation. I know why I did it, but that doesn't matter. I want you to know that I intend to marry you. You are a beautiful person inside and out. I'm not. I'm devious, manipulative, and dishonest. If you need to leave me, I understand. I deserve it. I don't deserve you, but I can change. I love you so deeply, so earnestly, but I'm fighting my fears. My fear that things won't last forever, my fear of being wrong, my fear that I won't be a success in life, a good husband to you. I do so deeply love you. I want to marry you. I want to be with you for the rest of my life. Love, Seth."

I stared straight into his eyes. I wanted Seth to see how much he had hurt me. My thoughts were spinning circles in my head. My heart and my mind were at war. I was beat down. I still hadn't found the courage to tell my family all that had happened. I didn't know where to find that courage. They still believed my fairytale. I wanted to believe my fairytale. I watched as tears welled up in his eyes and rolled down his cheeks. I wanted to believe him with every ounce of my being. The reality was, I felt stuck. I was four hours away from my hometown. I had given up my apartment, sold my furniture, and had no job to return to. I didn't have the financial resources to start over. I felt alone and limited in my options.

During dinner, Seth begged me not to leave. He promised that if I did decide to leave him that he would pay for my moving expenses and ensure that I got into a new apartment back in our hometown. He looked broken and sincere. He told me he was terrified of his feelings and being in love was new for him. He told me he had been in love before but now realized that wasn't love. Seth told me that his chest physically hurt at the thought of not having me in his life. He needed me.

I was scared. Scared to be with Seth and scared to be without him. He begged for me to come home that night and I did. I didn't have the energy to fight him nor did I want to. I felt numb inside. For the next four weeks, things were peaceful between us, and he told me repeatedly that he would again earn my trust and promised never to tell me another lie. I wanted so badly to believe him.

> Red Flag Reflection: One of the first signs of domestic violence is isolation. Seth had isolated me from my friends, my hometown and my former life. I was dependent on him financially and going into debt on student loans to make him happy.
>
> Oprah Winfrey once stated, "When people show you who they are, believe them the first time." Oprah then went onto say that there are two reasons why you choose not to believe the person: a) you don't see the sign because you don't want to; b) if you see the signs, you'd have to do something about them. In that card, Seth admitted that he was devious, manipulative, and dishonest. I am guilty of both "a" and "b." I saw the signs, but I didn't want to admit it. I didn't want to see the signs, because I didn't want to have to do something about them. I was hooked into a cycle of dysfunction and doing something about it meant revealing to my family that I was in yet another dysfunctional relationship. I made excuses in my own mind: compared to the past dysfunction, this was not as bad.

A Weekend Getaway Gone Wrong

After months of working long hours, Seth and I escaped for a three-day weekend adventure to Lake Tahoe with his older brother, Robert, and his friend, Ted. The first night was fun as we drank, gambled, and experienced the Tahoe night life. Seth became completely intoxicated and ended up shutting himself in our room and leaving me with Robert and Ted. We ended up in the kitchen doing shots and Ted asked me what I saw in Seth. Thrown off by his question, I didn't know how to respond. At first, I thought they were joking, but the mood quickly turned serious. "He doesn't see you as marriage material. You know that, right?" Robert asked. I was dumbfounded and couldn't understand why they were saying these things to me. Robert wrapped his arms around me to console me as I began to cry. "Cheer up, buttercup," Robert said. "I don't want to make you sad. I'm just worried about you." Shortly after, I dismissed myself and went to the room where Seth was passed out cold. I crawled into bed intoxicated, spinning, and downcast by the words that had been spoken in the kitchen.

On Saturday, we spent the day snowboarding, and not a word was mentioned about the previous night's conversation. That night, after hours of drinking, we were waiting outside of a club that was tucked inside a casino. A drunken man walked by with his friends and, using both hands, he squeezed my buttocks so hard that I screamed out in pain. Seth didn't see what happened but, within seconds of hearing my words, he was chasing the man through the casino with his brother following close behind.

The casino had two sets of doors leading to the outside and, as the drunken man went through the first set of doors, Seth violently attacked him. It was immediately apparent how drunk the man was because he couldn't defend himself. Seth reminded me of a pit bull as his eyes glazed over; there was no stopping him. I was screaming for him to stop beating the man, but he wouldn't quit. He was beating the man's head into the tile floor, over and over again for what seemed like several minutes. I stood by frantically begging him to let the man go. Blood was everywhere.

Someone began yelling for the police, which seemed to bring Seth back to reality. He finally stopped just before security guards and police officers surrounded us. When the officer asked Seth for his identification, he claimed that he didn't have it with him. He gave the officers his name, Peter Peterman. "Peter Peterman?" the police officer asked sarcastically, in disbelief.

I was trembling as I explained my story to the police officers. They checked my backside and found signs of ten deep fingerprint bruises beginning to form, which further corroborated my story. Seth talked to the police for several minutes and asked them what they would do if they had been in his shoes.

I was told that if I pressed charges for sexual assault, we would be free to go. I agreed. I tried to justify Seth's actions in my mind, but I was deeply disturbed by the brutality that I had just witnessed at his hands. While it was troubling, Seth smoothed things over by telling me that his reaction was a result of being my protector—that he was so in love with me that the assault pushed him over the edge. I struggled to erase my mind of the images of him being so savage.

> <u>Red Flag Reflection</u>: Being my fierce protector or not, violence to this degree is a glaring red flag and should never be brushed under the rug. Justifying Seth's behavior and sweeping things under the rug had become commonplace for me as time went on. While no one is perfect and one individual incident could be explained away, the incidents were piling up and painting a picture that I should not have ignored.

On our drive home from Tahoe, I brought up the incident that had taken place in the kitchen on Friday night. Seth was noticeably angry and stated that his brother had always been jealous of him. He said that Robert was jealous of his job, his college degree, his credit and ability to buy things and go on trips. Now, Seth said that Robert was jealous of his relationship with me and that, physically, I was Robert's type. My mind started to flash back to other odd encounters with Robert in which he mentioned to me that all our mutual friends thought that Seth and I were a strange pairing and that they felt that Robert and I were much more compatible. At the time, I had begun to think of him as my big brother, so these comments struck me as odd but laughable. Robert had also laughed about it at the time but, now, putting the pieces together, I felt uncomfortable.

Losing My Mother

I experienced a lot of hurt from my mother, who had been mainly absent from my life since I was six months old. I was born to teen parents and, due to mental illness, my mother had chosen a dark path that involved drugs and alcohol. While in her care as a child, I witnessed abuse of every type including her boyfriend beating her and raping her while I was in the adjoining room. I had been pulled into her suicide attempts on multiple occasions and, by the time I was in sixth grade, I had witnessed more dysfunction than anyone should see in a lifetime. I was intent on making something of myself in life to spite her. I didn't care if she lived or died. She had already died in my mind. I began calling my mom by her first name when I was 14 years old and, by that point, I was legally able to shut her out of my life. Every few years, I would send her a letter detailing everything she had done wrong. I wanted her to apologize to me. I was tired of hearing excuses from her. That was the extent of our relationship through my teen years and into adulthood.

Toward the end of November 2001, Seth and I were planning a trip to Chicago so that he could meet my family. I wasn't sure if I wanted him to meet my mom. The truth was: I didn't know if I wanted to see her at all. We had barely spoken in several years and, as much as I had delved into my childhood issues in therapy, I still carried a great deal of hurt. My mom caught wind that I would be visiting and called to see if we could arrange visits on her days off. I remember pausing and trying to collect my thoughts as she waited quietly for my reply. I then explained that I didn't know if I was going to see her during my visit. She was silent. I ended the call as quickly as I could.

A few nights later, on the evening of November 28, 2001, I was studying for finals at a Border's Book Store and received a phone call from my grandparents' house. "Hi, Grandma," I said, eager to tell her about my college classes. It was both of my grandparents on the line, and they were crying, "Tina, your mom is dead. She died this morning. It was drugs."

I heard the words my grandma said, but I didn't understand. I leapt from my seat and ran out of the bookstore leaving all my possessions behind. It was the call that I had anticipated my entire life. My mom overdosed. Thinking back to my last call with her just days before combined with her past suicide attempts, I suspected it wasn't an accidental drug overdose.

I was devastated. All my hopes for her to recover from addiction were gone. All my hopes for her to be healthy were gone. All my hopes for her to be my mom were gone; gone with a single telephone call. How could she be gone? I was in shock and unable to grasp what I had just heard.

The next hour was a complete blur. I ran out of the bookstore in such a panic that I left behind my laptop, my schoolbooks, and my purse. I was hysterical and I couldn't breathe. My world was spinning, my ears were ringing, and my mom was dead. I was standing up against my car sobbing, but I couldn't get in. My keys were still inside the bookstore. I was so distraught that logic was escaping me. I couldn't figure out how to open my car, but I desperately wanted to curl up in the seat and escape this horrific reality that had been handed to me.

A couple walking past me stopped and asked if I needed help. Yes. I needed help. I needed my mom to be alive. This woman, a complete stranger, hugged me tightly and then went inside to retrieve all my belongings. They helped me to get in my car and suggested that I call someone to pick me up. First, I called my Aunt Bev. I knew she was 2,000 miles away, but I just needed to hear her voice. Afterwards, I called Seth and he sounded confused. He was quiet and then said, "Okay, I'll meet you at home."

I drove home, yet to this day, I have no recollection of the drive. I waited for almost two hours, but Seth wasn't answering his phone. I was lying on my bed sobbing when he finally came home carrying a pizza. Seth walked in, looked at me, and nonchalantly said, "Do you want a piece of pizza?" I remember being shocked and staring at him in complete confusion. "No," I said. "I don't want pizza. I can't believe you stopped to get pizza! I needed you." He responded with words I will never forget: "I don't know what the big deal is? You weren't even close to your mom." Seth looked uncomfortable by my state of hysteria and remained distant all night.

> Red Flag Reflection: The coldness and lack of empathy was utterly alarming to me. No hugs. No feelings. No empathy. In my deepest despair, I questioned my own reaction to my mother's death because of how non-reactionary Seth seemed. Was I overreacting given the fact that I didn't even have a relationship with this woman? I received more empathy from the complete strangers at the bookstore and my neighbors than I did from my own boyfriend, which made me feel even more distraught.

After my mom's funeral in Chicago, Seth insisted that we needed to get away for a while. He made arrangements for us to travel to Maui; less than one month later, we were soaking in the beauty of the island. This was the first of many trips we took to Maui and my first time being in Hawaii. I was still in a fog after the death of my mom but relieved to escape my thoughts and my guilt. That last phone call from my mom was playing in my head on a continuous loop that I couldn't seem to shut off despite my best efforts. Her past suicide attempts replayed in my mind along with the reality that I had been so cold to her just days before her death.

The Engagement in Hawaii

During the second day of our vacation, Seth found a secluded spot on the coast to eat lunch. We hiked the rugged, rocky coastline to find the perfect spot. As I sat there finishing my sandwich and absorbing the tranquility of the ocean, I looked to my right and saw Seth kneeling beside me with a huge diamond ring. He proposed, and I accepted. Looking back, it seemed strange—not emotionally charged and not romantic at all. On our drive to the resort, we stopped for wine tasting and to take pictures of the ocean. Seth told every person that we encountered that day that we were engaged. He seemed elated, and I quickly chalked up the non-emotional proposal to a simple case of nerves.

As our car careened down the windy coastline, Seth suggested that we get married while in Maui. He wanted it to be private. He didn't want us to call our families with the news. He said that we would surprise them after the ceremony. I love spontaneity; we made arrangements to get married just two days later. On the eve of our wedding night, we sat down and decided to write our own vows. It was Seth's idea and, to me, it seemed incredibly romantic. I grew tired as the night progressed and decided to turn in early, but Seth explained that he wanted to stay up and finish the vows. I woke up through the night and realized he wasn't in bed. The hours passed, and he finally came to bed at nearly four o'clock in the morning.

New Year's Eve in 2001 was the morning of what should have been a very special day in my life. Seth seemed very anxious, which made me uneasy because, by this point, I was beginning to feel responsible for his moods. I had learned to be jovial to lighten Seth's moods, and I grew accustomed to putting on a happy face even if I didn't feel cheerful. Seth seemed restless, and I worried that he was having second thoughts. We drove to watch a surf event at Jaws, a popular surf spot in Maui where top surfers from around the world flew in to compete. Seth was ecstatic while watching the event and told me all about his early years surfing. His mood shifted by the time we had brunch and things felt normal again.

After brunch, we went to a copy center to print our vows, which Seth said he had carefully crafted until the wee hours of the night. He said that he wanted to make sure they were perfect. That's what I believed anyway, until Seth handed me sixteen pages of a typed document, which turned out to be a prenuptial agreement. "It's really not a big deal," Seth explained. "Everyone does a prenup these days, and it's just to make sure we are on the same page." As I sat outside on the curb reading this document, I couldn't believe what I was holding in my hands.

We hadn't discussed a prenuptial agreement and, while I am not an expert, this didn't seem like an ordinary prenuptial. Most prenuptial agreements discuss property and assets but we had neither. Seth stipulated that I was not allowed to gain an excess of ten pounds during our marriage. Exercise was to be a priority and needed to occur at least three times per week. If I had children, I had to return to my pre-pregnancy weight within one year. It also stated that I needed to finish college and graduate with a 3.0 or higher.

There were provisions for every aspect of our married life, and the prenuptial agreement even had stipulations about what would happen if we got divorced, such as if our marriage lasted less than five years, then I had to return the ring to him. If it lasted five to ten years, we would split the profit of the ring, and if our marriage lasted over ten years, I got to keep the ring. I was gripping onto 16 pages of sheer insanity, and I was speechless.

Everything in me screamed, "RUN!" Instead, I sat there on the curb crying and feeling frozen. I handed Seth the prenuptial agreement and told him that I couldn't go forward. Actually, I think I told him to go fuck himself. I refused to sign the document. I couldn't even bring myself to finish reading it let alone sign that packet. I couldn't marry Seth; I knew this in my heart. He begged. He pleaded. He apologized. We got married just a few hours later, on the coast of Maui. I did not sign the prenuptial agreement.

> Red Flag Reflection: Obviously, this was more than one red flag. There were flags of every color whipping in the Maui breeze, yet I still chose to marry Seth that day. I was still trying to convince myself that the percentage of good outweighed the percentage of bad. I was in a fog from the death of my mother and Seth pounced. He saw my weakness as opportunity. I have been told that this is called "trauma bonding." In addition, Seth maintained a sense of control by not letting me contact my friends and family in advance of the wedding. Even if I had contacted them, they wouldn't have tried to stop me, as they only knew about the good side of Seth.

Part 2: The Marriage

A few months into our marriage, we were driving through Napa Valley when Seth mentioned a business idea that we could start in our hometown. I am an entrepreneur at heart and saw this as a way for us to move back home, which I desperately craved. Within two months of that conversation, I was living in our hometown and working between 60 and 100 hours per week launching our new business. Seth kept his job in the city, and we commuted weekly between the two homes.

Seth and I became heavily entwined in the local business scene and were often called, "The Golden Couple." We started a young entrepreneur group and our life began to revolve around the new business and networking. We barely saw each other, as the business took every waking moment of our lives.

As we got our new business off the ground, Seth and I were living in a large home that belonged to his parents. Robert was maintaining the property, which was situated in a very affluent community, while his parents were overseas. We were paying rent on a wing of the house while Robert resided in the master suite. One day, Robert confided in us that his parents were struggling to maintain ownership of the home, which didn't come as a complete surprise as I had overheard rumblings about their financial troubles for quite some time. When Seth discovered that his parent's home was facing foreclosure, he immediately made a push to buy the house.

Seth's uncle owned a business in the mortgage and lending industry. With the help of several bank connections, Seth was able to purchase the home from his parents with a stated income loan. He signed the loan documents as a single male even though we were married, which he justified by saying that my credit was poor compared to his and he preferred to keep things separate. I was rightfully upset that he made this purchase without acknowledging our marriage or including me as his wife. When I held my ground by challenging Seth on the legalities of this transaction, his wrath came in the form of the silent treatment.

> <u>Red Flag Reflection</u>: This wasn't the first or the last of Seth's financial deviance, but it hurt that he was denying something that I considered sacred: our marital vows. It was another subtle reminder that I wasn't good enough. There were verbal agreements in place between Seth and his parents that he would never use the equity

from the home. The current equity belonged to his parents and was their only means of retirement income, when the time came. Seth's father expressed his concern regarding us starting a new business, but Seth promised that we would go the conventional route and apply for loans secured by the Small Business Association, should the need present itself.

Since we were increasing our living space from a 1,500-square-foot home to one that was over 4,000 square feet, Seth wanted to purchase new furniture. While the furniture we owned was brand new, it wouldn't even make a dent in this huge house, according to Seth. He explained to me in a condescending tone that the two home styles were completely different and that the new furniture that we recently purchased would look ridiculous if placed in a home with a more modern design. During a weekend in San Francisco, Seth wanted to go window-shopping for furniture but I was hesitant to even walk through the door of a furniture store with him.

We were not in a position to spend money. Money was extremely tight with the new business and the move. Financially, we were stretched ten feet beyond my comfort zone, and I voiced my opinion. I regretted my words before they even left my mouth. Now he was irritated, and I knew that the silent treatment would again be my punishment.

Seth parked the car with a force that was meant to emphasize his annoyance with me. I knew the unspoken cues, and I knew that this behavior would last for the rest of the day. We walked through a variety of art deco stores, and he seemed to loosen up as he pointed out various lighting options and furniture.

As a woman, I would normally jump at the opportunity to shop but not when I was with Seth. We had just taken out a mortgage that was over $5,000 per month with no solid plan on how we were actually going to pay for it. I gasped when I saw the price tag on the red art deco couch that he was now sitting on.

We left the city on Sunday night and made the four-hour commute back home without a single purchase. I was relieved and actually enjoyed the long silent drive for once. I had plans to stay on the California coast for the week so that I could work on our new business, and Seth was heading back to northern California for a weeklong work convention. I was looking forward to the time apart because the tension between us was quite elevated.

Seth was due back late that next Friday night and called to explain that he was running late. He told me to go to sleep and that he would see me in the morning. I woke up Saturday morning and realized that he was nowhere to be found, although I could see that he had been home evident by the bags in the doorway.

I called Seth's cell phone several times and didn't get an answer. When he finally called me back, it was mid-afternoon and he claimed to be working from a coffee shop. Seth was very curt in his answers and explained that he would see me in a few hours.

It was around eight o'clock in the evening when a large white moving van pulled into the driveway. I peered out the window just in time to see Seth step out of the driver's seat. I walked outside with a look of confusion on my face. Seth exclaimed, "I have a surprise!" as he threw open the door to the van. He had bought everything. The moving van was packed from top to bottom with the art deco furniture from San Francisco.

I stared in disbelief as the memories of each price tag flashed through my head. I needed to get out of there. I started walking as fast as I could up the driveway and onto the all-familiar looped street, which ran through my new neighborhood. I walked past the expansive, wealthy homes, and I knew in my heart that we couldn't afford this lifestyle. I felt like vomiting.

The tears began pouring down my face. I could hear Seth's footsteps catching up with me, so I began to jog. I wanted nothing to do with his insanity. I kept running into the darkness until I felt Seth grab my arm tightly from behind.

"Stop," he said in a gruff, low voice that terrified me. I spun around to face him and I was sobbing. "What is WRONG WITH YOU?" I yelled at him. "WHY are you doing this?" I asked. "You are psycho," Seth yelled back at me. "You are white trash…NO ONE acts like this in this neighborhood. I don't know where *YOU* were raised but we don't stand in the street screaming," he continued with his voice shaking with anger. Seth was still squeezing my arm, and the look in his eyes frightened me.

"LET GO OF ME!" I screamed as I pulled my arm free. Seth got in my face and said, "You are bipolar just like your mom, and you need help!" He said the words that he knew would kill me inside. I would never be like my mom. His words cut me to my core. No one had ever said such deep-seated, painful words to me. He crossed lines that night that I didn't even know existed. I sat on the side of the road in the dark of night with my head in my hands, and I sobbed for what felt like hours.

> <u>Red Flag Reflection</u>: No one had physically grabbed me before. I didn't know what to think. It was a firm hold on my arm, which let me know that Seth was in control. I eventually dismissed the incident and justified it by telling myself that it happened in the heat of the moment. He was angry. On the other hand, the words hurt much more than any type of physical pain that Seth could have unleashed on me. My deepest wounds were connected to my mother, and my greatest fear in life was to resemble my mother in any shape or form, especially her mental illness. The narcissist knows how to use your pain to inflict further injury in an effort to break you down. I began to doubt myself. Was my reaction over the top? Was I too emotional? Was there any truth to Seth's words? Today, I know beyond a shadow of a doubt that there was no truth to Seth's cruel words but, at the time, the fog was thickening.

Weeks went by and flowers, cards, and lengthy emails were once again a daily occurrence. The rollercoaster ride was becoming more predictable. Seth apologized. He only wanted the best for me and for us. He knew that I didn't have expensive things growing up, and he simply wanted to provide those things for me. He swore he didn't realize how much the furniture would upset me; stating that he assumed I would be excited once I actually saw it in the house. He claimed he called the store to return everything but it was a final sale policy. He even showed me the fine print on the receipt to prove his statement. Final sale: $11,402.

One Sunday morning, we were at a local coffee shop where Seth spent many of his mornings. He introduced me to an older gentleman whom he often spoke to in the mornings. Within minutes, the gentleman said to me, "You have to make him stop focusing on this blueprint life that he has in his head. That's no way to live."

I left the coffee shop thinking about these words of wisdom. Seth did strive to have a blueprint life, and any deviation from his plan never went well. The furniture was a façade and intended to impress people. It bothered me that Seth couldn't roll with the punches, and if something went against his plan, he would become angry, bitter, and sometimes downright frightening. It became my job to fix things. I walked on eggshells constantly being attuned to his mood barometer.

Fearing Robert

In addition to the financial and marital stressors that were engulfing us, we were living with Robert, which came with its own issues. Robert was doing construction work on the home in exchange for his living expenses, but there was tension surrounding this agreement. Seth was accusing Robert of overbilling him, and Robert was refusing to move out of the master bedroom suite of a house that we now owned. Robert locked us out of the entire upstairs portion of the house, and I was doing my best to stay out of the situation while remaining cordial. That became harder and harder as time went on and my concerns about him mounted.

While we were waiting in line at a grocery store one morning buying ice and alcohol, Robert opened his flip phone and discreetly took a photograph under a woman's skirt. While I did not realize what had occurred at the time, Robert showed Seth the photo as we climbed back into his truck heading for the lake. That was not an isolated incident, as he did this on other occasions with waitresses in restaurants and with unsuspecting girls at the lake who were in compromised positions. Seth and I conversed about Robert's behavior multiple times and, each time, he expressed his disgust; however, he repeatedly downplayed Robert's actions and stated, "Boy will be boys." I often questioned if this was truly what men did. Because I was in their inside circle, was I only just realizing something that was, in fact, commonplace?

Seth constantly tried to work on his relationship with his brother and often used the phrase "letting bygones be bygones," which seemed to be a theme in his family. One particular weekend, we tabled all the conflict and spent the weekend at the lake with Robert and Seth's youngest brother along with a few of his teenage girl friends. We were drinking, dancing, and having a good time on the boat, but I was bothered by the fact that Robert was giving these underage girls alcohol. Underage drinking was commonplace at the lake, so I knew that Seth and Robert would have quickly shot down any argument I made about the inappropriateness of the girls drinking.

After a day on the lake, a few of the girls came back to the house and Robert retreated to his room and returned to the kitchen moments later with a set of dice. Not just any set of dice but "sex dice." Rolling one die offered prompts such as "blow on" and the second die listed a body part. I boiled over and told Robert firmly that this was not okay. These were underage girls who had been drinking. I was furious.

Robert got in my face and was seething. "Shut the fuck up, Tina. This is MY family's house and you can leave if you have an issue!" I retreated to my room in tears. I could not believe this was happening. Any respect that I had left for Robert was now gone.

Shortly after this incident, things between the three of us went from bad to worse. Without even saying a word to us, Robert found a place just north of us and abruptly moved out. For quite a while, we had no contact with him. The financial issues between Robert and Seth had come to a head and they were barely speaking. It was a relief to have Robert out of the house, to reclaim the upstairs wing of our house, and to have the ongoing tension behind us.

One weekend in 2003, Seth and I found ourselves at a friend's wedding where Robert was also a guest. We spent the evening catching up with mutual friends and, at one point, we walked past Robert, who happened to be standing on the patio outside. It was dark as we passed, but we noticed that he was leaning up against a blonde girl, and they appeared to be kissing. I wasn't sure who the girl was; however, all hell broke loose the next day when we heard from multiple people who were irate because the girl he made out with was only 14 years old. Robert was 30 years old at the time. I was disgusted, and it further validated the decision we made to stay away from Robert.

Months went by and Cleo contacted Seth stating that she was concerned about Robert. According to Cleo, Robert had spiraled into a very dark depression and was suicidal. Cleo and Leonard were working overseas and felt helpless due to the distance. They asked if I would reach out to Robert since there was so much hostility between he and Seth. Cleo felt he would be more willing to talk to me. A part of me was hopeful that rock bottom would be a wake-up call for Robert to get his life together. Due to the history of suicide attempts with my mother, the word "suicide" is very triggering for me, and I took Cleo's words seriously. While I had very negative feelings towards Robert, I did not wish suicide or death on anyone.

I began communicating with Robert, hopeful that he would get help. He agreed to see a doctor for medication but only if I would go with him. I made the appointment and took him to be prescribed antidepressants. After a week of the medication, he seemed to be getting even worse. I was in daily communication with his parents, who asked me to move in with Robert until they returned home for the summer. I agreed to stay at his house on suicide watch for a few months, but I insisted that his weapons were removed from the home. I did not feel comfortable being out in a rural area with Robert if there were weapons in the house. I didn't feel comfortable being in the house with Robert at all, but I felt very conflicted. One of Robert's friends met me at the house to remove multiple guns, knives, and even a noose that I had found in the home.

One night, Seth and I were able to get Robert out of the house. We went to a local tavern for dinner, and the guys drank several beers. At one point, the restaurant atmosphere began to clear and employees started removing the tables to create an afterhours dance scene. Robert seemed agitated and dark suddenly. He got up to use the bathroom, and I decided to follow him as I felt that something was off. As I entered the hallway, I saw Robert slip out the back door, and I followed him. As I approached Robert, he looked scarier than I had ever seen him.

"I'm going to Jessica's, and I'm going to slit her fucking throat," Robert hissed at me.

"Please sit down, and let's talk," I said, motioning for him to sit down on the curb.

Robert sat down on the curb with force and was gripping his head with his hands. Seth came out and I gave him a serious look to alert him that there was a problem. My hands were shaking so badly that I could barely push the correct buttons on my phone as I dialed Cleo overseas. Cleo answered immediately, and I walked away from Robert and Seth to discuss the situation with her privately.

"Cleo, he's talking about murdering Jessica. He just slipped out the back door of Ivory Tavern and claims he was heading to her house. He is going to hurt someone; he needs help. I do not know what to do any longer," I stammered, as the tears began to flow.

Cleo begged me not to call the police, or anyone for that matter, and said that if I called the police, they would arrest Robert and it would only make matters worse. She assured me that Robert would never actually hurt anyone and that he was just angry. My gut instincts told me that he was, in fact, capable of hurting someone. Cleo asked that Seth and I take Robert back to our house when I stated firmly that I did not feel safe staying with him alone. She reminded me that it was a matter of weeks before she came home for the summer.

Seth and I brought Robert back to our house and he sat on the couch brooding. Within 15 minutes, Robert went out the front door and headed up the driveway on foot. Seth and I followed him as he walked down the street, through the neighborhood in the pitch black. Robert told us to go home as he sat on the curb, bent forward, and started crying a deep, guttural cry. He said he wanted to die. Once again, I dialed Cleo's number and explained to her that he was suicidal and needed help. She asked to speak to Robert, and he was hysterical while talking to her. While I couldn't hear what Cleo was saying, through sobs, Robert said, "Okay ... okay ... yes, I promise. I promise you I will not kill myself. Okay ... I love you, too."

I took the phone and Cleo asked me to get Robert back to the house and have him sleep it off. She asked if he could stay with Seth and I for the weekend, and I was relieved. While I didn't care if he stayed at the house with Seth there, I was afraid to be alone with him at his house in case he went dark again. I was afraid of Robert and did not know what he was capable of.

The next day, Robert insisted on going home, which meant that Seth would have to drive him back to his house because we had all gone out the previous night in Seth's car. During the 30-minute drive, I began to tremble at the thought of being back there with Robert, but I had given his mom my word. I secretly hoped that upon arrival, Seth would stay and I could return home to sanity and safety. We ended up cooking hamburgers on Robert's grill and, after dinner, Seth got up and said he was tired and that he would see me in the morning at our office. I couldn't believe he was leaving me there. I barely slept at all that night.

As part of the conditions of my stay, I was insistent that Robert see a mental health professional, which he reluctantly agreed to do. I found a therapist and made the appointment for him. At the request of Cleo, I attended the appointments with Robert, but Cleo forbade me from telling the therapist that Robert had made both suicidal and homicidal statements on multiple occasions. Cleo told me that she feared Robert would be hospitalized, which would make him spiral even further into darkness. I respected Cleo and believed that she knew best, so I kept quiet about the severity of the situation despite my strong gut feeling that he needed more intensive treatment. I sat quietly in the therapist's office during multiple counseling sessions, but I felt that being there was a waste of time if we weren't truly addressing the issues.

I pacified my own internal feelings and frustrations by reminding myself that Cleo would be home to take over Robert's care very shortly. On a phone call one evening, I overheard Cleo asking Robert again to promise her that he would not take his own life. He made that promise to his mother. Much of the time, I felt triggered by the history of suicide attempts with my own mother combined with the guilt of wondering if things would have been different had I been kinder to her on that last call. My guilt kept me firmly planted and committed to being on suicide watch.

> Red Flag Reflection: Leonard and Cleo were lifelong educators, and Cleo prided herself on her history of working as a counselor in schools. I looked up to them in many facets of life, from their long marriage to their standing in our small community. I respected Cleo's authority and guidance even when my instincts were screaming at me. I pushed my intuition to the wayside and reluctantly agreed to follow her action plan, which consisted of equal parts of denial and dismissiveness. I knew that going against Seth's wishes never worked well for me, and I couldn't imagine going up against the entire family unit or their instructions.

During my stay with Robert, I was disturbed by some of the things he was doing. One night, he spent hours on the computer creating a "lost dog" poster with his ex-girlfriend Jessica's photo. He planned to print it out and hang it around town. I confided in Cleo and Seth that I was worried for Jessica's safety and Robert's mental state. I was told that Robert had longstanding anger issues and depression but that he would never actually hurt anyone.

Robert then became obsessed with purchasing a Russian or Ukrainian bride and would spend hours creating folders meticulously labeled with each woman's name. Each folder contained their bio, height, weight, and measurements, along with photos. He began subscribing to Russian bride magazines and even began planning a tour of Russia through a mail order bride company. I relayed these things to Seth and his parents daily and, while Seth also seemed concerned, I felt that his parents were continuously dismissive of the severity of the situation, which left me questioning my own judgment. With his new Russian bride quest, Robert had a focus and seemed somewhat manic and high versus his previous state, which was increasingly dark and demented.

Because of Robert's mood shifting from dark to almost euphoric, I made the decision to return home to Seth, which was weeks ahead of the timeframe set out by Cleo. I was emotionally and mentally drained and ready to be back in my own bed. I let Cleo know that I was checking out earlier than planned, and she committed to being in touch with Robert daily. I felt as though I was drowning and looked forward to being relieved of the responsibility of caring for Robert.

Seth's Perfect Family Image Shatters

In the week that I was planning my departure, Robert had begun talking to a girl by the name of Savannah whom he met online. Savannah lived in Texas, and they were spending hours on the phone each night. Robert confided in me that he was sending her money for a plane ticket to visit him in California, and he began placing framed photos of her around the house. Savannah seemed much younger than Robert and, from the photos, she appeared to be an aspiring model—thin, gorgeous, and blonde. Given Robert's shift, I assumed the medication had finally stabilized him and felt relieved to be closing this chapter.

One evening that summer, Seth and I had plans to meet Cleo and Leonard for dinner. Shortly before we arrived at the restaurant, Cleo received a phone call from an irate Robert, and we overheard her trying to calm him down. She relayed that Robert was devastated after paying for Savannah's plane ticket and waiting to pick her up at the airport for their first official meeting. As it turns out, Savannah never boarded the plane and stood Robert up. She let us know that Robert was on his way to the restaurant to join us for dinner, and I instantly felt uneasy.

Robert arrived and was visibly angry while Cleo instantly began defusing the situation by telling Robert that there was surely an explanation for Savannah not being on the plane. Small talk ensued while Robert sat stewing and silent. I sat in disbelief when he broke his silence: "I'm going to fly to Texas tomorrow and rape and murder that fucking bitch!"

I had seen Robert rage before and he terrified me. Almost as a protection mechanism, I refused to make eye contact with him. Instead, I quickly looked to Cleo and Leonard for assistance, with tears in my eyes. I felt relieved that they were finally hearing how severe things were. Up until that moment, I questioned if they felt I was exaggerating because of their non-reactionary stance. Now, there was no denying it as they were hearing his chilling words with their own ears.

Cleo looked at Robert, concerned, but continued eating her spinach dip without missing a bite. I felt as though I was on a separate planet unable to relate to these people or their reaction to the words that just left Robert's mouth. Cleo was non-reactionary, which left me reeling. The rest of the meal was uncomfortable, as I could not bring myself to engage in Cleo's repeated small talk about their summer plans.

I relentlessly expressed my concerns to Cleo on multiple occasions that summer. Her son made a death threat, for God's sake. I felt a sense of desperation and wondered how I could get her to listen. Maybe if I waited until we were alone together in the kitchen, she would be forced to speak about this? Cleo continued to insist that Robert's new medication was to blame. This was the summer that I came to accept that I would get nowhere with Cleo, as my concerns fell on deaf ears. It was also the summer that I came to accept that this family was far from the picture-perfect image that they portrayed and, in fact, I struggled to grasp the magnitude of dysfunction and was left pondering how deep the cracks truly went.

Once I was home and the fog dissipated, I vowed that I would never again participate in Robert's care and verbalized this to Seth who, thankfully, agreed with me. The entire experience felt surreal, and I struggled to process all that had occurred. Seth and I completely distanced ourselves from Robert but heard through the family that he did embark on a tour of the Ukraine in search of a mail-order bride. Apparently discouraged by the rate of scams that took place, he shifted his focus to a Thai bride and began his research as well as his vacation there.

Ruining the Blueprint

In the early months of 2004, I began to experience a tingling sensation that radiated through the left side of my body every time I tilted my head forward. For months, I suspected a pinched nerve; however, a series of tests pointed to multiple sclerosis. I went through a two-week period of time in which I didn't even leave my bed and struggled to perform daily tasks. I was devastated. It felt as though I had heavy sandbags wrapped around my ankles and walking ten feet felt daunting. I ended up spending five days in the hospital undergoing a procedure called plasmapheresis where my blood cells were separated from my plasma and the plasma was then replaced with albumin. The treatment proved successful and I left the hospital feeling like a new person.

During my time in the hospital, I saw a very caring side of Seth. He brought my puppy to visit me through the back doors of the hospital after hours and showered me with books, magazines, and anything that I needed. Seth asked that we keep my situation within the family, as he wasn't ready to disclose the information to our friends. I agreed.

After I left the hospital, Seth was adamant that no one should find out about my diagnosis. He claimed that friends would treat me differently, and he didn't want that for me. It was the last thing that I wanted to fight with him about.

One night at a dinner party, I ended up telling a group of our most trusted friends about my diagnosis. Seth looked physically uncomfortable as people began to ask me questions and show concern. I knew from his body language that I had made a mistake in disclosing this information and, subsequently, received the silent treatment on the way home. When he finally began speaking to me, Seth accused me of craving attention and said that there were other ways to get it without depressing everyone. My diagnosis brought a shift in our relationship, which was noticeable on every level. We were no longer the perfect couple in his eyes. I was damaged in Seth's mind.

> <u>Red Flag Reflection:</u> Being that multiple sclerosis is a very unpredictable and terrifying disease, Seth's lack of empathy should have sent me packing my bags. Instead of caring about how I was processing this devastating news, Seth was myopically focused on his image in the community. I rightfully needed the support of my friends, yet Seth selfishly wanted me to withhold this life-changing diagnosis. Seth's need for the spotlight was overshadowed when our friends expressed their support and love for me at the dinner party.

Seth's blueprint did not involve multiple sclerosis, nor did it involve children. No room existed for the chaos that children would surely bring into his world. Seth said that he had watched his parents struggle for years and he did not want to follow that path. He felt like his parents settled in life and often said that they should have practiced law or medicine rather than settling into their chosen career paths. I was accepting of his plan to live life without children because I had never really experienced strong maternal instincts. I did not grow up with a mother in my life, and the mere thought of being someone's role model scared me.

A few months after my diagnosis, I was driving through town and began feeling nauseous. I had a strong feeling that I could be pregnant. I bought a pregnancy test, but I didn't dare tell Seth until I knew for sure. I couldn't even imagine looking him in the eyes because I knew how angry he would be if I told him about the pregnancy.

I took the pregnancy test upstairs in our master bathroom and read the box. The instructions claimed that it would take up to three minutes, but it didn't even take ten seconds. It was positive. I was pregnant. I stared at the test, and then I did what any other logical woman would do; I took another test. Sure enough, it was also positive. I was going to have a baby.

A rush of emotions filled my head. I couldn't imagine how I would share this news with Seth. The cute and creative ways that most women announced their pregnancy did not even register on my list of options. This was not a part of his desired blueprint life.

I walked out of the bathroom and tried to look at Seth, but I was afraid to meet his stare. I diverted my eyes down at the ground and said, through tears, "I am pregnant." I wanted Seth to grab me and hold me. I wanted to hear that it was okay and that everything was going to be fine. I wanted him to say, "I love you, Tina! It's okay! We will make this work!"

Seth didn't do any of those things. He stared at me for what felt like eternity. He had the look that scared me—the quiet, hidden rage. He turned and walked out of our bedroom. He walked down the stairs and out the side door without saying a single word to me. He was gone before I could stop him. I stood there alone gripping two pregnancy tests in my hand.

I was hysterical and climbed into my car. As my car careened down the road, I realized that I didn't know where I was going. I called my aunt, and she asked me to pull over. She told me all the things that I needed to hear from my husband. She told me that she loved me and that everything would be okay.

After about an hour, I began my drive back home. I was emotionally drained. I went home to an empty house and did an inventory of my life. I had a huge house that wasn't a home. I had a marriage that left me feeling empty inside. I was a part of a family that appeared normal to everyone on the outside but that was the furthest thing from the truth. Now, I was pregnant, and I was frightened beyond belief.

When Seth left the house, he went on a very long run. He ran for thirteen miles because running was one way he coped when his best-laid blueprint goes awry. Several hours passed and I grew concerned. I watched the sunset as I sat on our back porch. I was alone and scared. Sadly, my instincts told me that he wouldn't leave me because that would look bad to those around us.

What should have been a joyful celebration wasn't joyful at all. Seth finally reappeared that evening but barely spoke to me. Things remained quiet and uncomfortable for several days, and we both threw ourselves into work. After about a week of the silent treatment, he took me out to dinner and handed me an expensive video camera. Seth had three ways of coping: running, drinking, and spending money. As he handed me the video camera, he muttered, "I guess you will need this now."

> Red Flag Reflection: Any healthy husband would have been overjoyed (or, at the very least, supportive!) of his wife becoming pregnant. Seth was neither of these things. While unplanned, the reality was that we were a married couple, and pregnancy is supposed to be a happy event. Seth's reaction was nothing short of chilling.

Baby Makes Three

I went through my pregnancy alone. I wanted Seth to feel the baby kick or to put his head on my belly and share my excitement about this little miracle growing inside of me. My support system became an online pregnancy forum where I shared my milestones, doctor appointments, and anticipation. I sat back and read stories from random women about how excited their husbands were. I watched these women with envy for nine months.

In the local community, Seth and I were the glowing parents-to-be; in public, he played the role so well. He was physically present but he wasn't there. If he had an audience, he pretended to be excited about his new role as a father. In private, there was a great deal of silence and isolation in my world. I convinced myself that things would be different when he met our baby. I prayed every day that things would be different.

In addition to throwing himself into work, Seth became obsessive about training for triathlons. He started preparing for his first triathlon halfway through my pregnancy and I encouraged it wholeheartedly. Triathlons seemed to make him happy and eased some of the tension in our home. As I was leaving a friend's office one day, he said a few words that would stick with me forever: "Triathlons are a recipe for divorce." At that point in time, I had no idea how much the sport would take over my life but that statement should have been an indication. It became his drug and his mistress.

During the last four months of my pregnancy, Seth would disappear for hours at a time to swim, bike, and run. He devoted long hours to perfecting his swimming techniques, and the strict training regimen was the only thing that seemed to lift his spirits. I wanted him to be happy, so I didn't object. In a way, I was relieved when Seth was gone because I had become like a thermostat constantly trying to regulate his moods to no avail.

At the end of my third trimester, I began to object to the long hours spent at the gym or swimming at the lake. My main issue rested in the fact that the distance to the lake scared me. The lake was an hour from our home, and there was limited cell phone reception. I was terrified that I would go into labor alone. My due date came and Seth was growing tired of the pressure that I was putting on him. He was quick tempered and rolled his eyes whenever I spoke about the baby or my labor. In public, it was another story. He was the eager dad who couldn't wait to meet the new baby. It was a painful and confusing time.

I was now a full week overdue, and Seth was still driving to the lake daily. I was devastated and couldn't understand how he could leave me alone. I had stayed quiet during the entire pregnancy, but this was too much to bear. He offered a compromise: I could go to the lake with him and sit in a lawn chair while he swam, biked, and ran. I agreed. My contractions were growing worse daily, but being with him seemed like a better alternative than being alone.

As I sat in the rickety lawn chair hoping that I wouldn't go into labor, I watched Seth swim across the lake until he disappeared into the distance. It became an emotional rollercoaster as I watched him emerge from the lake knowing that he was going to disappear again on a bike for another thirty minutes and then reappear again only to leave on a run. The brief periods of relief that accompanied his returns were short lived. By the end of the two-hour period, I was emotionally spent and riddled with contractions.

Some days, the contractions were almost unbearable as I sat waiting in my lawn chair on the side of the lake. Upon our arrival at home, I told Seth that I felt like it was real this time. Seth didn't even attempt to hide his annoyance with me and responded by saying that he had been hearing "this was it" for weeks in a mocking voice and tone.

Seth proceeded to go to sleep, and I sat up alone throughout the night bouncing on a yoga ball to ease the contractions. I didn't want to wake him until I was positive that we needed to go to the hospital. Through the night, I recounted a time when I had been a Lamaze partner for a friend who was a single mom and, specifically, how much love I had for a baby that wasn't even mine. I was so hurt to think that the father of my baby, my own husband, couldn't even feel a twinge of love or excitement for his own daughter.

Morning came and Seth explained that he needed to drive to his aunt's house to borrow money. It was a forty-five-minute drive from our house, and I protested loudly. I begged Seth not to leave me. I was eleven days overdue and in active back labor. I had never experienced this level of pain in my life.

Seth explained that he had checks that were going to bounce if he didn't transfer money between accounts. He insisted that I get into the bathtub to relax. He set up a bouquet of flowers to be used as a "focal point" for relaxation. In the fog of this abusive relationship, I sadly felt a small sense of relief knowing that he had listened in Lamaze class and knew about focal points.

An hour passed and I called my doula due to the pain levels and the fact that I needed someone to calm me down. I was scared and had repeatedly called Seth's phone, but he was not answering. I held myself together as I spoke to the doula, who suggested that we should come into the office to be checked.

I promptly made an excuse for Seth. I couldn't bring myself to admit to her, or to myself, that Seth had left me and that I couldn't reach him. I told her that Seth was outside getting the dogs situated so that we could leave for the hospital. I told her that I was going to wait a bit longer before coming in. I didn't want her to be angry with him. My first reaction was to protect Seth's image.

> <u>Red Flag Reflection:</u> By this point, I was so heavily manipulated by Seth that this was a glaring red flag, too, but protecting his image was beginning to come naturally to me. I knew the doula would be in the room with us for the duration of the delivery and, if she knew the truth, she would be upset with Seth, which would lead to tension. I knew that if someone expressed any type of emotion toward Seth, I would bear the brunt of his anger. Seth would accuse me of seeking attention if I told the truth, so I didn't.

Seth came home an hour later, and I was waiting on the porch in tears with a cold rag pressed against my forehead and my bag packed. I felt clammy and faint and was so relieved to see him. I had been minutes away from calling friends to take me to the hospital. The ride was excruciating with every bump that we hit in the road. Seth was finally acting loving towards me, but he was manic at the same time. I knew it was because he had just completed a major financial transaction; therefore, all was right in his world.

After thirty-two hours of back labor, I was told that I needed a Cesarean section. On April 19, 2005, we welcomed an amazing little girl, Piper, into the world. Seth became the doting dad by helping to bathe and coddle her until I came out of the recovery room. My stepmother was present and was thoroughly impressed with how Seth stepped up to the plate and took over. She admitted that she gained a new respect for him that day. I was thrilled because it validated what I had hoped for all along. Seth would surely become the father Piper deserved.

I was released from the hospital four days after my Cesarean section and Seth stopped by my favorite restaurant to pick up a to-go order and drove Piper and I straight to the lake so he could get a swim in. He reminded me that he hadn't worked out for days due to our hospital stay. My four-day old baby girl nestled onto my chest in his truck as we sat in the parking lot and napped while Seth trained. The next day, Seth began packing for a weeklong camping trip, which was centered on his triathlon. Piper and I were to accompany him on this weeklong trek. He justified the entire trip by saying that it wasn't really camping because he rented an RV.

I had staples in my stomach and newborn Piper in a sling. The 100-degree heat was almost unbearable, but I stood at each transition point and cheered Seth on the entire day. By the end of the race, I thought I was going to faint while waiting in line for the shuttle bus. I flagged down a park ranger, who gave me a ride back to our campsite. The kind man looked at me in disbelief when I told him that my baby was a week old. I stayed in bed for the next two days with my newborn daughter, and I was barely able to walk.

During my pregnancy, my multiple sclerosis was in remission but six weeks after the birth of Sarah, I began experiencing horrible eye pain and double vision. Diagnosed with optic neuritis, which is common in those diagnosed with multiple sclerosis, I began traveling to see a new doctor in San Francisco in an effort to explore treatment options. Because I was breastfeeding, I was prescribed a treatment called intravenous immunoglobulin (IVig) which was donated blood plasma versus typical multiple sclerosis medication. Each month, I would spend a day at the hospital hooked up to an I.V. and then, I would spend the next four days experiencing flu-like symptoms. Seth asked me to keep this part of our lives private and I obliged.

More Truths Uncovered about Seth's Family

Seth's parents continued to live overseas. Their initial one-year contract turned into five years before we knew it. Because Seth had bought the family home, they were insistent on living with us during summer vacations and winter holidays. I particularly dreaded my father-in-law, whom Seth and I discovered was referred to as the "pervert principal" by several former students. My interactions with him seemed to confirm that title. At a recent family gathering, Leonard told my friend Christine that he would be "picturing her in Victoria Secret lingerie" prior to turning in for the night. He hit on another friend of mine during a wine-tasting excursion and grabbed my stepmother's butt at a family Thanksgiving Day dinner celebration. Seth and I continued to address these incidents with Cleo, who listened dismissively and always changed the topic with a polished skill that told me she had been dealing with these issues for years.

I carefully crafted an email to Leonard and Cleo begging them to find a summer home after I had given birth to Piper. I craved downtime with my new baby, free from the family dysfunction. I explained that having a new baby was a huge transition for us and, as a family, we would appreciate their consideration and that we would help them find an affordable option. Seth even agreed to help them pay for a summer rental, but our request was dismissed and caused a rift between Leonard and Seth. They insisted on moving in with us for two months whether we wanted them to or not.

Then came the trips to Thailand. Robert was actively seeking a Thai bride and, except for Seth and I, the entire family began vacationing there to support him in his quest. Cleo actively claimed that Robert's depression was a result of his yearning for a wife and children. She said that Robert wanted a family and craved fatherhood. His mission to find a bride became a family project that left me dumbfounded and disturbed.

Seth's younger brother, Carter, approached us after one such family trip to Thailand and voiced his concern about his father's behavior. According to Carter, his father went missing from their hotel late one night and didn't return until the next day. The entire family suspected that he had extramarital relations, and the boys had even encouraged their mother to leave him.

In a subsequent conversation that Seth had with Robert, Robert disclosed that he and Leonard attended a bar in Thailand where young girls are under the counter giving men blow jobs as they drink. I was beside myself with disgust and disdain. Shortly after, Seth sent his father a scathing email pointing out these indiscretions along with the rumors we had heard about him being called the "pervert principal." This email confrontation caused a permanent rift between the two of them; on return trips to the United States, Leonard resided with Robert versus our home, where he had previously stayed. For that, I was grateful.

Seth and I had little contact with Robert after giving birth to Piper, as we were both in agreement that he was not someone we wanted our daughter around. Despite a tremendous amount of pressure from Cleo, we were united in our decision. But, every holiday brought with it tension because she wanted us to come together and pretend to be one big, happy family.

On Father's Day 2006, Piper was just over a year old, and we succumbed to the pressure from Cleo and joined them at Robert's house for a BBQ. We were only there for about an hour when things went terribly wrong. One of Robert's dogs had recently had a litter of puppies, which were about 10 weeks old. The puppies were playing in the backyard, and Piper was standing at the sliding glass door watching them. Leonard came in and mentioned that the puppies were chewing on Robert's BBQ grill cover. Robert jumped up and ran outside, where he began systematically beating each puppy one by one.

As soon as my body caught up with my mind and with the reality of what was happening, I leapt from my seat on the couch and grabbed Piper while screaming hysterically for Robert to stop. I ran through the house and out the front door with Piper in my arms. As I ran, I could hear the tiny puppies screaming in pain one by one. I felt like I was in a nightmare. I was also screaming for Seth to make him stop.

I got Piper in the car, and I was hysterical as I yelled at Seth to call the police. I ran back into the house to grab my purse as Robert reentered. "You are SICK!" I screamed at him.

"GET THE FUCK OUT OF MY HOUSE, Tina!" Robert screamed back at me. He looked like a monster, and I knew in that moment that he was capable of hurting me. Seth and I left the house and made a pact that our daughter would never be around Robert again.

Piper, at 14 months old, came home and began hitting our dogs for weeks as she mimicked what she watched her uncle do on Father's Day. I personally vowed not to go near Robert ever again, and I absolutely refused to allow Piper anywhere near him. Cleo tried each and every Christmas to pressure us into celebrating the holidays as a family. She used good old-fashioned

Catholic guilt to persuade us to "let bygones be bygones." I remained firm and refused, and Seth continued to back this decision. Cleo could choose to live in denial about the issues in her family, but I would not subject my family to their insanity.

The Financial Rollercoaster

Being with Seth was like being trapped on a nonstop financial rollercoaster with death-defying twists, turns, and drops that made one's stomach enter the throat. I began to see a pattern. Every year, sometimes twice a year, Seth would sit me down and tell me that we were losing everything. The common denominators were overspending, poor planning, and living from one bank loan to the next.

My emotions during these conversations were equal amounts of terror and relief. The terror came because he was sure to remind me of my worst fear: we would have to leave the area and move to another city. My hometown was the place I wanted to raise my children and he knew that. I felt relief because it would force us into the life that I yearned for. I wanted a nine-to-five job with a regular paycheck. I wanted simplicity. I wanted a small home with a white picket fence in a quiet neighborhood. I wanted to enjoy life. I didn't believe that things needed to be this hard.

Our home was filled with a large black cloud of stress. When Seth would come home, our daughter, age two, would run from him. Seth had not become the father I had hoped for. Unless we were in public, he barely noticed that Piper existed. She could feel his tension, and she wanted nothing to do with him. His relationship with Piper was limited to photographs and the public spotlight. It was all for show.

Every time we were on the verge of financial collapse, Seth would pull off some great feat at the very last moment. I would usually be sitting at the kitchen table staring at an $800 utility bill, and he would rush through the door floating on cloud nine to tell me how he had saved us. That meant he talked the bank into another loan, or he would just tell me that everything was going to be okay. Many times, Seth wouldn't even share details of the transaction that saved us, and I would just be instructed to "trust him." He always seemed to make the impossible possible. He also had an uncanny way of turning it all back on me for not trusting him in the first place. He would often remind me that I worried for nothing. It was constant and it depleted me mentally, physically, and emotionally.

In the beginning of 2006, I was told once again that we were losing everything. We were losing our home, the cars, and the business. I was then told that everything was fine. Seth had met with a business-savvy group of investors, and he was able to convince them to come on board and save us. They agreed to a partnership. They agreed to pay off the past debts in exchange for a fifty-fifty partnership. He agreed. It was the answer to his prayers—these people were worth millions of dollars. These were investors who could finally support his endeavor. I was relieved as I held my daughter while he explained that I would never have to worry again. I was so tired of worrying. I was tired of a lot of things by this point.

Within days of the ink drying on the shiny new contract, Seth started spending. He was in an entrepreneurial frenzy and started plans to expand the business into other areas. Seth began staying up late into the night working on our business plan and spreadsheets.

Seth started buying things that concerned me. He quickly purchased a brand-new, thirty-foot Airstream recreational vehicle, new cars for us, and we began traveling to Monterey, California to look for a new office. He was buying office equipment before we had even secured office space. On one hand, his behavior scared me, but I quickly scolded myself for doubting him. Every time I doubted him, he proved me wrong. I was becoming numb to it all.

Some people would call it denial, but I had to come to a place in my mind that allowed me to stop the constant worrying. With my diagnosis of multiple sclerosis, stress was the worst thing for me. I decided to step back from the day-to-day operations of the business. I stayed on the sidelines and did my job, but I shut down in a lot of ways. I chose to believe in my husband and trust in his abilities; he reminded me so many times that as his wife, this is what I was expected to do. Seth reported that things were fabulous and that we were set for life. While that is what I was being told, it was far from the truth.

I was five months pregnant with our second daughter at the end of 2006 when our investors called a board meeting. I was firmly instructed to attend this meeting. We arrived at the downstairs banquet room of a local restaurant and sat down while waiting for the investors to arrive. You could feel the tension in the room from the very moment they walked through the doors. One of the partners dropped a heavy file on the desk with obvious intention. It was the financials for the business. I had a feeling that all hell was about to break loose from the looks on their faces.

The primary investor, Thomas, began yelling profanities. I had never been in a board meeting where the word "fuck" was used as an adjective in every single sentence. Thomas took a break from yelling and looked at Seth from across the table as he said, "What in the HELL is wrong with you?!" The investors proceeded to tell us that they wanted out of the business. They were writing us off as a loss and walking away. The business was over.

I left the meeting in utter and complete shock. I remember looking down at my pregnant belly and feeling like the worst mother in the world. What type of chaos was I bringing this innocent little baby into? I try to believe the best in people, but it was getting harder and harder to believe in my own husband with each passing day. I walked into a meeting with the understanding that we were on the road to being millionaires, only to leave wondering how I was going to buy groceries.

What were we going to tell our employees? My mind was racing. We were weeks away from Christmas, and they were dependent on us. I was devastated. I could barely look at Seth. Thomas' question echoed in my head. What in the hell was wrong with my husband? I couldn't handle the stress of sitting through the remaining board meetings that were scheduled that week. I didn't want to be in the same room with him anymore.

> <u>Red Flag Reflection</u>: What in the hell was wrong with Seth? Thomas' question validated how I had been feeling for a very long time. This was abnormal behavior. I felt like I was in a fog much of the time, so to hear someone else say there was a problem made things begin to come into focus. This wasn't just a case of overspending. This was living recklessly at the expense of others while lying, manipulating, and showing zero remorse for the damage left in his trail of destruction.

Seth was in negotiations over the next two weeks and, once again, he found a way to continue the business. This went against every piece of practical advice that we were receiving from our friends and advisors. Seth struck a deal with the investors to trade our house in exchange for their fifty percent of the partnership. They wanted our home, which sat in a very prestigious community, and Seth would get what he wanted: the business.

I didn't want to walk away from the home because its equity didn't belong to us. It belonged to Seth's parents, and it was their retirement savings. It wasn't his right to gamble this money, and I stated this to him multiple times. I wanted to close the business and walk away from it all. I was done. I could not handle another day on this rollercoaster. I wanted to pull up the safety bar and get the hell off this ride. Seth was essentially gambling nearly $400,000 of equity, and his parents' life savings were included in that total. I cried. I screamed. I begged. He did it anyway.

It was just two weeks shy of Christmas, and we were given fourteen days' notice to vacate our home. I was five months pregnant with our second child, and Piper was only 20 months old. It was all happening so fast that it felt like a blur. I sobbed as I packed our entire 4,000-square-foot house while stepping over my daughter's Christmas presents. I was so tired of Seth, the lies, the finances, and the stress.

I had lost so much respect for Seth by this point. He showed zero remorse or concern for his parents' retirement savings. I typed up a resignation letter and emailed it to him several days after Christmas. If Seth was going to continue this flailing business, I wanted no part of his decision. I wanted no part of the world that he was creating.

I hadn't just lost respect for Seth in terms of finances; I was at a loss for how to understand the way he treated our employees. We had an incredibly dedicated staff cheering for us and making great sacrifices to stand by our side. They worked long hours away from their families and were risking their own financial futures. Our loyal staff members wanted to believe in Seth, but it was becoming increasingly difficult to trust his promises. He began bouncing paychecks on a regular basis, which caused obvious concern and turmoil in the office. He had zero empathy for the staff members and seemed annoyed as they expressed their rising doubts. I needed to step back from all of it, or I knew our marriage would ultimately meet its demise.

We moved into a three-bedroom rental home in a normal neighborhood. It was nothing fancy, but it was perfect in my eyes. It was what I wanted. It was a neighborhood where children rode their bikes, and neighbors waived as you walked by. I was content. We could afford this house, and we could live within our means. I prayed the rollercoaster would come to a halt.

I could tell that Seth wasn't happy with the house, but I hoped that, with time, he would come around. My due date with our second daughter was just around the corner, and I was consumed with preparing for the baby. After a few months of being in the home, we had a baby shower, which he was strongly against.

Our first baby shower had been a very showy production at a local winery with about seventy-five people from the business community. There was wine flowing, catered cuisine, sushi boats, and presents. In some ways, I felt that the baby shower was Seth's way of coping with the drastic shift our life was taking. He could show off his pretend wealth.

This baby shower was different. Seth had nothing to show off, and it made him uncomfortable. Days before the shower, he took me car shopping, and we drove off the lot with a shiny new Mercedes. Buying new vehicles pacified him in many ways. The house may not have been impressive, but the new Mercedes in the driveway would let people know that Seth was still at the top of his game.

I was glowing at the shower, and it wasn't only because of my pregnancy. I was surrounded by my friends, and I didn't have to pretend to be someone that I wasn't. I could connect with people over real things. Seth didn't feel the same, which was apparent by the amount of alcohol he consumed that night and by the extreme hangover that lasted for the next two days.

I gave birth to my second daughter, Sarah, in the spring of 2007. She was such an easy baby and came into the world with a sleep schedule any mother would envy. When I thought about my baby girls, my heart was content and overflowing with joy. I loved every moment of motherhood. I threw myself into play dates, baby yoga classes, and every Mommy-and-Me class that I could find. When I thought about my marriage and my future, I felt desperate, hopeless, and filled with sorrow. I was petrified when I thought of my daughters growing up in such a dysfunctional environment.

Within two weeks of the birth of my daughter, Seth's mistress struck again. He packed us up and we headed for the weeklong camping trip at the lake for his annual triathlon. This time, I had a Cesarean section, a two-year-old, and a newborn infant. Surprisingly enough, this year felt easier because I had become more robotic. In addition, I had requested a pain pump at my incision site, which would allow me to be more mobile while camping.

Seth was very good at manipulations, and I was conditioned to buy into them. By the time we left for the camping trip, I was convinced that he was a hero with a brilliant plan to help me relax. Seth explained that if I were home, then I would inevitably be doing laundry, dishes, and cleaning. Being at the lake would force me into rest and relaxation. The week was nowhere near relaxing, and I ended up cooking a huge pasta feast for a group of fifteen triathletes.

We only lasted in the rental home for about six months before Seth began getting restless. He was drinking a lot on the weeknights and training for triathlons on the weekends. We barely saw him. I brought the issues up multiple times and was met with the same argument: he hated this life, and he needed something more substantial to show for his long hours and hard work. He felt like he was settling and hated not living up to his full potential.

Seth suggested that I move into our spare bedroom after Sarah's birth. He had insomnia, and our new baby was waking him up throughout the night. After two pregnancies, I was no longer the 115-pound trophy wife that he needed. The attempted prenuptial agreement flashed through my mind multiple times. The pressure to return to my bikini model body was overwhelming. Our relationship by this point was that of two roommates who barely spoke to each other. It was the unspoken things that hurt the most.

The next phase of our lives began over breakfast at our local coffee shop. It began innocently with Seth skimming through the real estate section of the newspaper and making comments on home prices. From there, it turned into looking at homes when we had time to kill. Within a few weeks, Seth had a real estate agent and was actively looking at homes. These weren't just any houses. They were very high-end, expensive houses.

We agreed to set a limit and eventually reached a compromise when it came to what we would spend on a home. I didn't want to be a slave to our mortgage, but Seth could no longer handle the embarrassment of living in our rental home. He began pointing out every minor thing that was wrong with the house, from the sound of the recycling center nearby to the cookie-cutter homes that all looked the same. I dreaded the negativity that saturated our home life.

One day, Seth came home and told me about a gated community that he had just discovered. He begged me to drive through the neighborhood with the real estate agent just to look. We were met with a magnificent gate and a guard who eagerly greeted this all-American family in a new Mercedes Benz.

We proceeded to drive through this mind-blowing neighborhood with tennis courts, plans for an equestrian center, lakes, trails, and million-dollar homes. As we made our way through the 550-acre neighborhood with rolling hills and breathtaking vistas, I felt like crying. It was happening again.

We pulled our car into the driveway of a house that sat on the highest hilltop of the community. The real estate agent parked next to us, and I realized that I needed to hold back the tears and put on the fake smile, on-cue laugh, and trophy-wife persona.

I followed them into the house, and I was in awe. Rich people lived in homes like this. Celebrities lived in homes like this. We couldn't live in a home like this. Seth lit up. He walked through the home room by room, and I followed behind him with newborn Sarah and two-year old Piper in my arms listening to our footsteps echo in the expansive home with sky-high vaulted ceilings.

Seth looked happy as he stood outside peering over the common folk from high on the hilltop. He never looked this happy anymore. I wanted to be happy again. I craved happiness. My happiness was dependent on his mood, his day, and his world. I had accepted my reality; if Seth wasn't happy, then my life was miserable.

Seth wanted the home and I knew it. I was smart enough to see the pattern at this point in our relationship. If he wanted this home, he would get it come hell or high water. If this were what it took for him to be happy, then I would support him. He claimed that he could make it work and told me all the reasons why this was such a smart investment and a turning point for us.

The Big House and a Fake Life

The house was currently listed at $1.2 million but appraised at $1.6 million. Seth talked over me, which I was accustomed to by this point. He used real estate lingo that he knew I wouldn't understand and rolled his eyes in annoyance when I questioned anything he said. According to Seth, we were walking into a home that had $400,000 worth of equity. That was what he owed his parents, and he knew that was a button for me.

Seth promised me that he would never touch the equity. He promised that he would never refinance the house again. I even made him say it out loud because I wanted a verbal guarantee. He sold me on a plan to repay his parents' retirement money with the purchase of the home. Seth continued to look irritated when I pressed him to understand how we could afford this.

It was the same look that Seth always gave me, which implied, "You are so stupid. Leave the money and business decisions to me." His perfect SAT scores, his pre-med background, and his college education—by this point, he didn't even have to remind me that I was beneath him. Who was I to question him? I wanted to believe Seth. One month later, we moved into the home.

Within a week of moving into the massive home on five acres, the spending spree began. Seth had a credit score of 800 and a lot of credit cards. He wanted to take a trip to my sister's house and shop for furniture along the way. He was on a wild euphoric high and was happier than I had ever seen him. Seeing Seth happy was a huge relief. He claimed that business was booming and life was good, and I bought every word that left his mouth.

We bought everything that we needed to furnish the house in one weekend: a massive dining room table, three huge chandeliers, a $10,000 bedroom set, couches, art, patio furniture, and everything else that we could find. Seth was unstoppable. If he was this confident in the business and in our new life, then I needed to believe in him. I needed to believe in him to make our marriage work. Many would coin this as denial. I had become just like Cleo.

I jumped right into our new life. I hired an artist to create a masterpiece fit for a princess on Piper's bedroom wall. It was a huge Candy Land™ mural, and it was truly spectacular. At two years old, Piper's bedroom was bigger than most living rooms. I kept myself busy decorating the girls' bedrooms and playroom with extravagant purchases. I threw myself into the role of a wealthy, stay-at-home mom but the reality was that I was too embarrassed to have other moms over to our house. Seth liked to rub his material possessions in everyone's face but I was the opposite. I was embarrassed by our lifestyle.

I started my own business in December 2007 and it became like another child to me. I put my heart and my soul into it. It was mine. One of the most difficult parts of my marriage was our mutual business. When it was doing well, Seth took all the credit. When it was failing, everything was my fault because I pushed us to start the business in the first place. I wanted something of my very own that he couldn't take credit for.

My business was a hit in the local media; it was on the front page of every newspaper in town. I had a dream home, fancy cars, amazing little girls, and a new business that helped me to forget the unhappy feeling that I had whenever I thought of my marriage. I kept myself busy and tried to compartmentalize the emptiness that I felt.

About six months after we moved into the home, my younger brother came to stay with us for a week. One night after dinner, we took a family walk through the community. My brother and I were walking up ahead of Seth and the girls when my brother said words that I will never forget. "You aren't happy. I hate seeing you like this. You need to make a change," he told me. I agreed with him, but I didn't know how to change my situation. I was trapped in a marriage void of emotions and, most importantly, love.

Seth hadn't hugged me in six months and our intimate life was non-existent. We had not had sex in almost two years because at 125 pounds, Seth no longer found me attractive. After two babies, I had retained ten pounds, but to Seth, it was one hundred pounds and it disgusted him. Most nights, he slept on the couch.

Gifts from Seth now consisted of exercise videos, books on how to get rock-solid abs, and a new bike. I didn't even ride bikes. The silence between us was deafening, but I was the only one who seemed to care. I didn't know how to escape, and my youngest daughter was only nine months old at the time. I could keep the fake, happy wife image up for our friends and the community, but I couldn't fool the people who truly loved me and knew me. My brother saw through it all.

Worse, I was beginning to doubt my sanity. I had always prided myself on my crystal-clear memory but I felt that slipping. I once walked into the kitchen and opened our junk drawer to discover it was filled with our silverware. I questioned Seth about it, and he looked at me like I was crazy. He told me that he had switched those months ago, which left me dumbfounded. I attributed it to stress.

One afternoon during a rainstorm, our roof began to leak and there was water pouring down the wall. I immediately called Seth to ask him what to do, and he unleashed on me, "God dammit, Tina! I told you to remind me to have the gutters cleaned!" What. The. Fuck. Was. He. Talking. About? I was frozen by the accusation and, at the same time, it gave me clarity. Seth had never spoken to me about the roof or the gutters. That conversation had never happened. I remembered the junk drawer incident, and I instantly knew that Seth had made that up. I didn't understand why but something clicked for me that day.

> <u>Red Flag Reflection</u>: *Gaslighting* was a term that I discovered years later; however, it was what I was living and, over time, it broke me down and made me question my sanity. There were several times that I wrote down Seth's instructions on projects just to ensure that my memory didn't fail me, which would result in his rage or silence.

Gaslighting is a way that an abuser psychologically manipulates to gain power or control. The abuser may move things in your home and then pretend you are crazy. They may turn on a light that you turned off and then claim it has been on all night. They may attack the foundation of your being or go for your deepest wounds. Seth's constant insinuation that I was bipolar like my mother wore on me over time, and I questioned myself anytime a single tear fell. Often the gaslighter will praise their victim one moment and tear them down the next, which keeps them off kilter. This was a part of the rollercoaster I was living. The praise was like throwing me a morsel of hope that I could win his approval if I was happier, skinnier, prettier, more loving, or worked harder. This dynamic gave Seth control and put me in the place of wanting to earn his approval at all costs.

Cleo: Queen of Denial

After two years of estrangement from Robert, Cleo realized that we were not budging in our decision to cut all ties with Robert. The dog-beating incident on Father's Day had been the last straw for me and, aside from hearing bits and pieces about his new Thai bride from family members, we had had no contact with him for two years. In fact, he had never even met our youngest daughter, Sarah.

One day, I was on Myspace, a social media platform, and happened to see Robert's profile. Out of curiosity, I clicked through to his pictures and felt nauseous, as his entire page was decorated with photos of my children. Was this real? Why did he have photos of my daughters? Some of the photos of Piper were from years prior, but he had current photos of Sarah that he must have taken from Cleo. I was on the verge of hysterics when I called Seth, and it took three attempts before he finally answered his phone.

"Your brother's Myspace is filled with young Thai girls and pictures of our girls. I am about to lose my mind. Make him remove every photo of our daughters immediately!" I snapped at Seth, who was in a business meeting and sounded puzzled.

Seth agreed to call his mom and take care of it right away. I rechecked Robert's online profile almost every hour all day long. My mind was racing. Finally, late that evening, I discovered that he had removed all the photos of my children. I questioned how twisted and deranged he must truly be while discussing the situation with Seth. Seth shared my concern but explained that

Robert must be attempting to create a public image of a loving uncle. While I wanted to believe Seth's explanation, my intuition was that it was deeper than that; however, I let it go because it was just that—intuition.

After two years of estrangement from Robert and upon Cleo realizing that we were not budging in our decision to keep our daughters away, she sent out an email to everyone in the family:

> Dear Family - Think about how you feel holding on to this sense of wrong, self- righteousness, anger. It's been two years and six weeks now. Is it making you feel better? Is it making you a better person? Is it in the best interests of you – really? Of your family – either immediate or extended? Is it based on love? Or is it based on disappointment in the other person, hurt feelings, pride that you have been wronged, treated with a lack of respect, based on the reality or perception that someone else did not honor you and your person?
>
> So, I am going to ask each of you to do something for me. I know that you are not yet ready to forgive one another for wrongs, real and perceived. I honor that, and so I am not asking that you do that – forgive one another – nor that you let bygones be bygones and go on like nothing has happened. LOTS has happened and it's real. I am asking however, just this:
>
> When Dad and I are home for summer or Christmas, can we please be a family for those few weeks? Can we get together once a week for dinner all together – I'll buy – I'll cook even!? Can we meet at concerts in the park, or go to Mass together? Thanksgiving together? Can we share Christmas– just for that one day? Can we celebrate Father's Day (scary, I know) and have a big old bash on the 4th like the old days? Can we suspend, for what will be no more than 10 shared times per year, our hurt and anger and mistrust? I really don't care at all whether you talk to one another or acknowledge one another's existence when we're not home – that is up to you. I realize I am asking a lot. But I believe in you. While we are home, I want us to be a family. I need us to be a family. – Cleo

Upon receipt of the email, I called Seth who had just read it and was also reeling from it. Seth had never stood up to Cleo, and I felt a sense of relief that we were on the same page when it came to this topic. All four of the boys in the family held Cleo on a pedestal and seemed to worship the ground that she walked on—admirable in a healthy family, but this was not a healthy family.

An hour later, and to my amazement, I was bcc'd on an email that Seth had written to Cleo on his own accord. I read it in disbelief. Seth stood up to his mom and confronted the situation head on, which earned him a great deal of respect from me.

> Hi Mom,
>
> I left Robert a message early last week on his cell. Once a year or so I encourage him to write an apology and let "bygones be bygones." His anger, comments about "fags" and fat women, resentment toward me (likely a deep-rooted jealousy of my career success, finding a cute blonde girl that he deliberately tried to sabotage, my credit ability, etc.), and his poor judgment. His beating dogs which our daughter repeated for two weeks. Scarier was at Applebee's where he talked about raping and killing Savannah.
>
> Cumulatively, any licensed counselor or psychiatrist would agree he needs counseling and maybe meds. Until he apologizes to Tina even in email, until he acknowledges and begins working on his anger and ending his redneck statements about gays, women, etc., we do not want his influence or interaction with our daughters. That is a simple reality. Uncles and aunts have tremendous influence on nieces and nephews. Attitude is an even stronger influencer. Successful families have successful offspring. Somewhere or sometime, he let anger interfere with his potential.
>
> I am sorry that you are the most affected. Robert was the Senior Class President. Yet, he has two friends left – what happened to all these friendships? He makes sure everyone who isn't on his agenda "is done." Certainly, he has described us this way yet his Myspace account and his Thai world painted an altogether different projection of Robert – our girls were all over his site.
>
> Robert is on a pathway to becoming a cantankerous hermit. His decisions cause the alienation – one friend or family member at a time. He needs counseling. Get him to go, and then we can get back to being a family. -Seth

The IRS Comes After Us

While Seth could fool banks and people, he wasn't above the Internal Revenue Service. I was in my home office one day, and I came across a notice from the IRS. It was partially hidden by one of Seth's file folders. The notice claimed that he owed a lot of money. The amount of arrears was over $150,000! I called him and demanded to know what was happening. Seth laughed at me with that condescending, evil laugh that I hated so much. The laugh that he used to remind me that I was nothing and that I was intellectually inferior to him. I was beneath him.

Seth said that I was crazy and accused me of overreacting. He loved to cite my childhood issues to deflect the spotlight off of himself. Seth again reminded me that my mother was bipolar and instructed me to calm down. He claimed that it was an error on their part, that the IRS had denied a carry-forward loss from 2003 that was completely valid and that he just needed to fax them a few papers to clear it up. I wanted to believe him.

Believing in Seth meant that I didn't have to live with that pit in the bottom of my stomach. It meant that I could focus on my daughters, my health, and my business. Sometimes, living in denial was easier and less painful than living in my current reality, but, unfortunately, the reality of the IRS was smacking me upside the head.

We had been living in our fantasy world for one year when I received a call from my nanny. Two women from the IRS had been to our house asking for Seth and left their business cards. I frantically called him and again; he dismissed it and said I was overreacting. He agreed to call the IRS but discovered that the agent was off for three days. Within hours of that phone call, we discovered that the IRS had frozen our bank accounts. Everything was frozen.

I tried to remain calm. I reminded myself that we had plenty of credit cards, which would get us by until he was able to clear things up. I started calling the credit card companies to inquire about our limits and interest rates. One by one, I discovered that every single card was maxed to the limit. Some were over the limit and some were past due. I dug deeper and discovered that our utilities were all past due and our water bill hadn't been paid in three months. All at once, it felt like I was being buried alive in a financial avalanche.

By the end of summer, Seth was still dealing with the IRS and nothing had been resolved, as he had promised. During that time period, I watched Seth lie to employees and string people along. I watched as the employee's financial worlds were crumbling down around them. I begged Seth to find a job and walk away from this lifestyle. I begged him to stop pretending and get real. I begged him to start being honest with people but he couldn't. Being honest and doing the right thing were never on the list of options for him.

Later that summer, Seth was scheduled to compete in a half Ironman® race on the east coast. He mentioned the race one morning, and I couldn't believe that the words were leaving his mouth. Our bank accounts were still frozen. We were borrowing money to pay our utilities and health insurance, yet he was trying to convince me to fly across the country to run a race? Seth told me I was being ridiculous because the trip had been paid for in advance. It was insane NOT to go, according to him. The plane tickets were paid for. The beach house was paid for. The race was paid for, and he was actively trying to justify the vacation. We hopped on a plane with the girls in tow and flew all the way across the country for his race.

The first two nights at the beach house were fine. Seth was in his element. It was his race and his mistress; it was everything that mattered most to him. He was a world away from the IRS nightmare. Seth lived and breathed triathlons. I was in second place in this race and, while that was unspoken, we both knew it as truth.

On the third day of our vacation at the beach house, there was a knock at the door. Seth quickly slipped out of the door to talk to the manager of the resort. Despite his best efforts, I could hear the conversation. The manager informed Seth that his credit card was declined. I then overheard Seth's lies. He claimed there must be a mistake. Seth went on to say that he had perfect credit and that money wasn't an issue. They walked further away from the beach house to discuss the situation, and I could no longer hear their voices. I was petrified. We were thousands of miles away from home, and we had no money. I sat looking at my babies, and sorrow filled my heart. They were so little and completely oblivious to this hell that surrounded them.

I could no longer deny my inner voice. What was I doing? I had two choices: I could stay in this marriage and pretend for the sake of the girls, or I could get out and protect them from this dysfunction. Could I really live with myself if I showed my daughters that this is what marriage was all about? How would I survive if I left Seth? He had beaten such self-doubt into my head for years that I felt completely dependent on him.

Seth came back into the beach house and was fuming. They wanted us out. They wanted us to pay or to leave. Seth grabbed his phone and his wallet and slammed the door on his way out. I started packing our things while trying to figure out whom to call. I was sobbing and knew that I needed to stop because I had reached the point where I refused to let him see me cry.

We didn't know a single person on the East Coast. I was cycling in and out of emotions. There was anger, sadness, fear, and then back to anger. How could he put us at risk again? How could he lie to me again? Why were we on vacation when our entire world was falling apart? What man would put their family at risk like this? Who was I married to? Seth returned thirty minutes later. We stayed that night in the beach house and flew home the next day, back to reality.

The IRS saga went on for over six months. We hired a top-notch accounting firm to represent us and, thankfully, we were assigned an IRS auditor who formerly worked in our industry and understood our books. Seth was correct in that we really didn't owe the IRS bill, but by the time that was proven, we had lost everything. In the end, we only owed the IRS a whopping $383 but had accumulated $20,000 in debt to the accounting firm who worked around the clock to save us. We hadn't paid our mortgage or bills in six months, and life as we knew it was over.

There was a period in which I couldn't even look at Seth. I was so hurt and so angry. He procrastinated on anything that involved paperwork unless it generated money. Had he just addressed the issue when the problem first presented itself, it would have never escalated to the point of no return. Had he not spent all his time at the gym or on the couch drinking beer, he could have dealt with this issue.

I was also angry because I knew that Seth felt more powerful than the IRS and had ignored their letters, calls, and notices just like he did everything else. He was above the IRS and that feeling only intensified when he was able to prove them wrong. We lost our home, our cars, and both of our businesses. He was myopic on the fact that he had been right and had no ability to self-reflect and own up to his part of it. Now he was bitter, angry, and drinking obscene amounts of alcohol each night.

They say that a crisis will show a person's true character. I sat back and watched as Seth borrowed money that he knew we couldn't pay back. I watched him write checks for thousands of dollars when his account was already overdrawn. I watched Seth give employees their paychecks knowing that they would never clear. I watched him manipulate, lie to, and cheat people I cared about.

One day, I overheard a bank teller accuse Seth of check kiting and had to look up the definition of this when I returned home because I was clueless. I officially learned the terminology for what had become common practice for Seth. I now knew that what he referred to as "transferring money" was actually an illegal practice that could put him behind bars.

My "a-ha moment" hit me like a ton of bricks. I was married to a con man. I had lost all respect for my own husband. The people who once trusted Seth were shown no mercy. Some people lost $500 and others lost $100,000. Not only did Seth fail to show remorse for his actions, he played victim to anyone who would listen. He blamed everything on the IRS and seemed to believe the reality-twisting, skewed version of the story that he was telling. Listening to him talk about it all once again made me question my own sanity.

Narcissistic Personality Disorder

I decided to contact a local therapist to start marriage counseling. I knew if Seth refused, I could personally use someone to talk to. Seth refused, so I made an appointment to see a local therapist and spent a full hour explaining the dysfunction of our world. I was trying to understand the deep deception and lack of remorse, along with the other pieces that kept me awake at night.

I wanted to understand Seth, and I wanted to help him. After an hour of talking to the therapist, she calmly got up from her chair and crossed the room. She took a book off her desk and walked back over to me. She opened the book and held it out for my review. The words she was pointing to read "narcissistic personality disorder."

Narcissistic personality disorder (NPD) is "a pervasive pattern of grandiosity (in fantasy or behavior), need for admiration, and lack of empathy, beginning in early adulthood and present in a variety of contexts, as indicated by five (or more) of the following" (American Psychiatric Association, 2013, pp. 669-670):

- Demonstrates a grandiose sense of self-importance (i.e., exaggerates achievements);
- Is engrossed in fantasies of unlimited success/power, brilliance, beauty, or ideal love;
- Thinks he is "special" and can only be understood by, or associate with, other "special" or high-status people;
- Requires excessive admiration from others;

- Has a sense of entitlement (i.e., expects automatic compliance with his ideas/behaviors);
- Is interpersonally exploitative (i.e., takes advantage of others for his own gain);
- Lacks empathy (unable to recognize or care about the feelings/needs of others);
- Is often envious of others or believes others envy him; and/or
- Demonstrates arrogant behaviors/attitudes.

I read the description, and it sounded a lot like Seth. It also described a striking resemblance to his father. A huge sense of relief washed over me. If I knew what the problem was, then we could solve it. I stared up at the therapist and said, "Alright, what do we do next?" I waited for her to give me the magic potion to fix him. Ann looked at me and shook her head. "This is a personality disorder," she explained. "You can't fix it. You can either accept to live with it, or you leave. He won't change," she said. I was confused and furious. How dare she say that he couldn't change? Everyone can change if they choose to. I left that appointment and cancelled my future appointments with her.

> Red Flag Reflection: I had fallen back into old habits of wanting to save the world. Even with everything that I had witnessed, I still wanted to help Seth. I went from feeling hopeless to feeling hopeful because I finally had a label and explanation for Seth's behavior. If he were to get help, I wanted to honor the vows that I had taken six years before. I still could not accept the reality of who Seth was. It was easier for me to find a new therapist than to listen to the truth. I was not ready to accept that my marriage couldn't be saved.

Decisions

I struggled for quite a while with the decision to stay or go. I verbally told family members that I planned to stay and pretend for the sake of my daughters. I saw that as my only option to protect the girls. As time went on, I knew in my heart that I couldn't pretend any more than I already had. Seven years of pretending was threatening to destroy me. Crumbling on the floor of my shower with tears streaming down each night once the girls were asleep became a common occurrence for me.

I didn't want my daughters to think that my marriage was normal. There was no affection, a lot of silence, alcoholism, and psychological and verbal abuse.

I cringed when I imagined Seth talking to my daughters the way he spoke to me, "Have you looked at the calorie content in that? When was the last time you ate a salad?" he would often say to me whether we were at home or in public.

I didn't even know who I was anymore. I doubted my ability to succeed. I believed what Seth had told me: because of my autoimmune disease, no one would ever want me. I worried about how I would survive. My business was very new, and I was dependent on Seth. One day, I sat down and wrote pages and pages of my thoughts in a journal, which was divided into four categories.

This is what I wrote:

1. What attracted me to Seth?
   - Stability: job, financial, family life.
   - Fun: going on trips and living a carefree life.
   - Thoughtfulness: cards, poems, driving 450 miles to see me on weekends, flowers, dates.
   - Being a gentleman: opening doors, etc.
   - Physical: constant hugs and affection.

2. The beginning signs that I should have paid attention to:
   - Buying the cars: Nissan 350z, Jeep, Subaru, Tundra, and Ford.
   - Borrowing money to "float" things.
   - Living in the future: I can buy it now because I will earn more on my next paycheck.
   - Elitist attitude: better than everyone around him, smarter, healthier, with more money.
   - Lying on multiple occasions: from little white lies to huge lies and false stories about his childhood.
   - Putting me down in subtle ways: lack of college degree, bipolar mother, and dysfunctional upbringing.
   - The way he treated our employees and people in general.

3. Why stay?
   - Stability for the girls: not wanting them to trek back and forth between homes.
   - Financial stability: one home versus two.

- The stigma of divorced families (for the girls).

4. Why leave?
    - Because my daughters deserve a better life.
    - Because I deserve to be happy.
    - Because I deserve to be loved.
    - The lies: I don't think he can decipher the truth from lies anymore.
    - The deception and the falsified stories relating to the past.
    - Because money isn't important to me. It's important to him. This life (cars, house, clothing) is what he wants but it isn't what I value.
    - Because I want to be in a relationship with someone who values the same things that I value: people, relationships, feelings, love, appreciation, and excitement for life.
    - The love that I once had is gone. He is not who I thought he was. I don't know who he is.
    - Saying that you love someone and showing someone that you love them are two separate things. I don't want to hear the words; I want to feel the feeling in my heart.
    - Zero physical intimacy: no hugs, no touch, nothing.
    - Complete loss of respect due to his conning people and showing no compassion or empathy.
    - Triathlons and selfishness revolving around training.
    - Drinking: I promised myself a long time ago that I would never be with an alcoholic.
    - His priorities were completely skewed.
    - Years of empty promises and zero change.
    - I am so miserable that I don't even know who I am anymore. I feel pathetic. I feel horrible that I brought my babies into this situation when I can look back and clearly see the warning signs.
    - His family: the thing that once attracted me to him is the most unattractive thing in the world to me. His family is so ill and screwed up, yet they cover their dysfunction with denial and a fake public image.
    - My daughters: I do not want them to feel like I feel in this moment. Unworthy of love, unheard, and judged.

- I want my daughters to have: compassion for people, gratitude for everything in life, and a mother and father who love each other. I want them to have fun without the constant negativity and harsh words from their father. I want my daughters to feel like they are being heard. I hate seeing the frustration in their faces when he ignores them or talks over them.
- I am so tired of the public image of the happy, kind father, and then the reality of whom we live with when the door shuts or the camera lens closes.
- I deserve someone who makes our family the number one priority. I want a partner who values me and my opinions. I am tired of being with someone so cold and selfish who doesn't take anyone else into consideration.

I needed to see the reality of my situation in black and white. I struggled to come up with any reason for staying. I didn't have writer's block when it came to the reasons for leaving. In fact, I found that the reasons for leaving were seeping out of me faster than I could capture them with my pen.

Finding a Voice

I asked Seth to go out to dinner with me. I looked him in the eyes and asked him not to interrupt me as I spoke. Any topic that was perceived as confrontational or emotional would be cut short by him speaking over me or putting up his hand and walking out of the room. I knew by taking him to a quiet restaurant, he would have to listen to me. He sensed that I was serious and did as I asked.

> "I am not in love with you," I said. "I don't know who you are, and I can't do this anymore. I want out of our marriage," I continued. "I am so desperate for love and affection that while cheating goes against every ounce of my being, I fear that I will sleep with anyone who even offers me a hug right now."

Seth looked panicked, and I saw tears in his eyes. This was only the second time that I had seen him cry. I was finally serious about leaving and he knew it. I told him that I felt alone and desperate. I was starved for love and affection. Seth finally wanted to enter counseling. I had been begging him for counseling for over a year. We started couples counseling the next week with a local psychologist. Seth was insistent upon two things: our therapist needed to be a man, and he needed to have a Ph.D.

When we began counseling, the psychologist told us that there would be both joint sessions and individual sessions. He wanted to get to know us individually and as a couple. At each couple's session, Seth would deliver a summary of what was happening in our world. He was careful to paint a beautiful portrait despite all that was really happening. I watched in disbelief.

For the first time, I stood firm and pointed out his lies and manipulations. Seth didn't know how to react because I had never taken a stand. The nervous energy coming from him made me physically uncomfortable. His jaw was clenched tightly, and his leg was shaking with an abundance of nervous energy. I was finding my voice and Seth knew it.

After several sessions, the therapist told Seth that he was unable to meet with him individually. He explained that he couldn't trust the things that Seth told him. The doctor needed me present to facilitate the truth. I had confirmation, validation, and further clarity in that moment. I wasn't the problem. Someone else saw through Seth.

We received the final notice that Seth's sacred home was in foreclosure. According to Seth, we could stay in the home free of charge until the banks bolted down the doors; but I couldn't do it. I did the calculations and the utility bills alone cost more than what it would cost us to rent a normal home. Our electric bill and gas bills each ranged between $500 and $800 every month.

Mentally, I needed to be free of this fake life. Seth was furious. He wanted to keep pretending. He wanted to stay in the home for as long as possible. I spoke to our therapist, and he agreed that it needed to end. I found a rental home and began to pack our belongings.

As I packed our things, I had a lot of time to think. I was moving out regardless of what Seth thought. I was standing up for my daughters and myself. I was finally putting my foot down. I wasn't going to live under his rule any longer. I wasn't going to live a fake life. I wanted a real life with real friends. It was empowering. I found my voice, and I stood up to him. The message was simple: we are leaving, and you are welcome to join us if you choose.

I yearned to celebrate life based on the things that matter most to me: love, gratitude, honesty, and kindness. I couldn't wait to experience those things, and I was willing to wait patiently for them to find me. I made a mental note to send the IRS a thank-you card for allowing me to shift the course of my life.

On the day of our big move, I had the equivalent of a pouting, volatile, teenage boy on my hands. Seth stomped around the house muttering under his breath how ridiculous this was and how a rental home was a waste of money. He didn't know how to handle my obvious defiance, and that was clear by his actions. On the same note, he knew that I was done, so he controlled himself more than he normally would have.

Without missing a beat, I continued packing as the movers took box after box to the truck. After seven long hours of packing and loading the truck, I was relieved to hear the moving truck door being rolled down and slammed shut. It was the sound of closure for me. It was the sound taking control of my own future for the first time in many years.

We all moved into the rental home together, and Seth began his new job search. After a few short weeks, Seth secured a job that was based out of state. We agreed that he would find a studio apartment or a bedroom to rent and that he would come home on the weekends.

Increasing Hopelessness

The week we moved into our new rental home, Seth had plans to attend a get together at his aunt Yvette's house in San Simeon. Our marriage was rocky at best, and I did not want to attend. Seth took Piper to the gathering, but he and Cleo both promised me that Robert would not be present. I ended up talking to Seth by phone and he mentioned that Robert was in fact at the event. I was so upset at the thought of my daughter being at the party with Robert present that I grabbed Sarah, got in my car, and drove 45 minutes to Seth's family's home to get her.

I entered the house, and I was fuming. I saw Robert standing with his Thai bride, Phonphan, on the balcony, and he smirked at me with that condescending look that the men in his family have mastered. I went into the kitchen and took Piper's hand, guiding her out of the house. Cleo and Lamia followed me to my car, apologizing for Robert's presence but, in the same breath, telling me that I was overreacting. I did not engage with either of them as I placed both girls in their car seats and drove home. Lamia sent me an email apologizing a few days later.

Seth and I were still attending marriage therapy together, but it was feeling more hopeless with each session. I didn't know which direction our marriage would take, but I knew that this living arrangement and Seth's new job would give me the time and space to think about what I wanted to do.

During this time, our world continued to crumble in a variety of ways. I had been in the dark about our finances for years. I knew that we had a large debt load, but the reality was hard for me to grasp. As our world began to unravel, it felt like complete and utter betrayal. I began uncovering lies and deception at every turn. There were lies to banks, lies to Seth's parents, and the worst one came when I discovered that he conned his younger brother out of almost $100,000 by using his credit to pay for business expenses. There were plenty of excuses, but the hardest part to swallow was the lack of remorse. It was never Seth's fault, and there was always someone else to blame.

The End of Our Marriage

While discussing my concerns about Seth's financial nightmare and lack of empathy for conning his youngest brother out of a small fortune, our therapist suggested that we consider a complete psychological evaluation for Seth. He advised us of the high cost, and while I saw the benefit, we agreed that it was not an option for us financially. Seth announced that week that our marriage was over. I saw how uncomfortable he became at the mere implication that something was wrong with him. This was Seth's cue to bow out of therapy and our marriage based on his need for self-preservation.

Seth called the therapist that afternoon just hours after the session and declared that our marriage was over. Seth also let me know that things had reached an irreparable level and that things between us were over. He snidely congratulated me on successfully manipulating our therapist and said he was done. The relief I felt in that moment was indescribable. Seth ripped off the Band-Aid that I so desperately wanted to remove, but I had been too paralyzed by fear of the unknowns.

One day, I ended up at a ribbon-cutting ceremony for my local Chamber of Commerce. I did not plan to attend, but when one of the Chamber staff members mentioned they were short staffed, I agreed to go. The event happened to take place at a new church in my town. I attended the ribbon-cutting ceremony and toured this amazing new facility. It was beautiful—the scenic views from the mountaintop were breathtaking. The pastor looked like the typical surfer down the street. The people were kind and very down to Earth.

I wasn't raised in a church. We went as a family when I was very young, but I barely remember the experience. As an adult, I did not attend church at all and some may have even described my viewpoints and lack of faith as atheism.

That Saturday night, I had a dream. In my dream, people were stopping me to tell me that two men whom I went to high school with were both trying to contact me. I had been out of high school for almost 18 years at that point, and I remember being very confused as to why these two people needed to speak with me in my dream.

I woke up and realized that the two people from my dream, Ben and Ryan, both had one thing in common: they were both heavily involved in their church. Ben was currently serving as a pastor in Texas, and Ryan was a musician and worship leader at a local church in my hometown. The only thing they had in common was a deep-rooted commitment to their churches and God.

As I climbed out of bed, I felt pulled to search for the service times for the church that I had visited the week before. Something was pulling me to go to church that morning. I walked into the service, and there was music playing. On the screen were the words, "written by Ryan Delmore." In my dream, Ryan was the person trying to contact me. While he didn't go to this particular church, they started and ended the service with his song. It was surreal, and I felt like it was a sign. I began attending services every week, and this church became my lifeline from that day forward.

Cohabitating

Despite everything that was happening, Seth and I were still sharing a home on the weekends. I stayed in the bedroom, and Seth stayed on the couch. We peacefully coexisted under the same roof with no formal agreement in place. For Seth, this was the perfect arrangement. He had complete freedom, yet he still got to pop in and monitor my life.

Seth and I discussed a very amicable split and nesting agreement for the girls. We weren't in a rush to start the legal paperwork, and things were so peaceful that we even went to Disneyland together to celebrate the girls' 2nd and 4th birthdays.

I soon faced the reality that not only was my marriage ending, but I was forced to close my beloved business due to finances. Within days, the local media began doing stories on my business failure and the money that I owed to customers. The press was relentlessly hounding me for interviews, and I vowed never to show my face in public again.

My plan of attack involved six boxes of Girl Scout cookies, wine, enough coffee to survive for the rest of the year, coupons for pizza, and a lot of sweatpants. I planned to pull the curtains closed and place a 'Do Not Disturb' sign on the front door while hiding under the covers.

Prompted by the media flurry, I sent an email to my clientele letting them know that my business was over. I wanted them to hear it from me before the story hit the paper.

When I was feeling down, I turned to my journals. One afternoon while I was waiting for my youngest daughter to awaken from her nap, I decided to make a list of the fifty things that I wanted in a partner. I penciled out the most desirable traits—those that would not only give me hope but would serve as my checklist for moving forward in my life. I looked over my list and knew that I would never settle again. I tucked my list away for safe keeping and promised myself that I would pull it out when the time was right.

At this time, Seth was living out of state, and I knew that he was dating other people. Surprisingly enough, it didn't bother me. I had no desire to date for the first time in my life. The knowledge of Seth dating only made the separation and impending divorce easier in my mind.

Hurting Piper

On one of Seth's weekends at home, we ended up running errands together in his car with the girls. I had just warned him that Piper, who was four years old at the time, hadn't taken a nap and was cranky. I knew Seth was in a bad mood, and it was the type of quiet anger that I had learned to fear.

I walked through the garage and into the house ahead of him carrying Sarah. Piper was upset about her jacket not being on properly and started to have a four-year old meltdown in the driveway. The meltdown wasn't the problem for Seth; it was the fact that she was threatening his image of the perfect family because neighbors were watching. He was angry because he couldn't control her.

Seth needed to stop her from being a disobedient child. He needed to remove her from the onlookers before his image was tarnished. Seth picked her up and carried her through the garage with his arms wrapped tightly around her chest. In his anger, he squeezed Piper's entire torso to make her stop crying.

I heard the commotion. I heard her cries and the garage door shutting to keep the world from seeing the imperfection. I turned to see Seth carrying Piper through the garage, and I saw the look of sheer terror on her face. I grabbed her from his arms and told him to get out of the house.

Our renter at the time, Shannon, was in the kitchen making tea. Shannon was our former nanny but she was also the girls' godmother. Shannon and I placed Piper on the counter, and she was in complete hysterics. She looked panicked and was inconsolable. I had never seen my little girl look like this. My heart shattered as I held her while she repeatedly gagged and tried to catch her breath.

I started a bath to calm her down, and Shannon and I sat and soothed her as the water filled the tub. Piper continued to gag during the bath and I felt desperate and distraught. We didn't see Seth for several days, and I made an appointment with our marriage therapist to ask for advice. I had never dealt with anything like this and was struggling with whether to report the incident to the police or to Child Protective Services.

I notified Seth that I was going to a counseling session and the chance existed that the incident might be reported. He attended the session and openly admitted what happened. The therapist told Seth to go home and talk to Piper. He said that Piper needed to hear Seth's remorse and also advised him to admit to Piper that he did something very wrong and that it wouldn't happen again.

Our therapist warned Seth that while he assumed this was a onetime occurrence, it would be reported if it happened again. I knew Seth had a temper, but I had never seen him take it out on the girls. Since I had never seen this side of Seth, I was also hopeful it was a one-time occurrence. I remembered the few times that he had become physical with me by grabbing my wrists, and it worried me.

For several months, we lived the weekend routine, and it was difficult. Seth arrived at 10 p.m. Friday nights and left on Sunday mornings. I didn't know how long that I could continue living this way but felt trapped due to finances and Seth's drinking. The biggest factor was that I didn't feel comfortable leaving the girls in his care.

With our current financial stressors and the inability to spend money on material items, Seth was only left with two coping mechanisms: exercise and alcohol. While those things seem counterproductive, Seth seemed to be able to do both in unison. I felt like I needed to stay home on the weekends even though tension between us was rising.

Out through the Back Door

One Friday night in May of 2009, I had just finished a three-day medical treatment for my autoimmune disease, which left me very ill. I was under the bed covers with the chills and a horrible headache. I was thankful that Seth would be arriving to take over with the girls. Sarah had a double ear infection, and I had been up with her much of the previous night.

I heard Seth come home around ten o'clock in the evening. An hour later, I heard his truck start up and drive away. He left knowing how ill I was. I stayed up most of the night with my little girl and her high fever. Seth never came back that night, and he failed to show up and take Piper to her gymnastics class the next morning. He called later in the morning with a horrible hangover and admitted he had stayed with a "divorcee" the night before.

I was so angry. I was angry that Seth had the luxury of choosing when to be around with no regard for me or our daughters. I was angry about the pure selfishness that had continued for nine years. I was angry about the alcoholism. I wanted him to start being responsible, and I wanted him to be a dad to Piper and Sarah. I had been waiting for four years for him to assume his role as a father, but it had not happened yet. I kept hoping that something would kick-start his desire to care about, and for, these little girls.

The Nesting Agreement

I knew our current situation had to end, so I came up with a plan that involved a great deal of sacrifice, but I was determined to make it work. I approached Seth and proposed that we begin the nesting agreement. I would wait for him to arrive on Friday nights and would then leave for the weekend. I planned to stay with friends, and I had a sense of security knowing that my children would be in their own beds at night versus bouncing back and forth between two homes. Shannon and her husband were still renting the upstairs unit above the girls and me, so I felt confident that another person would be there to keep an eye on things and alert me of anything alarming.

At the age of 36, I was officially couch-surfing on the weekends. I made the best of it. I stayed with my bookkeeper one weekend and a high school friend the next. I missed my daughters greatly. I cried a lot. I felt out of place and knew I needed to create my own support network. I needed to find friends outside of my traditional circle. I kept myself busy and my social calendar full because quiet time was my worst enemy, allowing my fears and anxiety to creep in and consume me.

I wasn't grieving in the way that you would expect. I had grieved over the loss of my marriage for two years before I left. Once I made up my mind that the marriage was over, I was done. I am an incredibly loyal person; however, I have a point of no return and I was there. I found that I was void of emotion for Seth and for the marriage. I didn't miss him, and I didn't miss our life together, but I missed my daughters greatly.

In June of 2009, Seth was going to pick up Leonard and Cleo at the airport and decided to take Piper and Sarah with him to greet his parents, who were returning for the summer. When Seth got to the airport, he ran into Robert. The girls were 2 years old and 4 years old at the time, and Sarah had never even met Robert. Seth relayed to his brother that I didn't want him around the girls and, moments later, I received a text message from Robert that said: "First off, don't make rules you can't enforce; you stupid cunt! Second, I don't need or want anything to do with your kids … you and Seth have obviously got them pretty fucked up already. So, go get a life … far away from my family; you greedy bitch!"

A Friendship Begins

After a while, a friend persuaded me to place an online ad. I kept it fairly simple and didn't include a photo. I made it clear that I didn't want a relationship but sought new friends for coffee, concerts, and laughter. Truth be told, I didn't care if they were male, female, or had three feet! I needed to create a circle of friends that were my own.

A man named Glenn answered my ad, and we exchanged multiple emails back and forth over the next week. I joked about cleaning my dryer vent, which had been taken over by sparkles and pink lint, and he joked that his dryer vent was full of sand from his teenage son. After a couple of weeks of email communication back and forth, he invited me to a coffee shop to meet in person.

I read Glenn's dating profile several times and wondered what we'd even talk about. Glenn was a park ranger, and my idea of camping was a 2-star resort. He was seeking someone who knew how to change into a wetsuit with ease and liked to hike on the weekends. He sought someone who didn't flinch at the thought of a "tick check" in the great outdoors. The thought of putting on a wetsuit weighed up there with root canals and, while I did own a pair of hiking boots, they'd never actually been on my feet. The mere thought of a tick on my body made me want to cry.

I actually felt a sense of relief because with nothing in common, the chance of us being compatible in a romantic way was slim to none. Regardless of my initial hesitations, my first coffee date in nine years was much easier than I anticipated. Glenn and I discussed our jobs and our social activities. He had been divorced for almost two years and, by most accounts, had a fairly uneventful parting with his ex-wife after 16 years of marriage and three sons. He seemed normal, pleasant, and respectful.

Glenn broke all the rules when he called me about two hours after our initial meeting and asked me to have lunch that day. Since I had just had lunch, we met again for coffee. I was more at ease over our second encounter and found him very attractive with a slight resemblance to George Clooney. Those two coffee dates were the beginning of a wonderful, magical friendship based on mutual respect, communication, and adoration. I felt more alive than I had felt in a long time.

In my heart of hearts, I believed that things with Seth would smooth out as we each found our grounding and started our new lives. I felt at ease knowing that his time with the girls would be under my roof and somewhat supervised with our upstairs tenants sharing the same kitchen and entry to the home. It gave me peace of mind to know that this was a new chapter, and I looked forward to earning my own income and regaining the power that I had lost over the years to Seth. When I told Glenn about my nesting agreement, he was impressed that two divorcing adults could actually pull off something like this. I was sincere when I told him that my divorce would be drama-free. As an optimistic person who avoids conflict like the plague, I believed this.

Part 3: Category Five Divorce Hurricane

By July, things were starting to unravel with Seth. I was increasingly concerned about leaving the girls in his care due to his out-of-control drinking. Seth's behavior was becoming worrisome. As fast as the tide can shift, Seth was alternating from telling me how worthless I was to begging for me to come back to him. The shifts and attacks were extreme, alarming, and exhausting.

At the house, there were some upcoming changes on the horizon, as Shannon and her husband were planning to move out of our upstairs unit. I didn't blame them. Thankfully, another one of our former nannies was planning to move in. Brooke loved the girls tremendously, and I felt at peace knowing that someone else I trusted would be at the home while I was away.

I was still couch-surfing on the weekends and trying to stay distracted every second that I was away from the girls. There were waves of emotions for me—a sense of freedom that I had not felt in ages, coupled with the ache of being away from my babies for the first time ever. Our finances and my health insurance needs were still preventing me from taking the legal action needed for our divorce.

Being emotionally divorced and legally separated would have to do for the time being. I felt the current nesting agreement still seemed better than shuffling the girls back and forth between two homes. Seth was still only physically present as a father, but at least he was spending time with the girls—something he rarely did on his own while we were together. I still naively held out hope that he could be a good dad to our daughters.

Shannon and her husband were just weeks away from moving out of our upstairs unit when she called me in a panic on a Saturday morning. She heard the girls crying downstairs and went to check on them around eight o'clock in the morning. She discovered that they were completely alone. Piper was trying to change Sarah's poopy diaper because she couldn't find Seth. Shannon discovered that the girls had even ventured outside, pajama-clad, looking for Seth. The girls had been left alone at 2 and 4 years old.

When I got that phone call, I was thirty minutes away and beside myself. Why would he leave two little girls alone? How long had he been gone? Where was he? What would have happened had Shannon left town for the weekend as she had done many times in the past?

I repeatedly called Seth's phone and, after three calls, he answered. I demanded to know where he was. I was waiting for his answer, and I was met with silence. I raised my voice and demanded to know where he was. "I left around 5 a.m. to work at the coffee shop and lost track of time," Seth responded calmly.

I was so accustomed to his lies that I was already one step ahead of him. There were no coffee shops in our area that opened that early. It was a lie. Tears began to flow. He seemed calm. He said that I was overreacting and that it wasn't a big deal. "Calm down … it was a few hours," he responded, in a very condescending tone. I was forced to accept the harsh reality that my daughters were not safe in his care.

His Twisted Family

On one of Seth's nesting weekends with the girls, I was informed that he had put them to bed on Saturday night, and then sat in the backyard drinking for hours. The girls began jumping on beds and playing with no supervision until our tenant noticed and alerted Seth of what was happening. Our tenant was concerned enough to notify me that this situation was becoming an ongoing issue, and she was worried about the girls being left unattended while Seth was outside drowning his sorrows. I emailed Seth to make him aware that this was unacceptable and unsafe.

Things went from bad to worse when I realized the level of manipulation that I was facing within Seth's twisted family members. Seth had given me his email passwords earlier in the year when I was sending out his resume to potential employers. One afternoon, I logged into his account and saw an email from Seth's aunt Lamia titled, "The Recent Rant: A Response." I clicked on the email and couldn't believe what I was reading.

> Seth- I think you also need to specify in your comments back to Tina that you were not in fact, "sitting outside drinking."
>
> Here is my suggested version to spin back:
>
> Tina- what you are now so upset about is not based on facts. Sad that you are so quick to jump into another of your angry rants. What you do not know is, I read the girls stories for 30 min. … and tucked them in with goodnight kisses. They were drowsy and sleepy. I remained in the house after tucking them in until all was settled and quiet. I was cleaning the kitchen … after about 25 min. of quiet, and

> a peek in their room, I went out back to do some basic weeding and to water the plants. The weather is hot. I was simply doing a little towards maintaining the yard. As I was watering the plants, I sipped on a single beer.
>
> I grow weary of your accusations and allegations based on what you wish to paint as a picture. The facts you choose to spin are false and mean-spirited.
>
> What you fail to appreciate ... is that if I am out back ... I do routinely check inside every 5-8 min. to listen for the girls. I did so on the night you are describing, and all was quiet when I went inside to check. The girls were not bouncing on the beds when I checked on them. It is clear to me that you are angry and grasping at anything to try to paint some self-serving profile of me.
>
> Let us just concentrate on an appropriate, fair, and reasonable settlement. For the record, I am just as responsible, caring, and loving towards the girls as you are. Yet, you seem to be attempting to create a wedge, and to paint me as being somehow neglectful. Your efforts to do so are very transparent. I am not in any way neglecting either of the girls' care or their safety. So, could we please move on without your vindictive attitude? - Seth (Lamia)

I felt nauseous as I read her fabricated rendition of the night in question. This was beyond lying; this was terrifying and, in that moment, I saw a glimmer of what my custody battle would entail. The next message that I clicked on was from Cleo and equally troubling.

> Seth- Regarding your letter to Tina's dad: Your first draft is heartfelt and true, but it's going to fall on deaf ears – and will very likely be used against you (inebriated at a friend's). Admitting fault in too much detail will be used against you. Think of this as a chess game; you have to outsmart her and if you react emotionally, you'll be feeding right into her game plan, NOT yours.
>
> You give them too much information, which they are not really entitled to. I know Tina has already bashed you to them, so you can't really think they are going to believe your version more than hers. - Mom

The third and final email that I saw was from Lamia. After reading it, I was paralyzed with fear by the calculating nature of this family. I wasn't embarking on a custody battle with one scary individual; I was up against an entire team of terrifying people.

> Seth, I have some steps that I think you should consider and think about maybe trying to implement ASAP! I think you should take away Tina's ability to paint you as a neglectful, alcoholic dad. So below are steps that I think you need to really ponder to salvage your personal well-being against her and relating to Tina's ongoing rants. She has clearly created quite a few issues that a court may use against you.
>
> I am suggesting these steps now to help you be prepared and totally proactive, no matter what. Given what she has been doing and putting out about you, I am having trouble trusting that she is capable of turning her feelings around. In order to defend against her charges regarding your drinking and endangering the children, I think that you would be wise at this time ... to do some things differently. *InnocentsDads.org* has listed out steps and one of them is, in fact, to stop drinking ... at least anywhere she can find out about it. More experienced dads who have been put through the divorce ringer found that mothers used this often to damn their ex-husbands. So, my advice, at least anywhere near Tina and her pals (spies) and anytime you have the girls ... do not drink! If you drink at the house ... put any and all evidence in your duffel bag and take it as trash away from the house. But even taking the bottles out, her paid spies will be reporting back to her.
>
> If Tina continues ... i.e. to destroy you emotionally and to destroy your reputation as a good dad, I think that you should be prepared to show a mediator, social worker, and/or a judge that you have done the following: 1) Do stop drinking anywhere ... Tina or her pals can see it or find bottles or caps. 2) Consider taking some evening classes RE: parenting. (I do not actually think you need these, BUT THE FAMILY LAW SYSTEM LIKES THEM.) 3) Do you have a friend/mentor who you can use to attest to your character and your great parenting of the girls? FYI: The family law system will discount family members as being biased to your side. So, you need to cultivate someone who sees you with the girls and who will attest to this if needed. -Lamia

I closed Seth's email account and could not bring myself to log into it ever again. It probably contained a wealth of information, but I had seen enough. I had seen more than enough. Those three emails provided incredible insight into this family, and the irony was that at the same time Lamia was emailing Seth with her sociopathic strategies, she was emailing me her "heartfelt support" and claimed that she was praying for me with her rosary beads.

The Involved Father

Seth was not involved as a father and had rarely attended doctor's appointments for the girls, which was a source of contention in our marriage. When our daughter had complex seizures, I had to beg him to attend the appointment with the child neurologist, and he didn't show up for her EEG or EKG appointments.

One afternoon, post separation, Seth and Cleo took the girls for the afternoon and, upon their return home, Piper mentioned that they had taken Sarah to the pediatrician. I was so confused. Piper went on to say that the appointment had to do with Sarah's hearing and speech. I was fuming when I called Seth and Cleo's phones to no avail and eventually sent them an email. They had no business taking my little girl to our pediatrician behind my back.

Cleo quickly responded with a carefully crafted email reminding me that she holds a master's degree in education and that she's worked with thousands of children over the years. She went on to diagnose my daughter, which is ironic given that a quick phone call to the pediatrician confirmed what I already knew: my daughter was developing perfectly normally, and there was no need for further evaluations or testing.

Seth was on a mission to paint himself as the involved father. Following his aunt Lamia's advice, Seth then began setting up play dates with Adam, one of our mutual friends who was a local chiropractor. Adam was a father of two children and one of the nicest people I'd ever met. Seth was doing exactly what Lamia instructed; he was cultivating a person who could testify for him. While I knew what he was doing, Adam had no idea and he took Seth's bait, hook, line, and sinker.

To someone who hasn't dealt with a narcissistic family, it may seem fairly benign that a father took his daughter to the pediatrician or that he scheduled play dates but it was so much more than that. Cleo and Lamia were trying to help Seth paint a picture of a very involved father. Cleo had advised him to think of this as a game of chess, because it was about winning for them. My fears mounted. To them, this was a game; but, to me, these were my babies.

The Sympathy Card

I opened my mailbox one morning to see a sympathy card from an old friend. It was a sympathy card for my loss — the loss of my marriage. It was one of the most touching cards I had ever received. At first, it struck me as odd but, the more I thought about it, it was completely appropriate.

I placed my daughters in the double jogging stroller and went for a run around the local college campus. Jogging had become my escape in which I was able to process the loss of my marriage, the loss of my home, and the loss of the life that I once knew. I also used this as a time to plan for my future and remember the things that I was most grateful for. My jogs allowed me to center myself and to prepare for whatever the day was going to throw my way.

One afternoon, I was jogging on my normal route, but everything looked different on this particular day. The campus was bustling with incoming freshman and their parents. I ran past moms who were walking and laughing with their daughters, and we shared the smile that only mothers can share. I could almost see a tear forming as one mother looked at my young daughters. It was an unspoken message in her eyes: time flies, so enjoy every moment.

As I ran past the college dorms, I felt a sense of sadness wash over me. This time, the tear was in my eye. There were many tears in my eyes as I ran. The reality of the impending divorce hit me like a ton of bricks. Was I robbing my daughters of the experience of walking hand-in-hand with two parents on the first day of college? Reality came rushing back to me: my family was broken. Seth was broken. I felt the weight of the world on my shoulders, and I felt guilt in a way I had never felt it before.

I continued running with more momentum and an intense urgency to be free of the college campus. I remembered the sadness in my marriage and the sense of despair I felt for so many years. I remembered the tension and the arguments, the loneliness. I cried as the memories flooded into my head and I allowed myself to feel the loss. I allowed myself to grieve for my failed marriage, but I also let go of the guilt in that moment. I knew I made the right decision.

With each passing week, my desire to form real friendships became more intense. I had many "friends" in the community but didn't have real friendships. My world had been one of pretend for so long. I was forbidden to talk about anything real during our marriage. I had been lonely and void of a real relationship for a very long time. I was like the plant that had been forgotten about in the corner—withered, frail, and barely holding on.

Seth's Bargaining Chip

Due to my autoimmune disease, Seth had convinced me that we should separate permanently but not file anything formal with the courts. He knew health insurance was his main bargaining tool to keep me in line. If I was going along with his plans, then everything was fine, but if I stood up to Seth, then he would threaten to call his employer and have me dropped instantly. My only fear in formalizing our divorce was my need for medical treatments.

I dreaded opening my computer because of the constant slew of harassing emails from Seth. I never knew what to expect. One day, I woke up to an email in which he begged me to reconsider. He had recently discovered my friendship with Glenn and he was beside himself. I was confused because I knew that Seth was dating and we had even joked about older "cougar" women being attracted to him.

In the email, Seth wanted to whisk me away to a resort for couple's counseling. Seth claimed that he saw a sign while running on a trail. He saw two doves at a 2,000-foot elevation. He repeated his victim story to me; he failed in every direction. He lost everything, and now he was losing his wife. Seth wanted another chance.

I had been in this position with Seth so many times. I would often fall for the emotional email, the charm, the apology, and the manipulation. Seth would whisk me away to Hawaii, Jamaica, Canada, Washington, Las Vegas, Oregon, Florida, New York, or Chicago to fix whatever relationship ailment that was affecting us.

If we had a fight, then I could almost count on finding plane tickets soon after. After the vacation, things would return to normal, which meant lonely, sad, and empty. Void of feelings. Void of affection. Void of love. That was what our normal looked like.

This email was different. Seth's attempt to charm me didn't work anymore. The link he sent to a high-end couple's retreat didn't work, either, and in fact,

I didn't even open it. This particular email from Seth arrived on the heels of a vicious email attack just twelve hours before where he told me that I hadn't looked good naked in four years. He then proceeded to tell me he was selling my bedroom set, and I could find a sleeping bag for all he cared. I was emotionally dead when it came to my relationship with Seth.

I also finally saw the manipulation in his words. How can you tell someone that you hope they choke on their breakfast and then flip a switch hours later and confess that you cherish them as much as the air that you breathe?

> Red Flag Reflection: Heavy manipulation had always worked in the past. Seth knew that doves have a great deal of meaning to me. When my youngest daughter had her first seizure, I was leaving my house to see a child neurologist, and I was an emotional wreck. As I was pulling out of our gate at an early morning hour, a dove flew straight up to my window and hovered there. Time stood still as the dove made eye contact with me and seemed to freeze in midair. In that moment, I had a sense of calm wash over me, and I knew in my heart that my daughter was going to be okay. Sure enough, her test results were normal, and there was no need for medication or further testing.
>
> Ever since that day, doves have been a calming force for me. I hear a cooing and it reminds me to stop, breathe, and be thankful. By sending me an email talking about doves and fuzzy bunnies, Seth was trying to tug on my heartstrings. He was trying to use doves to manipulate me.

Seth wanted one last dance. I didn't. I was the dove flying out of the cage of unhappiness.

The Downward Spiral

The weekend of Friday, August 14, 2009 was a special one for me. My friendship with Glenn was growing stronger, and I was excited to have him meet my sister and her family. I felt at peace leaving for the weekend because Brooke was moving into our house that day. I knew that she and her family would be around all weekend. Brooke had helped to care for the girls since they were very young, and I had complete confidence that she would keep an eye on things.

On Saturday afternoon, I received a chilling text message from Seth. The message read, "This is where I brought you from." Attached was a photo of the tiny, one-bedroom home where I lived when I first met Seth. He had driven twenty minutes out of his way to capture a photo of my old house. He often felt the need to remind me where I came from, but it concerned me that he went to this extent while my daughters were in his care.

That same evening, I received a panicked call from Brooke. She had snuck away to call me despite being threatened by Seth to remain silent. Through tears, Brooke informed me that the entire house had been stripped bare by Seth. He removed all my possessions and our mutual furniture. He took all the things that my daughters were familiar with in our home. This behavior was so bizarre that Brooke was scared to be in the home but even more afraid to leave the girls alone with him.

Seth had orchestrated a grand plan knowing that I was leaving town for the weekend. His aunt Lamia was on standby Friday night, and they loaded a moving truck almost as soon as I left the house. They took my bedroom set, my living room set, my dining table, my artwork, and they even took the photos of the children right off the walls. They took over $20,000 worth of my possessions, but it was the loss of the photos that hurt the most.

On Saturday morning, Seth insisted that Brooke meet him for coffee. This was the very day that she was moving in. Brooke said that Seth looked bizarre and manic. He was shaking and stuttering as he threatened to evict her if she told me what was happening in the home. He told her that I was cheating on him and all this promiscuous behavior was taking place in front of our daughters. She was afraid of Seth but called me anyway and began making plans to move out of our house on the very day that she was moving in.

I cried a lot that night. Some tears were over the material things, but the tears had more to do with the stark realization that I was beginning a terrifying journey with an incredibly unstable person. I cried for my daughters. At two and four years old, I couldn't imagine the confusion that they were experiencing while watching our entire house being stripped bare before their very eyes.

I promised myself that I wouldn't return to the house and react because I knew that was what Seth wanted. I found it ironic that Seth ruined our marriage by being so consumed with materialism and, now, material priorities were driving his actions in a sadistic way. He needed to win. He needed to show me that without him, I was nothing.

I had a full day to process the information before I returned home. I had mentally prepared myself before walking through the front door. I entered the house and hugged my daughters and, in that moment, nothing else mattered. While I felt like I had prepared myself, I wasn't equipped to deal with the twisted reality of what Seth had done.

Bizarro World

Seth had replaced my elegant Ethan Allen bedroom furniture with a toddler bed from IKEA and matching dressers. Not only did he purchase children's furniture for me; he had personally decorated my bedroom. I was in shock and disbelief. I felt like vomiting as I looked around. I could barely breathe.

In that moment, I believed he was more psychotic than I could have ever imagined. There were little pink dress-up boas hanging from my mirror. Seth bought stuffed animals and a comforter designed for a little girl. There were little pink, apple-shaped knickknacks lining my dresser. He had framed photos of me as a child and displayed them throughout the room. Under the glass that sat on top of a dresser, Seth had created a photo collage using photos of me as a child, photos of my siblings, and random photos of me dating back to the beginning of our relationship. Strategically placed on the pillow of my new toddler bed was a book titled, *The Proper Care and Feeding of Husbands*.

I yanked open the dresser drawers one by one and discovered that all my skirts, shorts, and undergarments were missing. Seth stole my underwear. What kind of a sick, demented person steals someone's underwear? The gears had shifted to the next level, and I was now scared for my personal safety. I prayed that this was a nightmare that I could wake up from, but I knew it wasn't a dream.

It took me several days to process what had happened. I felt as though I was in a thick fog. I then discovered a video that Seth had taken of the girls' reaction the next morning as they toddled out of their bedroom. Seth appeared to be more manic than I had ever seen him while speaking in a bizarre, *Mister Rogers' Neighborhood* type of voice, "GIRLS! This is ALL for YOU! Do you like it? This is YOUR furniture and no one else's! Isn't that neat?! You have your OWN FURNITURE!!!" Piper walked through the house appearing confused and made her way to the kitchen. Noticing that our beautiful, grand dining table had been replaced by an old, outdoor table and cheap folding chairs, she asked in a confused tone of voice, "Where is our table, though?" Seth quickly turned the camera off and the tape ended.

As the tape ended, a panic attack ensued. I wanted to run screaming from the house. I wanted to bundle my daughters up and protect them from this madman. I was frozen and traumatized and, for all I knew, Seth had hidden cameras to capture my reaction. A million thoughts rushed through my head that left me feeling paralyzed. I knew I had to file for divorce and that I needed to beg the courts to protect me.

Filing

On Monday night, I printed the packet to begin divorce proceedings and stayed up late into the night preparing them. I arrived at the courthouse 30 minutes after they opened and soon discovered that I was 30 minutes too late. As I took my place in line, I realized that Seth had beat me there. He was already at the window speaking to the clerk and didn't know that I was behind him. I watched him manically waive his arms around while talking to the court clerk. She was staring back at him with wide eyes while he was shoving photos up against the glass for her to see. He was showing her photos that he hoped would prove his wife's infidelity.

I stood there in utter disbelief. These were photos of me with friends. I had never cheated on him. He had downloaded my personal photos from my computer. Even scarier, Seth sounded like he believed this wild story that he had concocted. He filed for divorce minutes ahead of me and appeared startled when he finally saw me. He walked past me with an instantly smug look that had quickly replaced the victim mask he had been wearing just moments before.

I stepped forward to the window, likely looking as if I had just had the wind knocked out of me. I stuttered, "Umm…I…I…was going to file for divorce, but I think he just beat me to it." I motioned to Seth's paperwork that she was holding in her hand. She stared back at me with a look of compassion and concern, leaned forward to the small glass cutout, and whispered, "Do you want a restraining order packet?" "Yes," I stammered. "I think I do."

I walked to my car in complete shock. I opened the door to the backseat, climbed in, and curled up into a ball, crying hysterically for what seemed like an eternity. I didn't even know who Seth was. He seemed to derive pleasure from causing me pain. I hate conflict and Seth knows this. Seth thrives in conflict and seems to obtain a weird high from it. I thought back to the financial rollercoaster and recounted his manic episodes during heightened conflict, which increased even more when he had a perceived win. It was a terrifying realization to think that I was going to battle against this unstable man.

Seth had been planning everything for months. He had planned the weekend to strip the house bare. He had planned to play victim. He knew that taking the furniture while we were married would protect him from dividing the assets. Seth took everything and then filed for divorce. The deception ran deep and I knew that we were operating on two different playing fields.

My Stalker is my Husband

I quickly discovered the flaws in our system when beginning the outreach to obtain a restraining order. Each phone call was met with the same questions, "Has he threatened to kill you or has he physically harmed you?" The answer was "no" because he was too smart for that. I knew that he would slit my throat if given an opportunity, but that wasn't enough to get me a restraining order. Within a week, I began sleeping with a hammer under my pillow and an industrial-sized can of mace that my dad mailed me.

Beep. Beep. Beep. The sound of incoming text messages began to make me cringe. He loved to inundate me with messages that told me I was white trash. Looks were the only thing that got me anywhere. I was a slut. One text message said, "All I care about is making you answer to your conscience." The messages went on and on. Sometimes I could shrug them off; other messages left me on my knees crying and begging for someone to help me.

One night in August of 2009, I heard Seth's dog howling in the middle of the night. It was a specific howl that she only made when Seth came home. I sat straight up in bed with my heart racing. I sat silently in the dark holding my hammer and mace. Even though he was supposed to be four hours away, I knew he was outside my home. I was wide awake for the vast majority of the night only dozing off a few times here and there. I mentally reviewed my options and decided that calling the police to report that my dog howled in a way that concerned me would be met with the same resistance that I had with the intake operator at the women's shelter.

Morning came and I got my daughters ready for Sarah's doctor appointment. We were gone for just over one hour and, during that time, Seth entered the house and took every court document that I had. These were documents that I had worked on for two weeks straight.

In that surreal moment, my eyes shifted to the kitchen counter and I realized that something was missing. Seth took my computer. My computer contained everything that I needed: my court documents, personal information, photographs, evidence for court, and multiple email accounts. I frantically called the police, and they tried relentlessly to get my items back. Late that afternoon, Seth finally backed down to the police officers and agreed to drop my computer off at a neutral location, and then notified the police where they could find it.

My history files showed that Seth had accessed all my personal email accounts, Facebook, and other documents from 11:40 a.m. until 2:55 p.m. Seth downloaded my personal photos and erased any documents and emails that could be used against him in court. The police labeled it as a "domestic incident" and made a report only at my insistence. To my dismay, they wouldn't do anything to hold him accountable.

The Women's Shelter

In that moment, I knew that I could no longer be alone in my home. I took Piper and Sarah to a safe location for two nights while I cleared my head and tried to figure out the next steps. I sent an email to Seth and his family members letting them know that we were leaving the home. I was terrified that Seth would file false kidnapping charges if I took the girls without offering an explanation in writing. I wanted to document my actions for the court.

The reality was, I was afraid that Seth would hurt me, but I was even more terrified that he would kill me. Friday night was Seth's scheduled visitation with the girls, but that was obviously not an option with his escalating behavior. We stayed with friends again, and I notified Seth by email that I would not be honoring the visitation. Knowing that my daughters were safe, I turned my cell phone off for the night as I could already predict the mayhem that would ensue.

I woke up at before dawn on Saturday morning and checked my messages. Seth had left a total of three messages. Hearing his angry, drunk voice sent shivers through my body. I was physically trembling as I listened to each message.

> August 28, 2009 at 10 p.m.: Tina – I am going to very clear with you. Its 10 p.m. on Friday night. My daughters should be with me right now. Your behavior over the past six months has proven not only

that you are a bad mom but that you are a bad influence on my daughters. If my daughters are not at my house ... Do you understand this? My house! I pay rent on. I own this house. It's my house. Do you understand that? ... at 8 a.m. tomorrow morning, 8 a.m. tomorrow morning, Saturday, I will be emailing 3,000 people every picture that I have of you and, ultimately, Tina, you will be wrecked in this community. I do not care. I think you are white trash. I think you are a slut. And yes, you can record this. I think you are a slut! Do you understand that? You've slept with three people in three months while we were married and, yes, I think you are a slut. And, I think that before we got married you had slept with many, many people, and I really don't care, Tina; all I care about is the influence that I can impart on my daughters so that they have a good life without your influence. I think you have zero ability to impart a good perspective on them, and I will tell you right now that if my daughters aren't sitting here at 8 a.m. in the morning during the time that I am supposed to be with them, then you will be ruined in this community, and I will have no regrets for sending an email to 3,000 people of the pictures of you ... your own actions while we were married. 8 a.m. tomorrow ... have my daughters here or you are DONE.

August 29, 2009 at 2:16 a.m.: Tina – There is currently a court order where my daughters are at MY home that I pay for from 10 p.m. on Friday until 8 a.m. on Tuesday. The problem here is that you have not delivered my daughters to my house. I will be issuing an Amber Alert in the morning if my daughters are not at my house. I will be calling the police department if my daughters are not at my house. You are on thin ice, Tina, and I have a list of 3,000 local business people that I will email pictures of your infidelity and sleeping with three different men if my daughters are not here. Do you not understand that? If my daughters are not here at 8 a.m., I will email 3,000 people and show your infidelity, and the bottom line, Tina, is that you are a bad person. What you've done thus far proves that you are a bad person. There is karma in this world, and you will just have to deal with that. My daughters will not be influenced by someone who sleeps with 55-year-old men for money. Do you understand that? They will NOT be influenced by you. You have until 8 a.m. tomorrow morning before your world completely collapses. I want my daughters at my house 8 a.m. tomorrow morning … Saturday morning. Take care.

August 29, 2009 at 2:32 a.m.: Tina – You are a white trash bitch for letting my dog out of the fence. And I'll tell you what, Tina, I am going to file a restraining order, and you will not be allowed back at this house. Do you understand that? YOU are a LOSER. Do you understand this? And I am going to prove it in court. You are a loser, you are white trash, YOU ARE WHITE TRASH, do you understand this? You have been sleeping with three men in three months, and I am going to prove that as well. I just have nothing more to say to you.

The fear for my life intensified. I called my local women's shelter. It was by far the most humbling phone call that I had ever made. This was the very place that I had volunteered every year during Thanksgiving and Christmas. I packed two sleepy, pajama-clad little girls into my car, and we met an intake counselor at a hotel parking lot. After she accessed our situation, we followed her to a hidden residence in town, where we would receive reprieve from the insanity that was now my life.

Driving to the shelter was surreal. My legs were shaking so badly that I could barely keep my foot on the gas pedal. How did my life come to this? I thought I was making the right choices. I got married to someone who appeared stable and successful by all appearances. Seth was smart; he went to a good college. His parents had been married for thirty years. Nine short months ago, I was living in a brand-new home in a gated community. Today, I was taking my children to stay in a women's shelter.

I could barely look at the girls through the rear-view mirror as I drove my car across town. I felt like I was failing them. "Where are we going?" I heard a sleepy little voice ask from the backseat. "We are going to a hotel for a few days – it's a special hotel … it's a women's hotel. It will be like having a slumber party with other moms and children," I answered through my tears.

We were escorted to our room at the women's shelter. It was a little studio house away from the main house. We had privacy, but we needed to go into the main house to use the kitchen. I was grateful that we had our own space. Our little studio had three twin beds. The girls began jumping on the beds and were giggling. They thought we were on vacation. There was a little playground and a handful of mothers with their children. Even with people around, I have never felt so raw and vulnerable.

I sat in the cold, dark room of the studio and cried. The next two days were the darkest days of my life. I wanted someone to wrap their arms around me and tell me that I would be okay. I was overwhelmed. I sat staring at my laptop and thinking of the stacks of papers that I had to prepare. Seth had stolen everything from me. There was no internet at the shelter, so I had to strategically prop my laptop on the window sill to tap into a neighbor's Wi-Fi. I worked late into the night, standing up with my laptop crammed into the window, and poured my whole heart into my court documents.

The Family Court System

September 1, 2009 was our very first court date. I had never been in a courtroom, and the entire fifteen minutes was a blur. My paperwork had been reviewed and submitted by the attorney at the women's shelter. I sat there alone not knowing what to expect. The commissioner awarded me "exclusive use of the home," barring Seth from entering the house we shared. Now, I had a hammer, mace, and a court order. I checked out of the women's shelter and went home with a false sense of security.

In the court documents, Seth claimed that he sold all the furniture and used the money to pay the girl's preschool tuition through December. While I knew that the proceeds would have equaled much more than the preschool tuition, I didn't have the capacity to focus on the material items. I put the issue of the furniture and all my missing possessions on the backburner to be dealt with at a later time. Right now, I was in momma bear mode, and the girls had to be my first priority. On my gratitude list, I was grateful that I did not have to worry about tuition.

The very next day, I took my laptop and went to a local coffee shop to work. I had a strange feeling about being in the home alone and felt safer at public locations. I took my new stacks of paperwork with me because it felt safer that way. Within an hour of being at the coffee shop, I received an email from Seth stating that he was in my house dropping off food. I immediately called the police, who came out and took a report.

The police warned Seth that they would arrest him if he violated the order again. I was devastated. Seth sent me a very clear message that day: he was above the courts and he was above the law. He had no regard for either. My sense of security was short lived, and I felt discouraged that the police officers continued to label each incident as a "domestic issue" despite the fact that I finally had an order from the court. The police instructed me to put it back in front of the court because they couldn't help me.

The Visitations Begin

I took the girls to meet Seth at Starbucks for his court-ordered parenting time. As I got out of the car, Seth handed me a piece of paper detailing a new visitation schedule that he was proposing. It was centered on his triathlon schedule. I briefly looked the paper over and told him that I was not going to sign the document. I told him that we could address this situation in court on Wednesday. Seth looked at me and said, "You are an idiot." I responded: "This is inappropriate in front of the children."

I continued to ignore Seth while removing the car seats from the car. Seth continued, "You are a pathetic human being." At that point, Piper started to cry. She begged me not to go. She became hysterical, so I walked with her over to a bench. Piper said, "I don't like it when Daddy is mean to you, and I don't want you to leave." Seth had walked up on us by this point and said, "Tina, THIS is divorce and THIS is your fault." I replied, "Divorce does NOT need to be this way. You are causing this situation in front of the children. Please stop."

Piper continued crying for about ten minutes, repeating over and over that she didn't want me to leave. I explained to her that I would see her first thing tomorrow morning. I gave her a hug and had to walk away. She continued to cry for me as I struggled to place one foot in front of the other and walk to my car. My heart was shattering with every step that I took.

Our next court date was October 14, 2009. The anxiety leading up to the day was overwhelming. The anticipation of a man sitting behind a bench and making a decision that affected my daughters terrified me. How can someone make such an important decision about children after hearing twenty minutes of testimony? It was a difficult concept for me to grasp.

I sat quietly in the courtroom and, while waiting my turn, I watched case after case. There were drug addicts, abusers, and deadbeat fathers. By the time we were sworn in, I felt like the odds were against me. By all outward appearances, Seth looked normal. In his court paperwork, Seth looked like the star father, and I was naïve enough to believe that the courts would give any weight to the fact that I had been the only parent the girls had ever known.

The commissioner let Seth know that he needed to get a handle on his anger. Seth was reprimanded for violating the court order and entering the home. Seth's defense: he was simply bringing us lasagna and feeding his dog. The reality: the dog wasn't even living at our house at that point. Seth was reprimanded for threatening to veto my trip out of state with the girls for a wedding. I felt both discouraged and devastated by the proceedings. The commissioner closed by saying something along the lines of, "You two are crazy if you are already starting your divorce like this." I stared straight ahead in disbelief, because I didn't feel like I owned any of the craziness. Why couldn't they see through him?

Mediation

We were ordered to attend mediation through family court services. I went in desperate for someone to listen to me but I also struggled to put together sentences due to the trauma that I was experiencing. I prayed that the mediator would not be charmed by him but, even more, I prayed that she wouldn't believe the craziness that he was spewing about me.

Seth came into the room acting manic and crazed, which seemed to be the new norm for him. The mediator quickly realized that having us in the room together left me trembling and was extremely unproductive. She asked me to wait in the waiting room while she met with Seth alone. They were in the room for about forty-five minutes before she called me in.

The mediator didn't ask me any questions. She knew from talking to him that there were issues. Whatever Seth said or did caused her concern. I sat down and she said, "I am going to recommend a psychiatric evaluation. The courts can't order him to take it, but it will serve as a red flag to the judge. I will walk you back to the waiting room—take a seat and I will call him back in. After I take him in the room, go home."

I went home thankful and with a sense of peace. I could tell that the mediator was concerned for my safety. I had a glimmer of hope because if she saw through him in forty-five minutes, surely the courts would start to see through him, also.

The Parenting Evaluation

In court, the commissioner ordered a full parenting evaluation (3111 evaluation) to address my concerns about Seth's anger issues and his parenting in general. We were given thirty days to report to family court services and complete the paperwork that would kick off the process. While I had no idea what the evaluation entailed, I was thrilled to know that it was an in-depth look at what was truly in the best interest of our children.

The social worker who was being assigned to our case would interview everyone who knew us as parents: preschool teachers, nannies, babysitters, friends, and others who could testify to our parenting. I was hopeful that someone would finally see the issues relating to his temper, the stalking, and the parenting issues. In the meantime, his visitation remained the same: every other weekend. Our review hearing was scheduled for February of 2010.

I filed my paperwork, and I waited to schedule my intake interview. I called family court services weekly, but Seth wasn't complying with the orders. The evaluation couldn't start until both parties completed the paperwork. Month after month went by—November, December, January and still no attempt on his part to follow through. This had to be a sign to the court, or so I hoped.

Our New "Home"

Financially, I was devastated. I had $178 to my name. No retirement, no investments, no college fund for my children, and my car was slated for repossession. I had no idea how I would come up with the deposit for a new apartment, but I had the will so I knew I'd find a way. I began by reaching out to local churches in my area, Catholic Charities, the Salvation Army, and other community foundations. With no options for a co-signer and a bankruptcy fresh on my record from Seth's financial hurricane, I knew that the odds were against me while house-hunting.

With the help of a friend, I found a tiny little apartment for Piper, Sarah, and myself. I was sold on the fact that it was an upstairs apartment, which, in my mind, meant that there were no opportunities for Seth to be hiding outside and peeking into my windows. It was an old apartment, and it was designed as student housing, but it felt safe. I reminded myself that this was temporary because, otherwise, I felt like I was failing.

I pled my case and circumstances to the rental agency, and they agreed to give me a chance, but it was a month-to-month agreement. Glenn and two friends arrived bright and early on moving day. Even though the apartment was small, it was mine. I did it without Seth, and it was empowering. It was a step forward into my new life. The girls and I had a place of our very own.

I try to make the best of all situations even if they aren't ideal. We didn't have a kitchen table so I got creative. We ordered pizza more often than I'd like to admit. We used a small end table and explored the art of Japanese-style dining: cross-legged on cushions. Piper and Sarah thought it was fun, and we pretended that we were on a picnic.

I set a personal goal that we would move within a year. We had a roof over our heads and we had food on our table. I still slept with a hammer, but I felt a lot safer knowing that we had neighbors close by, and the upstairs unit made lurking more difficult.

The Disneyland Dad

Seth informed me that he was taking the girls to Disneyland for one of his weekend visits in November. The girls returned from the weekend, and I dropped them off at preschool on Monday morning. At 3:20 p.m., I arrived at the school for pick up and was stopped by one of the preschool teachers. They were concerned about a picture that Piper drew at school. Her teacher brought out a picture that depicted both girls and their father at Disneyland. In the picture, she was crying, and under the picture, she wrote: "Im fileeg (sic) sad so I want to call my mommy."

Later that night at dinner, Sarah said very matter-of-factly, "Daddy hurt Piper at the cookie shop."

I asked her gently, "Do you want to tell me what happened?"

Piper said, "I hit Sarah and Daddy was angry at me."

"How do you know that Daddy was angry at you?" I asked.

Piper replied, "Because he squeezed my wrist really, really hard and made me cry a lot."

I asked her to show me how her daddy squeezed her wrist. At this point, Piper took my arm and squeezed as hard as she could while scrunching her little face up and trying to appear as angry as she could.

"Ouch. That hurt," I said. "Did it hurt a lot or a little when Daddy squeezed your arm?"

Piper replied, "It hurt a lot—like when daddy squeezed me at the other house."

I couldn't believe what I was hearing. The school kept a copy of the picture. I copied the picture and filed it with family court services. I was confident that this would have a huge impact on the parenting evaluation. I was once again hopeful that they would be able to stop the damage being done to my daughters.

The Delusions

Seth had become obsessed with telling people that I had cheated on him. He had told this lie so many times that I think he believed it. He wanted the courts to believe that I was starting the equivalent of the Red-Light District in my neighborhood. At a concert with a girlfriend, we posed for a photo with a male friend. The entire interaction was less than two minutes in length, yet he saw a photo online and was convinced I was having an affair with this person. According to Seth, I was having affairs while driving down the freeway and with a random stranger in the produce section of the grocery store. California is a no-fault state; even if I had committed adultery, it wouldn't matter, but Seth was myopic on playing the victim in his fabricated, demented fairytale.

Seth sent an email out to people in our small town which was titled, "Three men in three months." In this email, he was the victim. He put pictures of men in the email, and his aunt Lamia narrated a story that they had concocted in her own handwriting. Lamia wrote little descriptions next to each photo such as, "Here she is with one man" next to one photo and the next photo would say, "Same outfit 12 hours later and a whole new man. She was with two men in one day!"

I was living a nightmare that didn't seem to have an end in sight. Everywhere I went, I heard stories about Seth being drunk in bars and acting in a disturbing fashion. Many people didn't even know that our marriage had ended but would pull me aside at public events and voice concern about Seth's behavior while intoxicated. One person told me that there were photographs circulating around town showing Seth passed out cold on the floor of a Mexican restaurant on Halloween dressed as Darth Vader.

An attorney by the name of Steve generously offered to help me by reviewing my paperwork and, subsequently, became Seth's next target. Seth called him and advised him to be careful because I would start throwing myself at him sexually in exchange for free services. The owner of a local car dealership who kindly helped me with a used car purchase received a message from Seth with the same warning. He was actively trying to ruin me in the community, and he really seemed to believe these delusional stories.

The Lies and the Deception

The court order stated that Seth was supposed to notify me of our daughters' whereabouts during his weekend visitations. As with all court orders, Seth felt above the law. He refused to provide me with a valid address despite my weekly pleas.

At one point, Seth provided me with an address in a gated community that he knew I couldn't access. A simple Google search revealed the address was an empty, dirt lot. To further verify what the internet showed, I drove to the address with a local realtor friend who had access to the community. As I suspected, it was exactly what was shown on Google Maps: dirt.

When confronted, Seth gave me another address in the same gated community. With the help of the same realtor, I was able to prove that this was also a false address. A third address supplied by Lamia also proved to be false. Over the phone, Seth laughed at me. I was forced to accept that he derived a sick, twisted pleasure from causing me pain.

For three months, I lived in fear over each and every visit. It was draining and exhausting, and I was desperate. I did not know where my daughters were staying or with whom. My daughters constantly mentioned that another male, Ryan, lived in the house, yet I had no idea who this person was. I agonized over whether or not Seth was going to return them at the end of the weekend. Only after he was reprimanded by the court did Seth provide a correct address.

In the midst of working overtime to find where Seth was keeping the girls, I received a phone call from Sarah's preschool; Seth had lied about paying the tuition through December. According to the school, he wrote a check for September's tuition that bounced, and we owed a small fortune. They told me that they could not continue with our enrollment but would allow us to stay through the end of the January, and they would not charge me for January. I was devastated to have to put the Sarah through yet another huge transition, but I was left with no options. We were forced to move schools, and I needed to cut her attendance greatly at the new school.

The Staged Home and the Evaluation

Our parenting evaluation was finally underway and, around that time, I discovered that Seth had rented and staged a home specifically for the evaluation. I knew this at the time, yet I couldn't prove it. It was difficult for me to listen to the evaluator, Elvia, discuss how nice Seth's place was and how it was completely dedicated to the children. She said that he even had photos of me displayed at his home so that the children would know that both parents loved them equally. How sweet. This was not the man that I knew. The man I knew needed everything to be perfect, and perfect wasn't defined as "child-friendly" nor would my photo be displayed unless it involved target practice at the local shooting range. I knew that Cleo and Lamia were behind this.

The following week during an internet search, I stumbled upon a photo that caused me to have the second panic attack of my life. It was one of Seth's family photos that had been taken at Christmastime; in the photo was Seth, his younger brothers, Piper, Sarah, Robert, and Phonphan. My head was spinning as I reflected on all the times that Seth and I agreed to keep our daughters away from Robert. I wanted to vomit.

I began to panic as the evaluation was underway, but I hadn't even mentioned my concerns about Robert in my paperwork because I felt it was one thing Seth and I were in agreement on. I printed the photo and prayed for guidance. I began to prepare myself for articulating my concerns about Robert to the evaluator.

The evaluator dug in and she spoke to people who knew us, such as nannies, doctors, teachers, and friends. Elvia came to our home, and she had us come to her office. She also interviewed Piper and Sarah several times during the evaluation. Elvia pointed out the issues she saw with Seth, specifically anger and dishonesty. She said that he seemed to go out of his way to torture me and to keep the girls' whereabouts from me. She stated that it was unnecessary and that he needed to let go of the anger. She was preaching to the choir.

- Elvia uncovered his lies: Seth claimed in court that he was in "intensive therapy" to deal with his anger. Elvia spoke to his therapist and discovered that she saw him one time and also found him to be angry.
- Elvia expressed her concern that Seth was knowingly driving the children without a license.
- Elvia seemed concerned about his alcohol issues and went so far as to subpoena his records from a local gym where he drank beer while watching the girls, which proved that he was violating the court order restricting alcohol consumption during parenting time.
- Elvia listened to my concerns about Seth's older brother, Robert. I told her about the incident where he spoke about raping and murdering women. She listened intently as I told her about the time

he made out with a 14-year-old girl at a wedding. She documented the incident in which he beat tiny puppies in front of our daughter.
- Elvia expressed concern about the incident when Seth left our daughters unattended in the house.

I was feeling hopeful about the evaluation and the direction it was taking. Maybe this woman would see through him. Maybe she would help me to protect the children.

The Stalking Continues

The girls and I woke up early one morning in February to prepare for our "Mommy and Me" class. Not yet caffeinated and operating on limited sleep, I opened my front door to take the trash downstairs. I immediately had a strange feeling that someone was watching me. I looked down the stairs and tried to grasp what I was seeing. Seth was sitting in his car staring up at me from the bottom of the stairs with an eerie smirk on his face.

Seth had lined my entire stairwell from top to bottom with 17 large photos. He had been court-ordered to return the pictures that he stripped from my walls at our former home. This was his sick way of following court orders while finding a way to wreak emotional havoc on me with one blow.

I stood there frozen, trying to grasp what was happening. I stared at him in total shock. Seth just sat there staring back at me. All I could bring myself to say was, "You are insane. You are completely insane." Seth replied, "Here are all of your picture frames." I ran into the house to grab my camera, and as I came outside, he turned his car on and quickly drove away. I was physically shaking. He thrived on intimidating me. Seth was deriving more and more pleasure from causing me pain.

A New Beginning

It was springtime, and Sarah, Piper, and I had been in the apartment for almost six months. Piper's Sunday school class had been told to draw a picture of their home: the place where they felt happy and safe. Piper proudly showed me her picture, and it was adorable. She then went on to explain that while everyone drew their home, she drew her *next* home. Piper drew a cute little house with a yard and flowers instead of the upstairs, tiny apartment where we lived. My heart sank as I smiled and complimented her artwork.

I immediately began looking for a new house or condo that I could afford, but it was discouraging given my credit issues. A few days later, I stumbled upon an advertisement for a two-bedroom condo with a garage and a fenced-in yard. I dialed the number and felt even more discouraged when I was told that they were insistent on good credit and references. I put together a rental resume with many references attached.

I met with the landlord, a kind, older man whose wife was dying of cancer. Mr. Montgomery showed me around and, when I expressed interest in the home, he placed a set of keys in my hand. He placed his hand over mine and shut my fingers. "Wait … there is a misunderstanding," I tried to explain to him that I hadn't even filled out paperwork.

Mr. Montgomery looked at me and said, "I don't need a bunch of paperwork floating around. I know a good person when I see one." I was in shock. As he walked out the front door, Mr. Montgomery told me to stop by his office in the next couple of weeks to pay the rent but that I was welcome to start moving things in that day. In that moment, I knew that angels existed.

I mailed Mr. Montgomery my first rent check along with the $1,200 deposit. He called me the very next day and said that he was ripping up the deposit check. I was confused. He went on to explain, "It must be difficult being a single mom. Don't worry about the deposit."

Piper got the house she drew in Sunday school with the fenced-in yard and flowers, and I met a person that I will never forget. Seth was always lurking, which kept me on edge at all times. He would call to talk to the girls and casually mention that he was four hours south of us. An hour later, we would pass him going down the street. I learned to always look over my shoulder and to always check my rearview mirror while driving.

As I was moving from my little apartment to the new condo, I unlocked my daughters' stroller only to realize that it wouldn't fit in my car. I rolled it back into the carport and then drove across town to my new home.

I was gone for one hour and, in that short timeframe, Seth went into my carport and stole my stroller. I immediately called the police and filed a report. The officer called Seth, who admitted that he had the stroller, yet the police officer sounded like a broken record when he called it a domestic dispute. I called it stalking, intimidation, and theft.

At a hearing that month, I begged the court to make Seth return my washer and dryer that he refused to relinquish. It sat in storage and Seth knew that I was being forced to drag my daughters to a laundromat each week after work but, to him, it was about control. In the hearing, the commissioner sternly reprimanded him and ordered that he give me access to the storage unit by 5 p.m. that same day. I hired someone to meet me there to load the washer and dryer, but also to ensure my safety.

After the washer and dryer were loaded into the truck and the delivery guy drove away, I began walking back to my car. Halfway through the parking lot, Seth pulled up beside me with his window down. I took a step backward to distance myself from his vehicle and then froze in my tracks, terrified of his next move as I had no way to quickly escape.

"This is my new girlfriend," Seth said, as he shoved a framed 5x7 photo out the window at me, which depicted Seth and a blonde woman posing for what appeared to be a professional photoshoot. "She's gorgeous, athletic, and stable, unlike YOU," he continued in a manic voice. I wondered, *is this really happening? He's insane.* "Stop. Please, just go," I said. Seth drove away, and I was left shaking.

Child Welfare Services

In May of that year, Sarah was rushed by ambulance to our local hospital after having a 45-minute complex seizure. I knew the severity of the seizure when I looked into the doctor's eyes. It was by far the worst 45 minutes of my life. Despite my little girl being given 10 mg of valium, they could not get the seizure to stop.

Seth didn't even show up to the hospital despite multiple calls to him. I discovered that the work event that he claimed to be tied up at was actually the Tour of California bike race, which he was obsessed with. Glenn arrived at the hospital to support me moments after Sarah's seizure ended. She had never met Glenn but, in her dazed state, she looked straight at him, stuck her arms out, and he held her in his arms. It warmed my heart on one hand, but on the other hand, it made me so angry that her own father wasn't capable of putting his children first.

After Sarah's release from the hospital, I met with a child neurologist and her pediatrician for a follow up. Seth's visitation was that weekend, and I was terrified to put her in his care. The instructions from the emergency room, pediatrician, and neurologist were very clear and provided to him in writing: she was never to be left unattended. Not for a single moment. The doctor's recommendation went so far as to say that we should sleep with her at night until further testing was complete. I reached out to Cleo to assist me in relaying the important directions to Seth, and she did as I asked.

As the weekend visitation came to an end, I was thrilled to pick up the girls on Sunday night. I arrived at the pick-up location, and Piper and Sarah climbed into my car.

"Mom, Daddy did something really bad this weekend" were the first words that I heard from Piper's mouth.

"What did he do?" I asked, with a lump in my throat.

"He left Sarah in the car alone for a very long time," she answered.

I immediately notified our parenting evaluator and Sarah's neurologist. Both women reported him to Child Welfare Services. Once again, I was hopeful that someone would help me to protect the girls, especially because we were in the midst of the custody evaluation.

I was expecting Seth to deny the allegations, but he didn't. He admitted that he took the girls to our local athletic club, where he watched the Tour of California on television. Seth claimed that he parked in the shade with the windows cracked and left Sarah sleeping alone in the car.

Reports on the timeframe varied from witnesses, but we estimated between 30 to 45 minutes. One written statement from an employee at the club stated that Seth checked on her "about every 10 minutes." Seth left her alone in a car, less than three days after being released from the hospital with strict orders that he had agreed to follow.

As if that wasn't bad enough, Seth also admitted that he drove to a sports bar and left Sarah in the car again. According to Seth, Sarah continued to sleep in the car while he ordered dinner. He didn't think it was a big deal because he went and got her when the food was served.

The very agency that was designed to protect my daughters failed them miserably. The following is what the social worker wrote in her report: "Seth was provided literature regarding leaving children unattended in automobiles. Assessment: No safety threats were identified, at this time. Based on the current available information, the children are not likely to be in immediate danger of serious harm. Seth demonstrated poor judgment when leaving his child unattended in the car. Seth expressed sincere remorse and has made a commitment to never do this again."

I couldn't believe what I was reading. What the fuck was wrong with this social worker? Was she a mother? Did she have a beating heart? I was speechless.

The Evaluation Continues

Elvia continued on, talking to those who knew us and collecting the information that I shared with her. I kept her updated on all the chaos that continued surrounding visitation, custody exchanges and co-parenting in general. I was caught off guard and panic-ridden when I followed up with her and discovered that she was scheduled to meet with Cleo that same week because I knew that Elvia was no match for Cleo's skillset.

I immediately expressed my concerns about Elvia talking to Cleo. I questioned why she was planning to talk to Cleo but not my aunt, who was like a mother to me. Elvia stated that it was protocol to talk to those who were involved in the day-to-day lives of the children. I countered her by reminding her of the facts; Cleo lived overseas and was only around for eight weeks out of the year. Due to her being split between her four sons who were spread out through California, our actual time with her was pretty minimal. As a compromise, Elvia agreed to speak to my aunt Bev.

While Elvia was interviewing my aunt Bev, my aunt broke down and expressed that fear about my safety consumed her. She told Elvia that I slept with a hammer under my pillow and that she worried Seth would kill my girls and me. The mother bear in her took over and, even though Bev had been a skilled social worker for over 25 years, this case hit too close to home and she struggled to find words to back up her fears. As the one person who had a front-row seat to my daily life over the past nine years, her fears were warranted but fell on deaf ears.

Elvia called me the next day and caught me off guard when she asked if I lived in fear for my personal safety and my life. While I did, I had been warned heavily about making statements like this, as it is often perceived by the courts to be a way to get a leg up in a child custody battle. The truth was, I did live in fear of my life. I knew to carefully navigate this subject with family court professionals. She asked me about the hammer under my pillow, and I confirmed that I did sleep with a hammer and mace under my pillow. In a condescending tone, she said, "If this is true, I find it odd that you are just now bringing it up." I was speechless.

Custody Evaluation Results

I received a phone call on June 24, 2010. The parenting evaluation was complete. This was the moment I had been waiting for and, based on my conversations with Elvia, I drove to her office feeling fairly confident. Seth, Elvia, and I all met in a room to go over her findings and her suggested parenting plan. There were the general items included in any parenting plan and then there were the following items:

> 1. The father will not transport the children until he shows proof of a valid driver's license.
>
> 2. The father's parenting time will be the first, third, and fourth weekends of the month from 9 a.m. Saturday until 7 p.m. Sunday.
>
> 3. The father will participate in weekly parenting classes for four months and will show the mother proof of completion. The father will also file in court a copy of proof of completion.
>
> 4. The father will participate in individual counseling to address personal issues specifically related to anger management, stress, and communication with the mother. Father shall file with the court proof of his attendance in therapy, inclusive of number of sessions and name of therapist.
>
> 5. The father will not drink alcoholic beverages until parenting classes and counseling is completed.
>
> 6. The father will ensure that the children are not left unsupervised at any time in the presence of his older brother, Robert, and they are only permitted to be in his presence on the following holidays: 4th of July, Thanksgiving, Christmas Eve, and Christmas Day.
>
> 7. Father will provide the address where the children will reside by the Monday prior to his visit.

When I read the portion about my daughters being around Robert in any capacity, I had to leave the room to compose myself. I stood in the bathroom with tears streaming down my face. Robert was my biggest button and Seth knew this. I could not grasp that the man who had been so firm in his desire to protect our daughters from Robert had completely flipped his position. I knew it was about control and winning. Nothing more and nothing less. He knew that this would kill me inside, and he was high on life that he had accomplished his goal.

I asked Elvia what would happen if I refused to agree to the terms. She told me that if I agreed, we would sign the document, avoid court, and not owe her any money. If I refused to agree to her terms, we would go to court, be charged close to $5,000 for the evaluation, and the judge would inevitably enforce the recommendations anyway. I didn't have $500 to my name, let alone $5,000. I was backed into a corner and had no one to consult with for guidance.

Against my better judgment, I signed the parenting plan and drove away in shock and in tears. Elvia knew everything that Seth had done and she knew Robert's history, yet this was her recommendation. This was the moment that I realized the courts do not act in the best interest of children. Nothing in that agreement was in my daughters' best interest. If Seth had squeezed the arm of a police officer or left a family pet in the car, he would have been in jail.

I was left holding an inadequate, useless parent evaluation and subsequent recommendations. In that moment, $5,000 was the same as $5 million to me. I couldn't pay it. I couldn't protect my daughters. I felt helpless and disgusted by this broken court system.

In the beginning of the evaluation, Elvia seemed to be genuinely concerned about my daughters. Toward the end of the evaluation, she had met with Seth's mother, Cleo. My greatest fear had come to fruition: Cleo used her charm and credentials to completely manipulate the evaluator. In one short afternoon, all the horrifying details of Seth and Robert's behaviors were erased by the same woman who helped mold Seth into the dysfunctional person that he is. Cleo was the one who taught him that all behavior was acceptable, as long as you remained perfect in the eyes of the world.

I wanted to have faith that Seth would follow orders. I wanted to believe that a simple parenting class and a series of counseling sessions could fix him. Instead, I knew that his entire portion of the investigation was staged. I didn't have an ounce of faith because I knew Seth. Twelve days after the custody evaluation ended, Seth moved out of the staged home never to return to it again. He was a master manipulator and had successfully fooled Elvia and the courts.

Failing His Daughters

At the end of summer, I received an email from Seth asking to be included in Piper's first day of kindergarten. I agreed, and we planned to meet in the parking lot at 8 a.m. We arrived on time and waited for Seth. He didn't show up nor did he bother to call.

Meanwhile, the harassment was constant. Seth had a tactic to deal with it in court: he lied. Seth deflected my accusations by saying that I harassed him. I would sit in disbelief as I read the text messages that I allegedly sent him. They were doctored.

The commissioner must have felt as though he were supervising two fighting toddlers. Seth was an expert at muddying the waters. I wanted to stand up and scream in court. I wanted them to sit down with me and go through the text messages. I needed an hour to show them what he was doing.

The problem was that I really was receiving these harassing texts, emails, and phone calls. There were many nights that I would cry in bed as I watched the text message light beep repeatedly. He would berate me and beat me down. I would cringe with every beep from the phone.

- "You should have never been lifted from-white trash status. Your looks are the only thing that ever got you anywhere. You are easy and out to get laid."
- "They say that nothing I have done or said constitutes a threat. All I care about is making you answer to your conscience. You seem hell-bent on destroying me."
- "You are a pathetic human being. Worthless. Uneducated."
- "Karma will take care of you. The beauty of my Karma is I have had mine delivered. I have lost everything. Wish you well Tina."
- "You lack so much ... and it's because of your upbringing and lack of cultivation. Lacking culture or a groomed skill. Just looks. So sad."
- "Have a good life Tina. I'd hate to be you. How do you sleep at night?"

Sometimes, Seth's text messages followed a simple request or an attempted update on the girls. Other times, they came completely out of the blue. Sometimes, they came in the middle of the night, and sometimes, they came while I was at work. Sometimes, I shrugged them off, and other times, I broke down. The attacks were constant, and I could not seem to find shelter from them.

The parenting agreement that we signed stated that Seth could have increased visitation (from three overnights per month to six overnights per month) if he completed these items:

- Four months of weekly parenting classes;
- Individual counseling to address personal issues specifically related to anger management, stress, and communication with me; and
- No alcohol usage around the children until completion of the above items.

Seth was to file proof of completion by October 31, 2010. If someone told me that I could double my time with my daughters by satisfying a few simple requirements, I would have signed up the moment I left the courtroom. Seth never completed any of the items, and I knew why. Seth's child support was based on the increased visitation (six overnights per month); therefore, he didn't need nor want increased visitation. Not only did he not do anything required of him by the court, he failed to show up to many of his already limited visits.

Throughout our marriage, Seth's alcohol problems had been an ongoing issue. Seth fluctuated between being a hard-core athlete who trained six days per week to a depressed alcoholic who would sit on the couch for hours on end watching television. I hated how he acted when drinking.

One Saturday morning, the girls and I decided to go to the pick-up location early for cinnamon rolls. We were scheduled to meet Seth at 9 a.m. On our way out the door, my phone rang. It was an area code that I didn't recognize so I ignored it. At 8:05 a.m., there was another call from another area code. I answered the call.

Me: "Hello."

Seth (in a tired, raspy voice): "Someone stole my phone last night, and I just woke up."

It was 8 a.m. and he was four hours north of us—in San Francisco.

Me: "Don't bother coming. We are going on with our day."

A slew of emails transpired over the next few hours. Seth arrived for the exchange nearly seven hours after his scheduled exchange time. He looked disheveled and smelled strongly of alcohol. I kicked myself for agreeing to meet him, but our court order didn't have a stipulation about being late to visits.

The issues with alcohol seemed to have no end in sight. One morning at 2 a.m., my cell phone rang, and I bolted upright and ran for the phone. The sound of a phone ringing in the middle of the night is never good news, and my heart was pounding. My mind was racing and my first thought was, "Oh my God, the girls!" before quickly realizing they were sleeping safely in the bedroom next to me. The phone number calling was Seth.

Me: "Hello?!"

An unfamiliar voice was on the other end of the phone, with commotion and music in the background.

Stranger: "I'm sorry to wake you, but I called the last number that was dialed on this phone."

Me: "Okay …"

Stranger: "I am concerned about the guy who owns this phone. He was extremely intoxicated and left his keys and phone behind. We are trying to make sure that he is alright."

By this point, I was annoyed beyond belief. I was annoyed that this is the father of my children. I was annoyed that we breathe the same air. I was annoyed that his antics woke us at 2 a.m.

Me: "I'm his ex-wife, so I can't help you. I will call you in the morning on this number when I can think clearly."

Over the course of our court trials, I had access to Seth's Facebook account through two different friends. On Facebook, Seth painted a picture of his fantasy world where he owned homes, businesses, and cars, yet failed to mention we had lost all of these things.

With access to Seth's Facebook account, I was actually able to see his wine-tasting excursions on the weekends, which he had actually attended after cancelling on the girls due to false claims of illness or work projects. His online profile stated the following: "I won't hesitate to drop everything for the promise of a great time with someone who I enjoy." That was probably the most truthful thing that had left Seth's mouth in years. Seth would even drop weekend parenting time with his own daughters. He would and he often did. In addition, Seth claimed that he belonged to his college triathlon club and the Surfrider Foundation. I wondered how he even kept up with the lies that he told. He derived a sick high by fooling people and creating an illusion.

As I was preparing for my upcoming divorce trial, I went into stealth mode. I found his online dating profiles on Fitness Singles and Match.com. I realize that many people stretch the truth online, but pretending to be a completely different person is another story.

- Seth's income was listed at $100,001 to $150,000, which didn't turn out to be a complete lie. He only lied about it in court paperwork pertaining to child support.
- Relationship status: Never married
- Education: Graduate degree (Seth only has a bachelor's degree.)
- Kids: No

The instability related to Seth's visits was affecting the girls, and it was getting old. The night prior to Seth's scheduled visitation in April, Sarah came down with a horrible cough and fever. I was up with her most of the night, as she is prone to seizures when ill. I packed the girls into the car early in the morning and drove to the exchange location. We left the house earlier than usual because I needed to buy an extra humidifier, thermometer, and medication to send with her, as I knew Seth would refuse to make the purchase on his own. I couldn't send mine because he would keep them to spite me.

We sat waiting in the parking lot after buying the humidifier, medication and thermometer only to receive an email seven minutes before Seth's scheduled pick-up time saying that he was not coming. I cried. I was tired and frustrated that I had dragged my sick little girl out of her bed for this man who clearly did not deserve to be her father. Reality set in within a few moments, and I was thankful that she would be home with me to rest. Seth's commitment at this point was only three overnight visits per month, yet he couldn't even follow through with that.

Laser-Beam Focus

While I followed the court order exactly as it was written, there was one area of the order that I followed with a laser-beam focus and that was the rule about Robert being around my daughters. There were four days per year that made me cringe and those were all major holidays. In my mind, it was less than four days because, every other year, we alternated most of those holidays with the exception of Christmas.

The girls were on a visit with Seth and he sent me a text message about a proposed meeting location at the end of the visit. The exchange location was different than the one in our court order, but it was more convenient for me.

The part that concerned me was that his suggested location was close to Robert's home. I had a sinking feeling and I knew my daughters were at his house, which was a violation of the order given that it was January 2, 2011.

I immediately called the sheriff with my court order in hand and asked for a child welfare check at Robert's house. Thankfully, I had connected with a very kind deputy who didn't brush me off but, instead, listened to my concerns and agreed to drive out there. Within 30 minutes, the deputy called me back and stated that he was at the residence and that my daughters were there along with Seth, Cleo, Leonard, Robert, and Phonphan. I knew it. That son of a bitch (literally). The deputy agreed to remain on the property until Seth could pack up the girls and leave the premises.

Seth arrived 30 minutes later at our exchange location and was irate. He informed me that I had ruined their family Christmas that they were delayed in celebrating and that there was a special place in hell for me. I ignored Seth's rants and got the girls and their belongings into the car and drove off. I knew how much Robert hated law enforcement and prayed that by sending the sheriff to Robert's house, I had created a boundary and sent a clear message: don't fuck with me or my children.

Closure

Our divorce seemed like it would never be final. There were constant hearings, and the preparation before each court date equated to a part-time job. I would estimate that we had had a court hearing every other month since the divorce began. Our trial date to finalize the divorce was finally set: May 27, 2011. I was desperate to put this nightmare behind me because I struggled to hold my head above water with a full-time job at an advertising agency and the responsibilities that come with being a single mom. I was naïve enough to believe that a stamped divorce decree was a milestone that would magically give us stability and begin to miraculously smooth out the road that we were traveling on.

I was becoming accustomed to bizarre statements and emails from Seth that defied logic. Shortly before our trial date, Seth told me that because we were married in Hawaii, he didn't believe that our marriage was valid. I was positive that I couldn't possibly be hearing him correctly. Did he not receive the memo that Hawaii had joined the union in 1959?

Shortly after that conversation, I received the following email from Seth: "Tina- I don't believe I was really even married to you since we didn't get married in California nor did we think it through. It was basically like a Vegas wedding; and what a mistake!! I may be seeking an annulment FYI. Of course, if there really is a marriage certificate, that won't affect how the court proceeds, but nonetheless it would be more accurate." I was left speechless that he put this in writing.

I arrived in court for our official divorce trial with my 3-inch-thick pink binder in hand. I had learned to document everything and, unfortunately, Seth provided me with plenty of things to keep track of. I had a total 154 exhibits to enter into evidence that day. That binder held the past 2.5 years of the nightmare that I was living.

That pink binder also held tokens of strength for me, including my biological mom's pearl necklace, a letter from my dad, a picture of my grandfather, an old email from my aunt, a card from my friend, a keepsake piece from my sister, a poem from Glenn, a bracelet, and photos of my daughters. My main source of strength was a handwritten card from my daughter that said, "I love you very much. You are the best mom ever." I packed my support system into that binder, and I went into court prepared to fight for my little girls.

In our trial, Seth was requesting additional visitation. Additional visits meant less child support. Securing additional visitation meant winning. Seth was set on winning at all costs. Seth's agenda in court was to prove that he had a stable, safe environment for the girls. He brought his cousin Chris into the courtroom to testify on his behalf. Seth grilled me on the stand and asked me what I thought about his cousin. I answered honestly, "I respect Chris and I respect his wife, Anna, both as people and as parents." At that point in time, I did.

The thought of our daughters staying at Chris and Anna's home on the weekends actually set my mind at ease. They were good people and their children were the same age as our children. Chris testified in court that Seth had total and complete use of a guesthouse on their property. I was relieved to know that my daughters would be in one place each weekend rather than a new bed each night. I wanted to believe their white picket fence story so badly for the sake of my children.

It had been one year since our parenting evaluation and subsequent parenting agreement. Our current situation was nothing short of a nightmare. In that year, Seth had failed to follow the majority of the following court-ordered items:

- maintaining a valid driver's license. Seth transported the children without a valid driver's license.
- completing the parenting classes. Seth never completed the required parenting classes.
- attending therapy. Seth didn't attend any of the required therapy sessions.
- arriving for scheduled visits. Seth repeatedly failed to show up for visits.
- no drinking orders around our children. Seth drank alcohol regularly around the girls.
- stay-away orders regarding his older brother. Seth took the children to Robert's house when it was against the court orders, and I had a police report to prove it.
- providing me with his physical address every time he moved. Seth repeatedly failed to tell me where the children were residing.

I was confident that these things would show that he didn't care about orders and felt above the law. I also felt that it showed a consistent pattern of behavior that was undeniable. I was wrong. The commissioner waived the requirements for parenting classes and therapy sessions. I sat there wondering what the purpose of a four-month parenting evaluation was if all the recommendations were waived?

I was dumbfounded with the ruling. Seth gained additional visitation time consisting of four one-week visitations quarterly and his monthly visitation increased to the first, third, and fifth weekends of each month from Friday afternoon at 3 p.m. to Monday mornings at the start of school.
Because Seth couldn't be trusted to show up, I was forced to pick up the girls from school at 2:30 p.m. and then wait at Starbucks for him until 3 p.m. I questioned why. If a parent isn't reliable enough to pick up his children from school, how could the court come to the conclusion that he deserved more time?

As the commissioner made his ruling, I looked back at my friends with tears streaming down my face. They were all staring blankly ahead and shaking their heads. I remember asking one of them afterwards, "What just happened?" They had no answer.

The Father-Daughter Dance

Friday, June 3, 2011 was Seth's first weekend visit after the court date. I picked the girls up from school, and we drove to Starbucks to wait. He never showed up. I called his phone repeatedly, and he didn't answer. Normally, I wouldn't have been shocked by his behavior. However, this was an incredibly important weekend to Piper and Sarah.

This weekend happened to be the girls' annual Father-Daughter Dance, which was organized by Piper's Girl Scout Troop. The girls had been filled with excitement for two months leading up to the event. By this point, I had learned to stay two steps ahead of Seth, and I had a backup plan.

Sadly, Piper was starting to see through Seth also. As we were driving from her school to the coffee shop, she asked me what would happen if Daddy didn't come. With a lump in my throat, I told her that they would still get to go, either with Seth's little brother or Glenn.

I was not going to let Seth have a negative influence on their special day. I got the girls dolled up in their finest Greek attire for the themed event and off they went on Glenn's arms. They looked so pretty in their white gowns, gold sashes, gold bracelets, and miniature up-dos. They danced, participated in hula-hoop contests, played games, and had a great evening. Glenn saved the night, and the girls were happy. That was all that I cared about. I craved peace. I just wanted to enjoy these precious childhood memories without the chaos brought on by Seth.

I was stuck in the vicious cycle of trying to make sense of Seth's behavior. I wore myself out by trying to rationalize with a man who was completely irrational. I wanted to get through to him so badly, but it was like trying to run in quicksand. It was exhausting and pointless. The rest of the summer was equally as bad.

Seth was not taking the girls to his cousin Chris' home as they had both promised in court. I had suspected that it was all a fabrication, but to watch it happen before the ink dried on our court documents was painful. The worst part was that I had already told the girls that they would have the stability of staying with Seth's cousins because I had wanted so badly to believe what they said in court. That first Friday night, they stayed at Seth's condo, which was four hours away, and the second night, they stayed at a friend's house. I had no idea who this "friend" was. The third night, they stayed in a hotel.

Three different beds in three nights, and I saw how this turmoil was affecting them upon their return.

I often referred to the days after Seth's visitation as a "Seth hangover." They would come back exhausted, cranky, sick, regressing in many areas, and suffering from nightmares. Their behavior sometimes left me baffled. My extremely sweet little girls were acting out behaviorally, and it was painful. I knew in my heart that this was because I was the "safe parent." They internalized a lot while with Seth but, like little pressure cookers, they needed to release, which they did for several days after each visit.

On Seth's next visitation weekend, Seth and the girls stayed with Cleo's best friend in Morro Bay, California. The girls returned home from Seth's parenting time with horrible sunburns, and Sarah had a horrendous rash from defecating in her pants at the beach, according to Piper's account of the day. Sarah had been potty trained for two years so that was not something I was accustomed to dealing with. To watch your children suffer, while your hands are tied by a broken system, is not something that I would wish on my worst enemy.

Seth's next visitation in mid-July was yet another hotel to add to the ever-growing list of unfamiliar places and unpredictability. At the end of July, I received a late-night email from Seth that his cousin's home was once again unavailable. According to Seth, he had driven the girls four hours north to his home in the Bay Area but, despite multiple attempts, I was unable to reach Seth or the girls all weekend and was beside myself with worry. I went so far as to contact the police and Child Welfare Services to check on the girls, but they were unable to verify the address that I had been given by Seth. He returned the children hours ahead of his scheduled drop-off time with no explanation.

Despite the picture that Seth and his cousin, Chris, had painted for the court, there was no white picket fence, and there was no stability. The court presentation was all for show. The lack of stability and the chaos my girls were being exposed to was causing anxiety and stress, which were presenting in the form of bed wetting, nightmares, night terrors, teeth grinding, and clinginess, which left me barely able to recognize the once confident, independent little girls that I once knew.

As a mother, my heart shattered week after week. I felt helpless and desperate for someone to save my children. I went into this battle naively believing that if I told the truth, my children would be protected. I was beginning to realize that I needed to be more strategic in my battle because, to date, I felt like I was failing at every turn. Seth thrived in conflict while I withered.

The Monster in the Parking Structure

One afternoon, Piper confided in me that her dad had been mean to her little sister. I asked her to tell me more. Piper described a situation that occurred late at night after returning to Seth's condo in the Bay Area. She explained that they saw a spider in the room where they were supposed to sleep, and Seth couldn't find it and became frustrated.

Sarah began to cry because she didn't want to sleep on the bed Seth had made for her on the floor. The material in the sleeping bag was rough and scratchy, and she was convinced that the spider was in her sleeping bag. At 4 years old, she was afraid to be in the unfamiliar room with the spider. Seth was growing increasingly frustrated with her cries and threatened her. He told her that if she didn't stop crying, he would make her sleep in the car overnight, which sat parked in a dark, scary parking structure. Seth knew that Sarah was afraid of the parking structure. According to Piper, Sarah then became hysterical and couldn't calm down.

Piper said she followed Seth out of the room and begged him not to put her sister in the parking structure. She promised Seth that she would keep her sister quiet if they could sleep together. He agreed. Piper went back into the room and comforted her little sister. At the age of 6 years old, this little girl was forced to become her sister's protector against her own father. She had taken on a role that even a grown adult would have struggled with. The same role was threatening to break me, and I was a 37-year-old woman.

At a subsequent therapy session, Piper shared this incident with her therapist, and I prayed that this would be the final piece that we needed to show his true colors. The courts had to see the damage being done to these little girls. How could they not? This little girl of mine was speaking her truth and speaking it loudly, but was anyone going to listen?

Cleo and Leonard's Court Declaration

A major source of contention in our marriage, Robert continued to terrify me. I felt like a freight train had hit me when I was served with papers in which Seth was asking the court to lift the orders that prevented Piper and Sarah from being in Robert's presence. There were strict guidelines in our parenting agreement that dictated when the girls could be near Robert, and Cleo had to be present.

It was difficult enough for me to navigate this topic while Seth and I were married, but the thought of me, as my daughters' protector, being removed from the equation was enough to push me over the edge. I couldn't grasp why now, during the divorce battle, Seth wanted this man around our children. Seth was back under the family spell of sweeping issues under the rug because, in their minds, anything kept behind closed doors doesn't exist. In addition, it was Seth's way to stick the knife in and twist it. He knew that this was the direct path to my jugular.

As I read the court declaration from Seth, I would have laughed except for the fact that this wasn't a dream, and my children's well-being and livelihood was at stake. Seth claimed that Robert had changed because he now had a wife and a son. According to Seth, Robert was officially a family man. Even worse was the joint declaration from Cleo and Leonard that read:

> "My husband is a 40-year educator and a past principal before we moved overseas, where he served a similar role. I am a lifelong educator as well, currently working as a school counselor. I do hold a valid and current teaching credential. I come home to California for about eight weeks in the summer and two weeks at Christmas, while my husband is here living with Robert's family. We have grown sons and are a close-knit family and have extended family with ties to the community since 1976.
>
> I respect Tina Swithin as the mother of our grandchildren. However, Ms. Swithin has decided that being in the presence of our eldest son, Robert, somehow presents a risk to her children. This has no basis in fact, and is the reason my husband and I would like to address the court today. I do understand Ms. Swithin's concerns. But while I understand them, I in no way agree with them. Robert has had some issues with depression in the past and has said and texted some terribly inappropriate things to Ms. Swithin. His intentions were to protect and defend his brother, "Seth": his methods were wrong and we do not agree or condone them. However, that does not mean he is a danger to Piper and Sarah. We resent the implication that we would somehow put our grandchildren at risk. We resent the implication that Robert is a terrible person and that merely being in his presence will damage the girls.

> Robert is now married, a father of a one-year old son and a respected contractor in this area. He would be here today if it weren't for the fact that he is required to be on a job. It has been difficult already to have so little time together as a family when I'm home and to further divide that time between Seth and the girls on their weekends together and the rest of the family. My husband and I share a home with Robert, his wife, and our grandson.
>
> We are simply asking you, your Honor, to modify the custodial agreement so that when Seth has custody of the girls, they can be in the presence of their uncle, Robert, and can grow up in a caring family-oriented environment with their aunt and cousin."

Stepping back into reality for a second, Robert did in fact have a wife, Phonphan, that he purchased from Thailand. As the family story has been told to me, Robert corresponded with two women in Thailand and scheduled times to meet with both of them. When he arrived with his parents for the first meeting, there had been a major understanding due to the language barrier, and Phonphan, was under the impression that they were to be married. In fact, before they knew it, Leonard, Cleo, Robert, and Kyle were thrust into a Thai village wedding ceremony where white bracelets were tied to their wrists as part of the celebration. Robert and his bride were officially married, and he called off his scheduled meeting with his second prospect.

Robert's wife left her first-born son in Thailand and, together, they had another child. The fact that Robert purchased a wife and was able to impregnate her does not mean he was miraculously cured. He was and still is to this day the same man who made out with a 14-year-old girl, beat tiny puppies, speaks of murdering and raping women, and spews racial slurs. He is still the same man that I will fight to protect my daughters from with every ounce of my being.

I worked feverishly to build my case and pour my heart out in court declarations. While I had always given 100% while fighting to protect my children, I was in overdrive on this topic. I reached out to countless people who knew Robert and who had witnessed his disturbing behaviors over the years. I quickly discovered that many did not want to be involved, or too much time had gone by and they did not feel confident that they could properly recount situations that would support my case. Despite the lack of witnesses, I felt very confident about the case I had built and I knew that, at a minimum, it would be cause for the court to err on the side of caution.

Minor's Counsel is Appointed

Our August court date came and, to my dismay, the court lifted the orders slightly as it pertained to Robert. The court order specifically stated that my daughters could be in the presence of Robert at any time, as long as they were in the presence of Seth, Cleo, Leonard, or Seth's cousin, Chris. I felt like screaming, "You can't trust these people! They don't respect court orders! They believe they are above the courts!" I was distraught and having a difficult time processing this news, given the substantiality of my accusations against him. I didn't understand how this happened and struggled to place one foot in front of the other while leaving to get to my car.

The only positive item that came from the order that day was that they also granted my request for court appointed minor's counsel. As the judge was handing down the orders, he gestured to the only attorney, Mr. Anders, who happened to be standing in the courtroom. Mr. Anders was waiting to be heard on another matter. I was hopeful, as Mr. Anders had the reputation of being a cutthroat bulldog, and he was the attorney that husbands in our town conferred with so their wives couldn't hire him. He was the most infamous, well-known attorney in our area, and I hoped that he would be the voice and the advocate that my children needed.

According to the court order, minor's counsel was ordered to investigate the allegations that I had posed and were assigned to make a recommendation in the best interest of my daughters. We were ordered to pay him $100 per hour, which was shocking to me as I knew his normal hourly rate was well over $400 per hour. I remained hopeful because this was what I had been fighting for. It was no longer my word against Seth's; there would be a third-party investigation. My only concern was that Mr. Anders was not normally appointed as minor's counsel and, in fact, other local attorneys were left scratching their heads when I relayed the news that he had been appointed to our case. One attorney commented that Mr. Anders was, "in the wrong place at the wrong time," implying that most attorneys would not want to be a part of my case and that he was appointed because he just happened to be the only one standing there in the scope of the commissioner.

The judge placed a new date on the calendar, which was August 31, 2011. This hellish battle had been going on for exactly two years, and I hoped that this would bring both closure and safety. At this particular court date, there would be a report of the finding from minor's counsel. I was hopeful, and these little victories gave me the fuel I needed to continue marching forward in this battle.

In the week following the court date, I met with Mr. Anders, who listened to my concerns. He asked all the right questions. I was incredibly organized because I had been waiting for this moment for so long. I had been prepared to show my case and documentation on a moment's notice to anyone who was willing to listen. He asked me to email him additional information on several topics that we discussed, and I agreed. His job was to call everyone who knew us: teachers, principals, nannies, babysitters, marital therapists, and friends.

Seth and his parents had met with Mr. Anders days before I met with him, but I was determined to stand firm in my truth and not let doubt creep in, despite knowing that they had likely laid a foundation of lies for me to walk on. In the initial interview, Mr. Anders asked me about Seth's brother Robert. I took a deep breath and poured my heart out to him. I outlined all my concerns, which were organized in bullet-point format to keep me on track. Mr. Anders leaned back in his chair, crossed his arms and with a smug look, condescendingly said, "I was told that you had an affair with him and that you are bitter."

What the fuck did he just say? An affair? My mind was racing. I had prepared myself for their lies but this? This was pure evil, and I felt nauseous. I stumbled to find my words and blatantly denied the accusation. The depth of dishonesty was something that I couldn't grasp. Everything after that was a blur, but I did manage to take notes on what Mr. Anders had requested of me. I stayed up until 1:30 a.m. the next morning compiling everything that Mr. Anders asked for and emailed it all to his office.

After weeks went by, I began to get increasingly anxious. The court date was fast approaching and my daughter's teacher had yet to hear from Mr. Anders' office. Our former nannies had not heard from Mr. Anders either. No one on my list had been called.

On one particular visitation weekend, Seth refused to tell me where the children were going to be residing while in his care. Seth was due to pick them up at 3:30 p.m., so I reached out to Mr. Anders for assistance. The attorney called me back at 3 p.m. and expressed frustration with Seth's lack of cooperation. Mr. Anders agreed that Seth seemed to thrive on making me worry over my daughters and their whereabouts. Mr. Anders expressed that he failed to understand why it was so difficult for Seth to simply tell me where my children were going to be staying during his parenting time. Once again, I was hopeful that he would continue to see through Seth.

It was the day before court, and no one on my collateral list had heard a word from Mr. Anders' office. I couldn't figure out what was happening. I didn't understand, and I felt desperate. This was the person who was supposed to be working in the best interest of my daughters. At 5 p.m. the night before court, I received a call. Mr. Anders asked if it was okay to postpone the court date; he wanted to ask for a continuance.

In a strange way, I was more relieved than I was frustrated. My greatest fear was that Mr. Anders would go into court with limited information. I was confident that now he would contact all the people who knew us. I was confident that he would contact the people who could verify my claims. I had to remain confident, as he was my only hope. Court was postponed until Wednesday, September 14th, 2011.

The Big Court Date

It was now two days before our big court date, and Mr. Anders had not contacted a single person on my collateral list. My anxiety was through the roof, and I knew I was walking a fine line. If I called his office demanding to know why he was putting zero effort into my case, it would surely backfire. As much as I wanted to hold him accountable, I was smart enough to know what a significant player he was in this equation. The last thing I needed was to anger the man who held my children's lives in his hands. Mr. Anders was making it clear that I was just another case on his desk but, to me, this was my daughters' well-being; their lives were dependent on this investigation.

Some people go to a happy place in their mind for stress relief. I picture "hurdles" in my mind. My counselor, Cindy, told me to picture myself jumping over hurdles, one after another. Ironically, the same week Cindy had given me this visual image, I received a letter from my sister. Inside the letter was an inspirational wallet card to carry in my pocket. It was a poem about jumping over life's hurdles. In my happy place, I am strong, driven, and I fly over hurdles with ease. I knew that *this* was the mindset that I needed.

The day before the court date, I received a call from Mr. Anders' paralegal. She nonchalantly asked for the names and phone numbers of my collateral contacts. I was confused. She was requesting the information that I had spent so many hours compiling weeks ago. I felt like I plowed straight into a hurdle. I took a deep breath and gave her the requested information for the second time and then, I began to pray.

I questioned myself: why was I feeling so powerless? I was giving my power and faith away to other people. It was clear that Mr. Anders was putting little to no effort into protecting my daughters. We were paying him a quarter of his normal hourly rate and, as such, he was giving us less than a quarter of his efforts. I was giving my power to an attorney who clearly didn't care and a court system that is overloaded. These people didn't have to go home and look my little girls in the eyes. These were *my* daughters, and I needed to take control and fight. I needed to awaken my inner momma bear once again. I needed to protect my children.

I rushed home and shifted into high gear reviewing my paperwork and refreshing myself for what felt like the millionth time. I divided my case up by categories, and I made bullet points under each of the key issues. I know from past experience that nerves can take over and the best-laid plans can go awry. I had a burst of confidence and a sense of calm come over me that night.

I arrived in court early to discover that Seth was not going to appear in person. He was going to appear via court conference call, meaning he was allowed to skip personal appearance and instead call into the courtroom via speakerphone. I was relieved to hear this, as being in the same room with him often knocked me off kilter. I sat at the table as Mr. Anders reported his findings.

Mr. Anders had spoken to Sarah's school principal and Piper's therapist. He had also called Seth's cousin Chris, who gave him rave reviews as a father. He called one of Seth's friends, who also gave him rave reviews. He didn't call the people who actually knew us. He didn't speak to our live-in nannies or the teachers who interacted with us every day. Mr. Anders didn't call my cousins or my family members, nor did he call my friends.

I sat there and waited patiently for Mr. Anders to finish. I checked the items off my list as he addressed each one. Mr. Anders closed his report, and the commissioner asked me if I had anything to add. I did. I had so many things to add, largely because Mr. Anders had not done his due diligence.

I brought up Seth's drunk-in-public offenses that were uncovered during the investigation but, shockingly, weren't even mentioned by Mr. Anders. These items substantiated my ongoing claims of alcohol abuse. Getting arrested for being drunk in public is one thing if you are a college student but a 35-year old man? I addressed Robert and the disturbing issues associated with him that weren't mentioned nor were they even investigated, which left me dumbfounded given that this was the very topic that caused Mr. Anders to be assigned to our case.

I focused heavily on the fact that Seth was continuously lying about the children's whereabouts during the visits. I addressed the most recent visitation of September 3-4. He claimed they were in San Diego, but I knew they weren't. In the past, it would have been my word against his but not this time. Something came over me in court; it was the same sense of calm that I had felt the night before. For the first time, I felt like I was in control. Prior to walking through the courtroom doors, I mentally visualized myself grabbing ahold of God's hand, and I felt his presence with me in the courtroom.

The commissioner seemed to be listening to me and asked Seth over the court speakerphone where the children were residing during the last visitation. Seth replied that they were staying at his condo in San Diego. The judge asked him to describe the weekend visitation, specifically, what time he picked them up, what they did after that, and so on. Seth claimed that he picked them up at 3:30 p.m. This was true. Seth claimed that he took them to our local farmers' market. This was true. Seth claimed that they had dinner and drove to San Diego afterwards.

The commissioner pressed more—what time did they get to San Diego? What did they do Saturday morning when they woke up? What did they do during the day on Saturday? Saturday night? Sunday? Seth painted a huge mural using a colorful palate of lies.

Seth said they arrived late Friday night, and he carried my sleeping daughters to his condo around 11 p.m. They woke up the next morning and went to a Starbucks and then to a park. According to Seth, it was an entire weekend of fun and games.

I waited for Seth to finish and then I said, "Your Honor, that's not true. What he is saying is not true." The commissioner asked, "Does anyone have GPS to prove where the children were and who is lying?"

"I do," I answered, and I did.

Everyone in the courtroom stared at me. Mr. Anders looked uncomfortable as he peered at the paperwork I was fumbling through. I pulled out my very detailed GPS reports, which showed my daughters' location every hour on the hour all weekend long. They weren't where Seth claimed they were and, in fact, they were staying at Robert's home the entire weekend. It was just another lie in his huge barrel of lies. The difference this time was that he was lying to the commissioner, to the court, and to the minor's counsel.

Two months prior, at the advice of two friends in law enforcement, I had purchased a GPS device. It was a small flip phone, but it allowed me to log in and see where my daughters were at any time of the day or night. Seth had no idea that I was tracking them; no one knew.

The commissioner called a recess, and we were all dismissed for a 15-minute break. While we were in the hallway, Mr. Anders looked annoyed and demanded to know why I hadn't told him about the GPS prior to court. He was fuming because he hadn't done his job, and it was apparent to the court. He looked like a fool, which didn't sit well with his elevated ego. Truth be told, I had called his office and emailed multiple times but received no response. I also knew that my only chance of proving that Seth was a liar was to catch him in the act, in a lie, and in the courtroom.

Court resumed and we were asked to take our seats. The commissioner started the proceedings by saying, "I have told you on multiple occasions that you were losing credibility in my courtroom. Today, you lied to me, you lied to the court, and you lied to Mr. Anders. There will be sanctions for this. I am awarding full legal and physical custody to Ms. Swithin. There will be no overnight visits. Visits are restricted to 10:00 a.m. to 4:00 p.m. on Saturdays and Sundays for the first, third, and fifth weekends of each month. Ms. Swithin will be able to go to sleep at night knowing where her children are—they will now be in their own beds."

I stood up and tears started to stream down my face. I could barely see through my tears to open the little wooden gate that led into the viewing area of the courtroom. As I walked out, the people in the courtroom were silently clapping their hands and smiling. One woman was holding her heart, and I could see tears in her eyes, as well. I completely forgot that these people were there. I had gone into my warrior zone, and I became Mama Bear. These complete strangers were cheering me on.

This was a monumental victory in my plight to protect my children. After over two years of fighting, I had succeeded in getting full custody, which is virtually unheard of, and I successfully ended overnight visits. I could go to sleep knowing that my daughters were safe. As hard as this journey was, I never lost sight of the goal: to protect my daughters. I knew that they weren't safe with Seth and his family at any time of the day or night, but at least the girls were with me at night. I was going to sit in gratitude and celebrate this major victory.

The Saga Continues

Six weeks had passed since the last court appearance, and I still had hope that Seth would start pulling himself together. I wanted to believe the recent court date would serve as a wake-up call. I got the girls ready for their Saturday visit, and we made the 30-minute drive to the designated location. On the way, Piper asked if Daddy was going to show up. "I'm not sure, but it is his weekend, and I hope that he will be here. I haven't spoken to him, so I'm not positive," I replied. I knew in my heart that there was a 50/50 chance that he would actually be there. We arrived for the exchange and waited; he didn't show up.

I wanted to buy a huge bubble to protect my daughters. I wanted to find a way to shelter them from these disappointments. I knew in my heart that this is their path, and my job is to give them the coping skills they need to deal with the disappointments. My job was and is to model what a healthy, loving parent is and to provide stability and love when they are with me. I can't control Seth, and I can't force him to be the dependable, healthy role model that I want him to be. Controlling Seth would be a full-time job that I don't want.

The next day was once again Seth's daytime visit, and I was willing to bet that Seth would be a no-show. I knew it would be another one-hour, round trip, wasted drive; but my hands were tied by a court order that required me to show up. Sure enough, Seth was not at our designated meeting spot and, for the first time, I decided to tell Piper and Sarah the truth. I gently let them know that I, too, was frustrated and didn't understand the choices that Daddy made. We went home and went on with our day.

Up until that day, my normal mode of operation was to have a back-up plan in case Seth didn't show up. I usually verbalized my plan to the girls by saying, "If Daddy comes today, fabulous! If Daddy doesn't come then we will do X, Y, and Z." My definition of "X, Y, and Z" usually involved some type of fun activity or a treat. I would jump through hoops to prevent Piper and

Sarah from feeling an ounce of disappointment. I came to realize that by overly protecting them, I was doing them a disservice.

A few weeks later, at one early-morning custody exchange in a coffee shop parking lot, I saw Leonard drive up and noticed that Seth was not in the car. I rolled down my window, and Leonard explained that Seth was running late and that he would take the girls. "No, you aren't taking the girls," I replied. "I do not feel comfortable with you taking the girls and have previously consulted with an attorney on this matter. I will not set a precedent that you are an acceptable caretaker for them. Have Seth call me when he gets into town." Hours later, Seth contacted me sounding hungover. He arrived at our exchange location with a smirking Leonard driving the car.

In a two-month period of time, there had been a total of six scheduled visits. Seth was a no-show on four of those visits, and he was hours late to another. These are not good odds in Las Vegas, and they are not good odds when you are betting on the hearts of two little girls.

The Narc Decoder

Carrying pepper spray around my house became a part of my everyday life. While I loved my little condo, I didn't feel safe in my house. I had been feeling very on edge because, upon returning home one day, I discovered a videotape of my wedding in Hawaii that Seth had perched against my front gate. Seth loved to leave subtle reminders of his presence in my life. This type of bizarre, psychopathic behavior kept me operating in a constant fight-or-flight mode.

I often said that from a clinical perspective, Seth's emails and text messages would be fascinating to read. Because I was being hit from every angle by Seth's verbal and behavioral assaults, they were often debilitating. There were times that my aunt would read the messages for me and tell me how to respond because his attacks were slowly destroying me, and merely the sight of his name in my inbox would cause my anxiety to soar.

In between the fury of emails and text messages, I was often left hanging when it came to making important decisions about what school I would be enrolling the girls in and holiday schedules, and the worst were his attempts to derail me from making medical decisions by completely ignoring my emails. There were no resources to guide me, and I was often left feeling defeated on how to proceed in a court-approved fashion.

Over time and with a tremendous amount of research under my belt, I became savvier about how I responded to Seth. If I needed an answer about a medical or educational decision, I would give Seth a deadline such as, "If I don't hear from you by December 8th, I will assume that you are in agreement with signing Piper up for soccer, and I will proceed accordingly." Another example was, "If I do not hear from you by Wednesday the 11th, I will take that to mean you have no problem with the changes proposed." The key was to give him ample time to respond but not let his non-response control my life.

Through my extensive research on Cluster B personality disorders, such as narcissistic personality disorder, antisocial personality disorder, and borderline personality disorder, I uncovered a new language that took quite a bit of insight to understand. As it turns out, Seth and I were speaking completely different languages. I spoke English while he was speaking "Narc-ish." I am convinced that there is a Narc-ish manual somewhere with step-by-step instructions on how to inflict fear, confusion, and despair. The narcissist's secret language can only be decoded by those who aren't fooled by the narcissist's stealth ability to inflict confusion and chaos.

I invented a machine that I affectionately refer to as "The Narc Decoder," and it has restored my sanity, empowered me, and given me a good laugh on occasion. Seth's attacks once brought me to my knees begging for mercy; now, I can successfully scrub down the projection, lies, attacks, and ulterior motives.

> Original Message: Tina- The beauty of my karma is that I have had mine delivered. I have lost everything. Wish you well, Tina. -Seth

> "Snap, fizzle, pop" and out comes the decoded email: Tina- I get my jollies by threatening you with karma. For me, it's like mind masturbation. Oh, how I love it! It's a way for me to threaten your life without crossing legal limits. What I am really trying to say is, I hope to see you in a dark alley where I will promptly slit your throat. Wish you well, Tina. Sleep tight! -Seth

The slew of messages seemed never ending. Seth thrived on tormenting me. I quickly learned not to ask Seth to make changes to the schedule because a simple request invited insanity into my world.

> Original Message: Tina- We will switch to 2:30 pm – 8:30 pm so that you can go to the birthday party with Sarah. That being my

compromised position. There has been a minimum of 6 birthday parties on Saturday I have brought the girls to over the past 3 years. I am only to assume that your libel and slander about me and my family to the other mothers that will be at the party would make it an uncomfortable situation for every parent there that you have gossiped negatively to about me. Personally, I would have no problem meeting everyone and showing the other parents that I am just a good dad and a pleasant person.

My Mom and I would like to bring the girls to San Diego Zoo and Legoland. We would like to do this August 1st- August 4th. Would you agree to this short summer vacation now so we can make hotel arrangements? Also by Tuesday AM, I will be giving money to the Child Support office. Best regards, Seth

<u>"Snap, fizzle, pop" and out comes the decoded email</u>: Tina- I need to tell you what a victim I am by no fault of my own and how you have wronged me.

Let me just slip in a quick request for overnight visits out of the county when the court and judge have found that I am not trustworthy enough to have the girls overnight. Maybe we can just let bygones be bygones and you can forget that you've been fighting me in court for three years? It comes down to the fact that I need new photos of our daughters having fun at so that my friends on Facebook will believe that I am the great father that I claim to be. Oh, by the way- I will pay you the child support that I've been neglecting to pay for the past year if you agree to what I want. If you don't agree then you can forget it. Best Regards, Seth

Sure enough, this wasn't the end of the topic by any means. The next email from Seth rolled in by the end of the week:

> Tina- I accommodated your request to change the visitation time this Saturday to 2:30 p.m. to 8:30 p.m. I do look forward to seeing the girls on the 21st at 2:30 PM and the 22nd at 11 AM. You will recollect that following the custody evaluation, that the recommendation is that the girls spend three weekends with overnights with me as well. The other agreement was that I could take the girls on a five-day vacation. I kindly asked you to grant a vacation to San Diego with my Mom and the girls.

> I do not want to have to go request a hearing with court to spend Wednesday the 1st of August through Sunday the 5th of August with the girls to bring them to San Diego Wild Animal Park and Lego Land. Would you please say this would be fine? Best regards, Seth

Stepping back into reality for a moment, the evaluation and court order that Seth referred to was from June of 2010. A lot had changed since that time. Mainly, the court had seen through him, and he was caught lying about the girls' whereabouts on multiple occasions. Seth's lies resulted in sanctions that stripped him of his overnight visits.

I think that Seth truly believes he can choose whichever court order fits his needs in the moment. It doesn't matter that the order is over two years old or that there have been five to ten new orders that supersede the one that he is referencing.

My response to Seth was short and simple:

> Seth - As you know, there is a court order in place that supersedes the order from 2010. You are asking me to violate a court order, and the answer is "no." I do not feel comfortable with you taking the girls out of the county for overnight visits. I plan to adhere to the court order as it is written. Tina

I had studied the Gray Rock style of communication, which basically states that your communication is so cold and boring that the narcissist or sociopath loses interest and stops looking to you as a source of their narcissistic feed (Lovefraud Reader, 2012). While this is a highly advised style of communication for dealing with a personality disordered individual, it often reflects poorly on the healthy parent in court as it seems cold and rigid and goes against the Kumbaya-style of co-parenting that the court expects from both parties. I became skilled at my own style of communication, which weaves common courtesy and pleasantries into the Gray Rock communication. I wanted the court to know that I was not the problem in this equation.

Back to Court

In mid-November 2011, I placed another court date on the calendar for December 14th. As much as the thought of court made my stomach turn, I needed to make changes to the current court order. Out of the past eight visitations, Seth had only shown up for four visits. He didn't call, email, or text. We were spending hours driving to these visits, and then the court order required us to wait 30 minutes for him to show up before the visit was cancelled. This meant buying an item at the coffee shop upon arrival, and then purchasing a second item after 30 minutes so that I had black-and-white evidence in the form of receipts to show that I was following orders. By this point, I knew the he-said, she-said didn't hold up in court and that Seth's dishonesty stretched far and wide.

I called Seth at one parenting exchange when 15 minutes had passed, and he hadn't arrived. To my surprise, Seth answered and said, "I didn't realize that it was my weekend."

"I'm sorry. I don't know what that's like. I don't know what it's like to forget that you are a parent," I replied before hanging up the phone and scrambling to find childcare. I was scheduled for an important work event.

On one of the four visits, Piper and Sarah came home and told me that Seth had slept for a long time while they were at the beach building sand castles. The girls were walking to and from the ocean alone to collect water for their sandcastles while Seth slept on a blanket. As he only sees them for a total of six hours each visit, I have a hard time comprehending how he could spend a single moment of that time sleeping; but, I knew the reality: he was hungover.

Was the commissioner going to be frustrated and annoyed to see us back on the calendar? Absolutely. I wanted the court to know what my daughters were going through. I wanted the occurrences to be on court record, and I wanted Seth to be held accountable. I was thankful that I didn't have an attorney to hush me or to tell me "this" or "that" wasn't *enough* to put in front of the court. As long as I was breathing, I planned to put everything in front of the court until someone decided to listen.

One Mom's Battle Begins

In November of 2011, I looked over at my (then) boyfriend Glenn and said, "I'm going to start a blog and I'm going to call it, 'One Mom's Battle.'" I needed an outlet to share my journey and I also wanted a place where those closest to me could follow court proceedings without me having to repeat my story over and over again. It was a way for me to release and purge the craziness that had become my life because the alternative was for me to drown in the madness.

I felt as though I was constantly overloading my friends and family with my trials and tribulations. I felt guilty that Glenn had to constantly hear about the drama unfolding in my life. The blog gave me a place to heal by telling my story. It provided me with incredible insight as I put together a timeline, and it allowed me to see the issues that were present from the week I met Seth. It was my place of refuge, and it allowed my friends and family to follow my journey at their discretion. In the first two months of writing, the blog gave me more healing than two years of therapy had provided. It also allowed me to see my truth in black and white.

I left my house on the morning of November 17th to drive Piper to first grade. We drove, sang songs, and talked on the way to school. I pulled my car up in front of the school to let Piper out and, as I opened my car door, a car flew in beside me and blocked my car. I saw that Seth was driving the car, and my life flashed before my eyes as Robert got out of the car from the passenger side. I didn't know what was happening, but I was trembling. I knew in my heart that they were both capable of taking my life, and I couldn't make sense of what was happening or why they would be at Piper's school.

Robert stood at only 5' 9" with a very thin build, but I lived in fear of him. As I faced him, I quickly scanned him for a gun. I felt as though I was in a bad dream, one that had haunted me on a regular basis. With a dark, evil smirk on his face, he was physically blocking me from exiting my car as he handed me a large stack of court paperwork. I grabbed the papers from Robert, threw them onto my front seat, and continued helping my daughter out of the car. I couldn't believe that they were doing this in front of Piper.

I drove away from the school and pulled over to review the paperwork. I was shaking so badly that I didn't feel safe driving. Seth had scheduled an emergency hearing for the very next morning. As usual, the paperwork was rambling and strange. Most of it didn't even make sense. The bottom line was, Seth's aunt Lamia found my blog, "One Mom's Battle," and wanted the court to order me to remove it from the internet. They wanted to silence me, as abuse thrives in silence and darkness.

Seth accused me of parental alienation syndrome, defamation, and slander. He wanted to take my blog away from me. My blog wasn't about him. The blog was my healing. It was about my desire to one day help other women walking in my shoes. It was my journey, and it had nothing to do with Seth.

I printed every page from my blog and submitted it all to the court for review. While I knew in my heart that the hearing request would be denied, I was still concerned. I drove to the courthouse to wait for the paperwork and was incredibly thankful to read the commissioner's words: "Denied- No Hearing to be set."

T-Rex

Around Thanksgiving in 2011, I was driving with the girls and Piper asked me if the upcoming weekend was Seth's scheduled visitation. When I confirmed that it was, indeed, her weekend with him, she informed me that she didn't want to go. She then questioned whether she had to go, and I explained that she did have to go. I went on to say, "Mom and Dad work with a team of people who decide what is best for our family. I may not always agree with the decisions that are made, and Dad may not agree with the decisions that are made, but we all have to follow the rules."

I am very cautious about how I approach these conversations because I never want to be accused of persuading her or speaking poorly about Seth. I keep those thoughts tucked safely in my head. I asked her why she didn't want to go with her dad, but Piper became quiet and didn't respond. I took my cue and let it go. I want my daughters to know that I am here if they wish to speak, but I never want them to feel pressured. It pained me to know that this tiny 6-year old girl was feeling angst.

As I was pulling my car into the driveway, I heard Piper's voice from the backseat: "Dad calls you 'T-Rex."

"What?" I asked.

"T-Rex. Dad says bad things about you to everyone, and he calls you T-Rex, so I won't know who he's talking about," she explained.

"Who is everyone?" I asked Piper.

"To Grandpa, Uncle John, Uncle Robert, and other people in the family. He says really mean things, and I don't like going over there anymore. I wish I could just stay home," Piper confided in me.

What I wanted to say in that moment: "Dad says mean things because he is a mean, sick person. He is a selfish man-child who couldn't care less about the damage he inflicts on his daughters. He's as much of a psychopath as O. J. Simpson!"

What I said instead: "I don't understand why Dad would do that. It's a poor choice, and I will talk to him about it."

I'll gladly claim the title T-Rex. I'll claim it as my role in protecting my children. Tina Rex: fierce and fearless against the evil predators of the world. I will claim it—but do not use that term in a way that will hurt our daughters.

I emailed Seth about calling me T-Rex in front of the girls. My email was very brief. Obviously, he is entitled to feel any way he wants, but I asked him to please refrain from speaking poorly about me in front of the girls. I didn't email Seth because I thought he'd have a "come-to-Jesus moment" and repent; I emailed him mainly to document the incident. Seth responded and actually acknowledged that he called me T-Rex. True to form, Seth then dove straight into his normal ramblings and threats.

Seth accused me of quizzing the girls about their visits to the point that they feel like they must tell on him. Seth said that I was a parental alienator. He said that he was planning to report me to Child Welfare Services because the judge didn't agree with his *ex parte* motion pertaining to my blog.

I realized in that moment that I was stronger. I could finally see right through Seth. I could almost predict his emails. I wasn't affected by his emails any longer. In fact, I opened the email and only felt pity for Seth. I knew the sick high he received from believing that he had successfully pushed by buttons.

Seth has a knack for spinning everything back on someone else and is unable to accept fault or responsibility for anything. He admitted to calling me "T-Rex," but then spun it around so that it was actually my fault that my daughter told me about it. I watched Seth skillfully do this for years, whether it was in our marriage or in our business, but it was empowering to see through his manipulations. As clear as day, I saw through him and he hated that.

Seth isn't capable of sending an email without adding a personal jab or dig. He ended the email by pointing out that because our divorce was final, I should not be using an email address with his last name. He ended the email by saying, "Do you have another email that does not have (married name) in the address? The judge gave you back your maiden name months ago."

I saw the email and closed it. No feelings were elicited, and my heart wasn't pounding. I knew that my healing was in progress.

Reclaiming My Identity

The girls came back from their weekend visitation the first week of December and, during a six-hour visit, Seth found ways to inflict further damage on the girls. We met at the coffee shop for our exchange, and the first thing I heard when Piper entered my car was: "Mom, Dad was calling you 'T-Rex' to Popi [Leonard] again yesterday, and they were laughing and saying mean things."

Seth sees his daughters for a total of 24 hours per month, so he has roughly 696 hours of free time per month to talk about me to whomever he chooses. That's a lot of time to play victim or wallow in self-pity, mixed with a shot or two of negative energy. I do not understand the need to waste a single moment of his already limited time on openly bashing me to two innocent little girls. But alas, I have to remind myself whom I am dealing with.

I struggled to find the right response when the girls told me these things. I was torn because I don't want the girls to feel like they need to tell me these things but, more importantly, they shouldn't be hearing these things in the first place. How do you teach your children that it's not nice to call people names when their own father chooses to do that very thing?

When Piper and Sarah got into the car and told me that Seth spoke poorly of me, I chose not to turn it into a huge ordeal. I quietly said, "That is Dad's choice to do that. However, I don't think he should be saying those things in front of you. I also don't want you to feel like you have to tell me these things. If you want to talk about it, then I am happy to do that. However, it isn't your job to worry about this. Your job is to be a kid and not to worry about adult things. I know my truth and I know who I am, so when people say unkind things, I don't allow it to bother me."

By leaving our marriage, I received the opportunity to walk away from our pretend world and reclaim my identity. The material possessions were all symbolic of a fake, empty, and lonely existence. I wasn't fake, empty, or lonely; I was happy to be free of Seth's world.

Through the trials and tribulations of my divorce and custody battle, I learned that life was really about the little things. In early December, I spent an entire day reclaiming my identity. While most people normally cringe at the mere mention of the DMV or Social Security office, I was ecstatic to be there. I walked out of the government offices holding papers that left me feeling more empowered than I could have imagined. I was so thrilled that I then drove to the bank and ordered new checks. I reclaimed my identity as Tina Marie Swithin. The name I was born with and the name that I intended to keep for the rest of my life. These little moments filled my tank, and I was grateful to leave Seth's name in my rearview mirror.

Refusal to Follow Court Orders

Our next court date had arrived. On December 14th, I woke up feeling confident and strong. I was requesting a change to our drop-off and pick-up location. It was frustrating to spend an hour driving when Seth didn't feel that showing up for his parenting time was a high priority.

- I asked that the exchange location be changed to a place five minutes from our house. Verdict: granted.
- I asked that Seth be ordered to notify us if he planned to exercise his visitation. I prefer to shelter the girls from the disappointment if Seth doesn't plan to show up. Verdict: granted. Seth was ordered to notify us 24 hours in advance *if* he planned to exercise his visitation.
- Minor's counsel issued a request that Seth be prohibited from calling me names in front of the girls. Mr. Anders passed out copies of emails in which Seth admitted to calling me T-Rex. Verdict: the commissioner agreed that it needed to stop. The attorney agreed that it needed to stop. I agreed that it needed to stop. The commissioner stated that there is already an order in place preventing Seth from this behavior and appeared frustrated but made no further orders on this topic.

I questioned the significance of a court order if Seth faced no consequences for violating it. I was flabbergasted that the commissioner didn't hold him accountable for behavior that was clearly not in my daughters' best interest. Did parental rights carry so much weight that the court would allow this behavior to continue sans consequences? Apparently so.

I emailed Seth on a Wednesday night prior to his visitation to recap the details from court, specifically the 24-hour notification order. Seth was required to notify us on Friday morning if he planned to exercise his visitation. Friday morning came and went with no notice. I finally sent Seth an email on Friday afternoon around 4 p.m. asking whether he planned to pick up the girls. I received no response.

I awoke Saturday morning and checked my emails again. There was still no notification. At 10:05 a.m., five minutes after his court-ordered parenting time, Seth began calling my phone. At 10:30 a.m., Seth emailed me one of his normal, attacking rants.

I was torn. Do I follow the court orders or do I let Seth continue to operate with no regard for the judge, court, or orders? If I didn't hold him to the orders, then, in essence, I was also violating the orders. Cleo began texting me. Seth began denying that the order existed, and he created his own version of the order. I sent him an email stating that I would make an exception this time; however, moving forward I planned to follow the order as it was written.

I went to the courthouse on Monday morning to verify that my memory was serving me correctly. The order stated: "The petitioner shall email the respondent 24 hours in advance to let her know he will exercise visitation; if no email is received, visitation is cancelled."

The new court order protected Piper and Sarah from the constant disappointment of waiting at the exchange location when Seth didn't show up for visitations. It allowed us a sense of normalcy and prevented Seth from creating havoc in our schedule. If Seth didn't email to confirm visitation, the order allowed us to make other plans and go on with our life. It stopped Seth's ability to rule our lives, which is what he thrives on.

Out of the Mouths of Babes

I was talking to Piper and Sarah at breakfast about the New Year (2012) and my aspirations to have more joy in my heart and to live in gratitude. We talked about things that we hoped for and things that we wanted to work on. Piper looked straight at me and said, "Do you know what I wish for but I don't think it will happen? For Daddy to be nicer to you." I didn't know what to say. I leaned over and gave her a hug.

A few days later, I picked up Piper from her counseling session and, on the way home, she said, "Mom, do you know another reason why I don't like going to Robert's and Dad's house?"

"Why, honey?" I said, with that sinking feeling in the pit of my stomach.

"Dad and Robert have the photo from your wedding in a frame on the fireplace, and they covered you up with blue tape," Piper said. "But Dad isn't covered in blue tape ... only you. It's your wedding picture."

I took a deep breath and prayed for composure and wisdom. *God ... can you hear this? Can you tell me what to do? What do I say to this?*

"Wow, that doesn't sound very nice at all," I answered while trying to figure out what to say next. What do you say to your 6-year-old daughter when she tells you that her father keeps an enlarged photo of you covered over with tape? My mind was racing. In my humble opinion, the word "psychotic" was designed for people like Seth and Robert and the behavior they exhibited.

Piper then went on to say, "I didn't want to tell you because I didn't want to hurt your feelings. It isn't up on the fireplace right now, because I think Noni [Cleo] made them take it down when she came for Christmas."

Drunk Driving

Shortly after the New Year, I found myself standing in the criminal court division at the local courthouse. Seth's younger brother, Carter, informed me that Seth had been arrested for a DUI. The most recent disclosure was that he had received a DUI in October, which meant that he was driving the girls on a suspended license. The date that Carter provided also lined up with the morning that Leonard had shown up on his own to pick up the girls. Now, it made sense why he showed up driving a hungover Seth just hours later; he had just bailed him out of jail that morning. I also knew about a 1997 DUI arrest while he was in college so, together, these infractions were painting quite a picture in addition to his drunk-in-public arrests.

I was struggling with the computer's outdated instructions, and an attorney who happened to be waiting in line offered to help me. We entered Seth's name into the public computer, and several items popped up, which were also foreign to me. The attorney looked at the screen and said, "Someone you know has quite a drinking problem." Seth does have quite an alcohol problem, which was a source of contention throughout our marriage; while that was bad enough, now I wasn't around all the time to shelter the girls from his substance abuse issues.

The following week, I was able to obtain the arrest record, which went on to describe the night of Seth's arrest. The arresting officer actually pulled up upon Seth's vehicle, which was stopped in the middle of the southbound lane at 2 a.m. He wasn't pulled over on the side of the road, he was dozing off in the middle of the road. The officer immediately smelled alcohol on his breath and noted that his eyes were red and watery.

Seth went on to tell the officer that he hadn't drank any alcohol and that he was a triathlete. He asked the officers if he could just lock his car and walk home but upon further questioning, he was disoriented and didn't even know where he was. In the field sobriety test, they had to explain the instructions five times and he still failed. Two different officers attempted to give Seth breathalyzers multiple times and failed, as he was blowing saliva into the device.

I reflected back to a time that Seth had bragged about beating a breathalyzer by blowing small amounts of water into the device so while he was obviously impaired during his arrest, he was also very calculated in his plan to hinder the officers and buy himself time to sober up. He finally agreed to a blood test, but he had bought himself five hours from the time of his arrest until his blood was drawn. The test at 7 a.m. showed a legal blood-alcohol level: .08%.

Hurting Piper Again and the Broken System

While in the bath one evening, Piper told me that Seth continued to call me T-Rex but that he had shortened it to "TR." He had also told her that what happens at his house stays at his house and that if I ask the girls any questions, they are to tell me that it's none of my business.

One afternoon, Piper approached me and divulged even more disturbing information after a visit with Seth. Piper claimed that Seth had hit her over the weekend. Piper had never been hit before, and it was confusing. It upset her, it scared her, and it hurt her physically.

According to Piper, Seth took the girls on a hike with his cousin Chris' family. Piper claimed that her dad acted nicely when her cousins were around but wasn't nice when they were alone. Apparently, Piper was getting into Seth's new car after the hike, and she stepped on the seat of his car. Seth yelled at her. Piper then became nervous while trying to navigate into her car seat and stepped on his seat again. Her shoes were dirty, and he became angry and hit her across the arms. I asked Piper to show me how hard Seth hit her. Her response: "Mom, I can't show you because I can't hit that hard."

After Seth hit Piper, he gave her the speech about keeping it a secret. That is what Seth is accustomed to. In his family, they pretend. They pretend to be healthy, and they pretend to be normal. They sweep issues under the rug. You can only pretend for so long before things start to unravel, though. The problem was that it was all unraveling at the expense of my children.

Piper told me that after he hit her, she cried hysterically in his car until they arrived at a restaurant. Seth then instructed her to stop. Sarah was also crying, and she explained that it was because she was, "sad and scared for her sister." Apparently, Seth took the girls' cell phone so that they weren't able to call me. Piper told me that she cried so hard that she couldn't breathe.

I sympathized with mothers who took their children and fled. Had I possessed the financial resources to do so, it would have been on my list of options. Canada, Mexico, and Timbuktu were just a few places that went through my head. I felt like I was going to break. Why was it so hard to protect children? It seemed that logic had escaped the family court system. In addition, I discovered that the local court calendar was booked until the end of February, and Mr. Anders informed me that he could not even begin paperwork for a full week due to his packed calendar. What that really meant was that paying him a fraction of his hourly rate placed my daughters very low on the totem pole of his priorities.

According to the court, we did not qualify for an emergency hearing, as physical abuse was not life threatening. My takeaway was that unless my daughters were in a life-or-death situation, no one would act. The reality was that if it ever reached that point, it would be too late for anyone to act. I struggled to understand this broken system. I knew that Seth was in a downward spiral and that he had very little to lose.

I couldn't bring myself to verbalize my deepest, darkest fear, which was that I believed Seth was capable of taking my daughters' lives and making it appear to be an accident. Verbalizing that would bring it from the darkness into the light, and I didn't feel strong enough to process this thought that often jolted me out of bed in the middle of the night. Every time this thought entered my mind, I pushed it back into the darkness.

It was because of this unspoken fear that I made a vow to put each occurrence or violation in front of the court. When I went to sleep each night, I had to know that I had done everything in my power to protect my daughters. I didn't have sufficient time, energy, or resources to do this, but I didn't see an alternative. If something happened to my little girls, it was a burden that the court would need to bear.

My frustrations with the family court system kept me awake at night. The very system that was designed to protect my children was failing my children. Where's the common sense? My natural instinct as a mother to protect my children was overshadowed by this flawed system. My daughters' right to enjoy a happy, healthy childhood was stripped from them because parental rights carry more weight than children's rights in family court. "In the best interest of the child," is supposed to be the guiding light of the family court system, but those are just meaningless words. The court's actions proved otherwise.

In the meantime, I was struggling financially and needed to take on a second job but couldn't imagine how I could add anything else to my plate. I was already working full time while a full-time single parent. As someone who needs eight hours of sleep, I was lucky if I got half of that most nights. I was doing everything in my power to hold on but, most days, I felt like I was losing my grip. I was in survival mode.

The sweet receptionist at my church knew how much I was struggling and began emailing me every Monday morning to inquire about the groceries that I needed. I would then drive up curbside and she would bring the groceries out to my car, so I could avoid the embarrassment of running into members from my local business community who volunteered their time to help those less fortunate. As much as I was learning to accept help from others, it was still a humbling time in my life.

An Emergency Hearing

To my surprise, and contrary to what Mr. Anders had told me, I received the news on January 18, 2012 that he had, in fact, set an emergency hearing for Friday morning to address Seth's recent DUI charges. He also planned to address the fact that Seth was driving the girls without a license. My unrelenting badgering of his office must have lit a fire under him.

As soon as Seth discovered that we knew about his DUI, he began having Leonard drive him to the custody exchanges at our local coffee shop. They would then drive back to Robert's house, where Seth would promptly put the girls in his car and continue about his day, which meant driving them without a license. While I knew he was doing this, I didn't have evidence to prove it until I saw him driving with my own eyes and thoroughly documented and reported it to minor's counsel.

I was sitting in the park working on my laptop as Sarah was pushing the merry-go-round structure around and around the day before the hearing. She yelled over her shoulder, "Love you, Mom," and my heart melted. Tears filled my eyes, which seemed to be a recurring issue on this particular morning. I should have been pushing my daughter on the merry-go-round but, instead, I was in survival mode preparing my notes for the *ex parte* hearing and Monday's court date for child support. There I sat in a tiny park, barely able to see my computer screen due to the glare from the sun and trying to keep my court papers from flying away. I hadn't showered, was hopped up on a breakfast of Red Bull, and had bags under my eyes that grew deeper and darker with each passing day.

There were so many mixed emotions. I felt hopeful that supervised visits for Seth could finally be a reality. I picked up a declaration from my daughter's therapist that morning and felt physically ill as I read it. The therapist spoke of the confusion and anxiety that Piper expressed over her father hitting her. She went on to discuss that my wedding photo being covered up in blue tape and displayed on the family's fireplace mantel caused Piper to have additional distress. Piper was a 6-year old little girl who should have been consumed with how fast she could run on the playground, yet she was carrying burdens that many adults are not even equipped to deal with.

So many sleepless nights, I prayed that Seth would hit rock bottom and realize what he was doing. I hoped that Seth would see the two amazing little girls in front of him and choose to do the right thing. I hoped he would stop seeing the girls as possessions. I hoped he would stop trying to win and simply be the dad that they deserved. These hopes mirrored many of the same ones I held six years before while pregnant, praying that Seth would be a good dad. My mind was in a constant battle between false hopes and reality.

I normally went through a rollercoaster of emotions in between visits. The Monday morning after a visit brought forth relief that the girls were home safe. I was usually emotionally drained by the time the girls piled into my car. The following few days involved the girls re-acclimating to normalcy and routine, which was always difficult. The rest of the week was typically peaceful and happy. The week leading up to the next visit generally brought anxiety, fear, and uncertainty, due to the damage Seth could inflict in a short window of time and what he's capable of.

That afternoon, I received a card from my church, as I had asked them to pray for me after a service on forgiveness. The card said, "May you always have the courage to set boundaries and do whatever it takes to protect your daughters. God will give you great strength and boldness." Often, my feelings toward Seth oscillated between anger and pity—because he will never know true love; he is incapable of truly loving another human being. He is incapable of self-reflection and honesty. For what he continued to put my daughters through, I despised him.

I needed to hear that message from my church that day. Fighting to protect my daughters is what nature intended for me. As their mother, it's my job. I stayed up late that night completing my court declaration, and I filed the paperwork first thing in the morning. In the paperwork, I spoke from my heart. I didn't speak out of anger or hatred but as a mother who is doing what she is supposed to do. I went to sleep knowing that it was in the hands of the court and God.

Another Hurdle Cleared in Court

Family court is a series of intense ups and downs, highs and lows. I've always struggled with the word "victory" in family court because I am triggered due to the narcissist's mindset and driving force, which is about control and winning. I believe that any small step in securing my daughters' safety is a victory and the *ex parte* hearing turned out to be just that. For me, winning means that my daughters are safe and have peace.

I arrived at the courthouse early in the morning for the *ex parte* hearing. In our courthouse, *ex parte* hearings are handled by paperwork alone. The commissioner makes his decision based solely on the declarations and evidence in front of him. In the paperwork submitted to the minor's counsel, he asked that an order be put in place that stated Seth couldn't drive without a license. What seemed like common sense to me obviously needed to be spelled out legally. It would be laughable if it weren't my life. Mr. Anders had pulled Seth's criminal record and painted a picture for the court that I was previously unable to prove:

- 1997 – DUI (did not appear on his record but the court is aware of the charge);
- April 2000 – drunk in public;
- June 2010 – drunk in public; and
- October 2011 – DUI.

My request to the court was for supervised visits, but the commissioner took it a step further by cancelling all visits pending the next hearing. He set a formal review hearing for February 8, 2012 at which point the accusations and situation could be reviewed in greater detail. While I knew the reality of the system, I decided to focus on gratitude and the fact that my daughters had just gained a few weeks of peace and normalcy away from the madness.

Child Support

I found myself back in court just a few days later on Monday, January 23, 2012, because Seth filed a motion to lower his support. I arrived at 8:30 a.m., and the commissioner put off our case until the very end (11:30 a.m.) because it always took longer than the normal cases.

I was prepared and had done a bit of research on my own. While I never claimed to be a mathematician; I struggled with the equations and word problems that Seth created. Seth only worked for two of the past eight months and paid less than $1,500 in child support during that time yet managed to spend $16,000 on rent and was able to purchase a brand-new car. Something didn't add up. Thankfully, the commissioner was also confused by the math and asked Seth to explain.

"My mom and my roommate cover my expenses," Seth stated.

"So, your mom and your roommate are running around paying your rent and buying you new cars yet no one is paying child support?" asked the commissioner.

Seth has an innate ability to talk in circles when he is caught being dishonest, which is exactly what he started to do. He claimed to have a job then backtracked. He then claimed to have a job offer with a start date of February 15. Seth gave the commissioner the name of the company, the address, and the salary that he would be making. The reality was that without a private investigator, I was in the same position that I was before I walked into that courtroom. I was at the mercy of the overburdened Child Support Services to collect from Seth.

The court date was a waste of time, and there were no repercussions for Seth's ongoing charades. Two court dates within three days is too much for anyone. The ups and downs wear on your mind, body, and heart. I was completely spent by the end of the court hearing. I went home and slept for a solid hour but could have slept for the rest of the day if I had that option. It was one of those deep sleeps where you don't know your name upon waking.

The Next Battle Begins

The next few weeks had flown by, and the next court date was already upon us. It had been a peaceful few weeks with minimal drama due to the cancelled visitation schedule. My request was for a reduction in visitation and permanently supervised visits. I was praying that the courts would put my daughters' best interest first.

At around 11:00 a.m. on February 8, 2012, the commissioner looked through the evidence and made an off-the-cuff statement about supervised visitation. The commissioner then ordered a recess. I was hopeful. I went to the bathroom and prayed.

When court adjourned, Seth went into his sales mode. He makes a six-figure income as a salesperson, and he is a master manipulator. This was his stage, and he thrived when the pressure was on. Seth read a statement, which was clearly written by Lamia. In the letter, he admitted to his drinking issues and claimed to have enrolled in a DUI course. He spoke of parenting classes that he planned to enroll in.

It was remarkable to me that Seth could hold himself together in court. I knew his state of mind, and it frightened me. Somehow, he was able to pull himself together in court and appear to be a normally functioning human being.

I was then able to read the statement I had prepared:

> I would like to go on record and state that I am extremely concerned about the safety of my daughters while in Seth's care. I have watched Seth spiral out of control over the past four years. I am concerned about his mental stability. I am so concerned about my personal safety and my children's safety that I have retained a private investigator.
>
> Seth has no regard for the court orders or the laws. He has no regard for the well-being of my daughters. I plead with the court to order supervised visitation.

Minor's counsel recommended supervised visitation or shorter daytime visits.

Verdict: The commissioner ruled that visitation was reinstated. There was no supervision required for his visits.

"Nothing to date warrants supervised visitation" was the answer that I received when I pushed to understand the ruling. I wanted to scream, "What *does* warrant supervised visitation?"

I was devastated and in a state of confusion. I had sat there in court and listened as Seth read a clearly rehearsed statement prepared by his family. I sat with my chin held high as Seth's dad chuckled under his breath while the judge addressed the photo of me that Seth and Robert had taped over "as a joke." It's not a joke. It's sickening. The commissioner bought into Seth's sales pitch. No one addressed the fact that Seth was driving the girls without a valid license, and they downplayed the fact that Seth hit Piper.

My Sanctuary Tarnished

It had been so long since Seth and I had any sort of email communication that I had conveniently forgotten how truly bizarre he could be. We exchanged emails due to his visitation restarting. The new Sunday visitation conflicted with our church schedule, so I sent a simple email asking to change the time by one hour. I knew better but, because my church had become my lifeline, I took the risk. Two normal, healthy co-parents could easily navigate a one-hour time adjustment, but when you are dealing with a high-conflict narcissist, it opens you up for World War III.

> Seth- On Sunday morning, the girls and I attend church from 9:00 a.m. until 10:30 a.m. I propose that we shift the Sunday visitation schedule to 11:00 a.m.-5:00 p.m. (versus 10:00 a.m.-4:00 p.m.) which would allow me to bring the girls to the designated pick-up location. If you'd like to shift Saturday and Sunday to this (11:00 a.m.-5:00 p.m.) time, I am fine with that to be consistent. -Tina

> Seth's response: Tina, I am not sure about this. Up until you moved in with your new husband, the girls were attending Rolling Acres Church which they greatly enjoyed. Then you changed to a Bible church in Dana Point and didn't even tell me. –Seth

I looked from side to side in utter confusion. My husband? I changed churches? What was he talking about? Glenn and I had recently moved in together, but I was not engaged let alone married. I had been attending the same church for three years. I had never even been to another church during my entire adult life. This is a delusional man whom the court deems competent enough to be around children.

Church isn't always a place of peace and love, especially when you are divorcing a narcissist. Seth had his visitation at the ordered time, as he refused my request to change the schedule by an hour. I met him at 10 a.m. and continued on to the 11 a.m. service at the church I'd been attending for three years.

Seth mentioned that he would bring the girls to church at 11 a.m., which I thought was odd. Seth walked into the service about 20 minutes late and marched Piper and Sarah right though the main service instead of placing them in their regular Sunday school. To my dismay, he sat directly in front of me. I instantly knew what he was doing and kicked myself for not seeing it sooner: he was playing the good dad and bringing his daughters to church for the world to see.

Piper and Sarah saw me and came running to where I was sitting with a friend. The girls both sat with me during the entire service and, halfway through, I mentioned to Piper that I needed to leave 15 minutes early for an appointment. I told Piper that she could stay sitting with my friend, or they could go sit with her dad. She whispered that she didn't want to go with Seth and that she wanted to stay with my friend. I was concerned because she looked worried when we made eye contact.

Close to the end of the service, I told the girls that I needed to leave. Piper started crying. She said, "Please, Mom … don't make me go with him." I walked her into the church lobby, and she said it again, "Please don't make me go, Mom," but she was crying harder by this point. Seth was furious and started in on me, "PAS (Parental Alienation Syndrome), PAS—this is YOUR doing. You are causing PAS!!!" He had a look of rage in his eyes that scared me. I begged Seth to stop over and over. I begged him to stop doing this in front of the girls, but he wouldn't quit.

By this point, we were all outside in front of the church. I was trying to explain to my daughter that it was only a few more hours before she came home. Seth kept interrupting me and yelling over me. He said to Piper, "This is RIDICULOUS. Knock it off." I continued to plead with Seth to stop.

Seth grabbed Sarah and began walking up ahead of us in the parking lot. By this point, Sarah was hysterical. Seth continued to yell over his shoulder about PAS and about my blog. He was yelling about how ridiculous this was. I was trying to hold it together for my girls because I didn't want them to see me cry. I didn't want to scare them even more.

Seth placed both girls in his car and sped out of the parking lot like a madman. I immediately sent Cleo a text message asking her to contact Seth and calm him down. I was terrified by how upset the girls were and that Seth was acting so crazy. I cancelled my plans and went looking for Seth's car at a park he said they were going to.

When I couldn't find them, I drove 40 minutes back to my house to track them with the GPS phone they carry. I needed to know that they were okay, and I was able to track their drive back to our meeting location, which set my mind at ease. They were coming home. I reached out to my local police station for assistance with the exchange because I was scared of Seth's state of mind. I also left a message with my daughter's therapist because this was more than I could handle, and I wanted her guidance.

Another Emergency Hearing

It was the end of February 2012, and I had come to accept that the bags under my eyes came with the territory. I wondered how many late nights I had stayed up typing declarations and other paperwork. There were too many to count. For someone who hates conflict, this battle was eating me alive most days.

I watched the clock turn to midnight while preparing for an emergency hearing to stop Seth's next visitation. I found myself wondering why it was this difficult to protect my daughters. I felt my confidence swell as I reviewed the powerful declaration from a woman who witnessed the incident at church and several others who offered to submit testimony in support of my case.

I was finally gaining strong voices in my corner, such as therapists and others who had vowed to help me protect Piper and Sarah. In the past, I was constantly met with the same answer from mutual friends and community members: "I will tell you anything you want to know, but I don't want to be involved." There are no words more frustrating when you are in the midst of a custody battle. I came to discover that, often, the people who should lend their voices won't, and the people who have no business weighing in are the first to step up to the plate.

With our review hearing already on calendar for March 7th, I knew I was taking a risk with this emergency hearing, but Seth's state of mind was horrifying; I was still unsettled from the church incident. I could not stomach the thought of him having the girls until the court had time to properly review things in March.

For our emergency hearing on February 29th, I was requesting all visits to be cancelled. My argument was Seth's state of mind that led to the event that transpired at my church. I submitted over 20 pages of declarations and evidence. It was strong evidence, and I felt hopeful. The commissioner granted my request. It was small victories like this that refueled me and filled my cup back up. These small leaps restored my faith in the system. I felt hopeful once again.

Six-Month Review Hearing

Back in September 2011, I sat with tears streaming down my face as the commissioner handed down the verdict: sole legal and physical custody to me, and Seth was stripped of all overnight visitations. The commissioner then set a six-month review hearing, which was on Wednesday, March 7, 2012.

I received another one of Seth's bizarre, rambling emails on the heels of court, where everything is again my fault. Seth is the victim, and he takes no ownership for any of his mistakes. Seth takes no ownership for what he does to the girls. In this round of court, I was asking for a psychiatric evaluation and professionally supervised visits in a public place pending the evaluation.

The six months in review: there had been a total of ten weekend visits. Of the ten scheduled visits, there had been:

- Two weekend visits (4 days total) where Seth was a no show with no advance notification;
- Two weekend visits where Seth was 45 minutes late for pick up or to drop off the girls;
- A drunk driving charge;
- One weekend that I cancelled Seth's visitation due to his failure to follow court orders;
- One weekend where he hit Piper across the arms for getting his car seat dirty;
- Several weekends of Seth calling me names in front of the children;
- Several weekends of the girls having to see a photo of me on his fireplace mantel in which I was completely taped over in blue electrical tape; and
- The incident at church, where Seth traumatized the girls and me.

At our review hearing, Seth was caught in another string of lies. I addressed the court and stated that the Seth I witnessed in courtroom hearings was not the Seth that I interacted with outside of the courtroom doors. I explained that we would be in court all afternoon if I went through every lie that he told in court and in declarations. I addressed the fact that this was our six-month review hearing, and it was Seth's chance to start behaving like the responsible father he claimed he was. He did the opposite. Seth continued in a downward spiral. I pointed out that Seth's words—that he was a fantastic parent—were not in alignment with his actions.

The web of lies was thick and hard to stomach. There were little white lies and half-truths, and then there were blatant lies and elaborate stories. The huge lie that was told in court (this time) had to do with my church, the very place that had brought me comfort, security, and even groceries when I was in need.

In Seth's version of reality, this was *his* church. According to Seth, he attended this church every week and sat in the exact same spot. He claimed that I came to his church and that I purposefully sat in his section. I was dumbfounded. I sat there listening with my mouth wide open. I couldn't quite grasp what I was hearing. There have been so many lies but this one was almost too hard for me to believe. Seth was talking about my church. He was lying about my church. I was waiting for the sky to open and for lightening to strike. I began shaking. How dare Seth invade the place where I am able to reconnect each week and find my strength! These are the pastors who would pray for me on a random Tuesday if I emailed them about a bad day. These are the people who provided bags of groceries for the girls and me when we were in need and unable to depend on Seth. These are the people who helped me get into my first apartment after I left the women's shelter. These are the people who ensured my daughters received Christmas gifts one year when I couldn't provide them.

I watched as the commissioner raised his eyebrows in disbelief. The commissioner pressed him further on the topic. How was it possible that he lives four hours away from the church he claimed to attend regularly? He became evasive when pressed for the number of times he attends. He was evasive because he had been caught lying. The commissioner stated, "I don't care whether you go to church or not. That is your business. What I do care about is when someone lies in my courtroom."

Tears began to flow again as I hung onto every word leaving the commissioner's mouth. I was awarded supervised visitation. I finally received protection for my daughters and peace of mind as a mother. The commissioner set a new hearing for April 10, 2012. Minor's counsel was ordered to uncover the truth, specifically, whether or not Seth attended this particular church every week as he stated in court. If he was lying, the order was to become permanent. In my mind, this was a slam-dunk.

True to form, I discovered that Seth called my church within minutes of court ending. Seth wanted them to say that he was a member and that he attended regularly. They couldn't say that because he wasn't a member, and he didn't attend regularly. In fact, I estimated that he attended twice in the past year. They couldn't do what he asked because of one simple thing: it wasn't the truth.

Supervised Visitations

Mid-March of that year went down in history as the week I was able to take a deep breath. The constant emotional rollercoaster from court tended to wreak havoc on my soul. I woke up on the Friday after court with a feeling of peace. I learned to embrace those moments as they come and appreciate them greatly. This calm tide gave me the strength I needed to push through the next rough but inevitable storm.

It was a welcomed relief to have a few weeks without worrying about court but even more of a relief knowing that the girls were protected from Seth, Robert, and their entire family. It took me a full week to figure out how to best explain our new reality of supervised visits to Piper and Sarah. I explained that they would now have a "buddy" with them at their weekend visits and that they would have visits at fun places like parks or children's museums. I explained that their new buddy was like Anna, their therapist. Piper said, "Good. I think I will feel safer going with Dad from now on."

Near the end of March, I found myself in the place that I had worked so hard to reach. I sat waiting for my appointment with the woman who was going to supervise the visits: Susan, the program director of Safe Harbor Supervision Services. We discussed the policies and the next steps in the process.

I felt at ease as Susan laid out the ground rules. Visitation would take place in a public setting with many boundaries and limits. She would be with my daughters at all times and not simply observe from a distance. No visits were conducted inside of homes, and visitations near bodies of water were prohibited. As I walked outside, I heard doves cooing right over my head. That was my sign that everything would be okay.

The very first visit took place in a pizza parlor, and I was instructed to meet Susan exactly 20 minutes before the visit to allow the girls to become acquainted with her. The guidelines were given in advance in writing and verbally. In an effort to limit the stress on the children, I would leave at 1:00 p.m. and Seth would arrive at 1:05 p.m. The visit was two hours in duration and Seth would leave at 3:00 p.m. and I would be there five minutes later.

The rules were crystal clear to me, but Seth was above rules as I discovered at every turn. Seth makes his own rules and I often wonder what happened in Seth's childhood that stunted his growth and his soul in so many areas. Although I have lived this for years, Seth never ceases to amaze me with the choices he makes.

Our first day of supervised visits went sideways before it even began. I arrived at 12:40 p.m. as instructed and, as we walked into the restaurant, we saw Seth inside. The director of the program wasn't there yet. I opened the door to the restaurant, poked my head in and said, "You aren't supposed to be here yet." Seth's response was, "It's a public place!" as he threw his hands up in the air as if to show how annoyed he was with my mere existence.

Piper, Sarah, and I waited outside the restaurant and, upon Susan's arrival, I explained to her that Seth was in the restaurant, and she directed us into the restroom. She then went back out to tell Seth to leave the premises and return at the proper time. The girls were confused, and all of it was avoidable. The rules are in place to prevent these exact situations. Seth didn't care how he affected the girls that day, or any day for that matter.

One of Seth's future visits fell on Easter weekend, and we were both notified that the supervision agency would not be open on Easter Sunday and, therefore, there would be no visitation. The court order reads that his visitations are the first, third, and fifth (if applicable) weekends of each month when/if the supervision monitor is available. They told me that they were closed, and I noted my calendar.

Seth sent me a text message asking, "Can we just plan to meet on Easter Sunday at church so that I can see the girls?" I responded with a simple, "No." The next morning, I woke up to the following message from Seth, "What about Easter Sunday? I want to see the girls for a while."

These are the exact situations that previously left me questioning my sanity. Did I miss something? Weren't you the one I've just spent three hellish years fighting in court? Do you really believe that after all we've been through, I would just say, "Sure! Let's meet and hang out on Easter and violate court orders! That will be great! Can you pick me up a cup of coffee on your way to church with no sugar, extra cream?" Sometimes I could relate to what Alice must have felt like when she was visiting Wonderland.

My response to Seth: "The visitation monitor's office is closed on Easter, and I know you have already been informed of that."

The Girlfriend

Several friends had encouraged me to reach out to a former girlfriend of Seth's because, according to them, she was living in fear of him. From a social media search, I realized it was the same girl from the framed photo that

Seth had tried to taunt me with several years earlier. I made contact with Clarissa and, to my surprise, she was not only willing to talk to me, but she was willing to write a declaration for the court to help me protect my daughters.

> My name is Clarissa Davis and I dated Seth Collins from October 2009 through January 2010. After dating for about two months, I became concerned with his irrational and disturbing behavior, which became even more apparent and frightening while drinking alcohol.
>
> One such incident that I can remember was New Year's Eve 2009. This was the night I started my new job as the hostess for the VIP clientele at a local nightclub. He came out to "support" me in my new job, but upon realizing that I could not give him much attention, he proceeded to drink heavily and stumble around to the various tables, which caused multiple guests to ask that he be removed from their area. His reaction was to forcefully grab my arm and yell into my ear that I needed to be with him at all times that night. I quickly directed him to leave, which he finally did so after over an hour and "encouragement" from the security staff. The following morning, he proceeded to come back to my place of work, at which point my boss requested he be denied entry to the building when I am working. His irrational behavior only intensified once I ended my relationship with him.
>
> Shortly after New Year's Eve, our relationship ended. When I told Mr. Collins that I no longer wanted to see him, he became completely irrational. He would not accept the fact that I was breaking up with him and tried to physically fight one of my male friends. He then began calling my employer and disparaging me in an attempt to make me lose my job. I became increasingly concerned about Mr. Collin's behavior and my personal safety. I began receiving multiple hateful voice messages, text messages, and long letters. I was so concerned and fearful of him by this point that I was forced to change the locks on the doors to my home. During our very brief relationship, I found him to be delusional and emotionally irrational by jumping from fake happiness to extreme anger.

Setting Boundaries

Monday night, Seth called to talk to Piper and Sarah. He immediately dove into his manipulations. Sarah got on the phone and Seth said, "Hi, Sarah. Remember when we were at the children's museum together yesterday?"

"Yeeesss," Sarah answered.

"Do you remember when you wouldn't let Daddy go and you were holding onto me?" Seth asked.

"Yes," Sarah answered.

"Daddy had to drive all the way back to San Diego. I'm far away now …" Seth went on and on. The conversation was so bizarre that, as I listened to him, I wondered two things: who was sitting next to him that he needed to impress, or was he recording the conversation?

Two nights later, Seth called back. Sarah had been running a fever for the previous 24 hours and didn't feel well. She answered the phone, and he started off by saying, "Hi, Sarah. I miss you."

Sarah was silent as she just stared at the phone.

"Do you miss Daddy?" Seth asked.

"Yes," Sarah answered uncomfortably.

"Do you remember when you didn't want Daddy to leave and drive back to San Diego?" Seth asked.

She stared at the phone without answering.

At that point, I picked up the phone and walked into the garage. I explained to Seth that there are boundaries and that he can't continue with these questions that make the girls so uncomfortable. I came back into the house and explained that Daddy could call back in a little while. At that point, I sent him a message:

> Me: Seth- you are absolutely welcomed to call the girls. I have never prevented that. There are boundaries, and I will not allow you to emotionally manipulate the girls. You are welcome to call back if you can refrain from that type of behavior.
>
> Seth: I'll be reporting your interruption. In every phone call, Tina. You lied in court about what happened at church. I never uttered parental alienation syndrome. I said "PAS." This is my church, too. I

took the girls there every weekend you were out partying. I never sped away. You have endlessly lied in court. I am going to prove you have lupus not MS. You lie about your income. You lied about your rent.

Me: They will be awake until 8 p.m. You are welcome to call back; however, you are not allowed to put them on the spot and continue with the bizarre questions that you were asking Sarah. She was visibly uncomfortable.

Seth: You should not be listening into every phone call. Sarah was hugging me and said, "I won't let you go. I am going to steal you from San Diego." The supervisor had to tell her to let go. You don't have any clue what your selfish, money hungry behavior is doing to OUR daughters not YOUR daughters.

Unless you've experienced a narcissist in your life, you may be scratching your head right now. The entire experience makes you doubt yourself and question your sanity. If you have ever experienced a text message from a narcissist, then you understand every line of it. Prior to understanding this disorder, I felt the need to respond and defend myself against everything that he said.

My old instincts would be to remind Seth that he did in fact speed out of the parking lot recklessly with the girls in the car. I would want to tell him that I've never lied in court. I'm not money hungry—I've supported my daughters without regular help from him. I would normally rush to contact my doctor for a form that says I was diagnosed multiple sclerosis and not lupus. That cycle is never ending and utterly exhausting.

Thankfully, I had begun making the conscious decision to be a survivor and not Seth's victim, no longer feeling the need to defend myself to him. I knew the truth, and I would not waste my time trying to remind him of the truth. It's pointless. His messages show that he is a disturbed person with a distorted sense of reality. The phone call to my daughters and the text messages show nothing but a twisted mind.

My response was, "Your attempt to portray me in a negative light is noted."

More Lies

While I did not think Seth could wiggle his way out of the issues at hand, I wanted to be prepared. I had made all the appropriate contacts and received supporting documentation, and it was simply a matter of filling out the forms and going through the motions. It should have been fairly simple to prove his lie about church.

I then discovered that there was another lie on the table. Seth was backtracking to get out of his lie to the commissioner and the court. Because Seth couldn't get the church receptionist to say he was an active member, he stated he was a member in the church's hiking group. If this didn't involve my daughters, it would have been somewhat humorous. A mental health professional would have had a field day studying Seth and our case.

Being a self-taught detective, I found that the church group hikes on Saturday mornings at 9 a.m. and all hikes take two to three hours. Seth's visitation had commenced at 10 a.m. for the past six months, and he lives four hours south of our church. I found it odd that he would be driving four hours south on his off weekends to hike with a church group when the area he resides in is known for their trails and outdoor beauty. I sent all the information to the girls' attorney to prove that his new claims were not true, either.

I also contacted my church for the dates the girls attended Sunday school. There are two dates that Seth picked the girls up from church, and those were on the dates that I took them to church. He only agreed to meet me there for his scheduled visits. In the past six months, Seth could have taken them to the 11 a.m. service every single Sunday yet he never did.

I pulled out my shovel and began digging for the truth, which was buried under Seth's lies and manipulation. That truth was held inside 55 pages of court documents that would hopefully show the judge the type of person that I was dealing with. The commissioner's words about making supervised visits permanent echoed through my head, and I knew the stakes were high.

In preparation for court, I contacted the company monitoring Seth's visitations. There had been a total of three visits, and each were only two hours in length. As the visits were only two hours in length, I didn't anticipate a goldmine of information. Apparently, I was wrong. A lot can go wrong in a total of six hours. It left me wondering even more about Seth's mental state because he didn't try to put on a show for the supervisor, which is unlike him.

- Seth was 20 minutes early to the first visit, which started everything off poorly for all of us. He had strict orders to arrive on time. He had to be asked twice to leave the restaurant.

- Seth ordered his favorite pizza (chicken garlic pizza) without thinking of the girls, which means they barely ate anything. They only like cheese pizza.
- Seth had to be reminded that cell phone usage was strictly prohibited during the monitored visit.
- Seth was late to his second visit with no explanation.
- Seth sat and drank coffee while socializing with another father for 20 minutes of his two-hour visit.
- Seth had to be reminded that there are no cameras allowed when he tried to take a photo.
- Seth arrived late to the third visit with no explanation.
- On the report, it was noted that, "Dad does not interact much with girls as they play."
- Seth brought Robert's , Thai bride to the visit with her son and had her pretend to be a stranger at the park. It was against the rules to bring family members to the visits. He lied about being related when asked three separate times. The girls confirmed to the supervisor that they were in fact their aunt and cousin.

Once again, it was a bag of mixed emotions. If you were to reach in the bag, you would find sadness because my daughters deserve SO much more than this. You would also find shock because even when I don't think I could be stunned anymore, I am proven wrong. You would also find confusion. If I hadn't seen my children for six weeks, you wouldn't find me drinking Starbucks and socializing with a random adult for twenty minutes. Inside my bag of emotions was also anger because I had and still have no hope for him to change; therefore, my daughters must endure many more years of his damaging ways.

Manipulating Others in My Small Town

I live in a small town where nearly every family has 2.5 children, a Subaru station wagon, and a happy golden retriever standing guard at the white picket fence. I was walking to the local gymnasium where my daughters were in spring break camp. A minivan pulled up and someone said, "Tina, can I talk to you for a minute?"

I knew what was coming before the words even left her mouth. Less than an hour before, I had received the court paperwork from Seth and discovered that he hired a very well-known local attorney. In addition, Seth went into church on Easter Sunday and cornered this woman's husband into writing a declaration about his attendance at church. While the declaration was vague, he manipulated them into verifying he attends my church. I could see it in the woman's face. I could tell that she felt horrible and didn't realize the damage that had been done.

We talked for a bit about the situation, and she took down my contact information. How do you describe three nightmarish years of insanity in a 15-minute conversation without appearing insane yourself? I must have looked shaken because she got out of the car and hugged me. While I love living in a small town, I hate that people are manipulated by Seth just like I once was.

I later discovered that Seth had preyed upon several people who ended up writing letters for him. One of those letters came from the pastor of my church. He didn't do anything to be malicious; he did what Seth asked. The letter stated that Seth had been attending church since 2009, when we first enrolled our children in Sunday school. This was true. We were married and began going to church as a family at my insistence.

The declaration went on to say that Seth has attended periodically since then. In 2011, Seth attended on one date in November when I asked him to meet us there for the visitation exchange. It didn't say "regularly." It said "periodically," but it was vague enough to move the situation into a gray area. Narcissists and gray areas seem to go hand in hand. It's an area in which they thrive.

After receiving the declarations, I immediately approached the church and explained the situation in further detail. Once the Pastor and his receptionist understood how their declarations had been used to manipulate the court, they offered to write updated declarations. The new declaration took the situation from gray to black and white. The revised declaration included:

- Tina is a member of our church since completing the 101 Class in September of 2009 along with regular attendance. Tina also completed the 201 class in 2012.
- Seth is not considered to be a member of the church due to the requirements of the 101 Class and regular attendance.
- The requirements of membership were then outlined in detail.

Pro Se Against the Big Attorney

I was thrown off when I found out Seth had hired an attorney to represent him. We had both been pro se (representing ourselves) until this point. It shouldn't have surprised me because the hole he dug was so deep that only a powerhouse attorney could bail him out of his self-inflicted disaster. Seth's new attorney, Mr. Hanson, was well-known and respected by our community and our family court professionals. I would be lying if I said that I wasn't nervous.

In his impoverished state, I questioned how Seth could afford a luxury lifestyle, a new car, a criminal attorney for his DUI, and then a family law attorney. I hoped that the court would also question this. I came to the conclusion that I could waste my time worrying about being pro se against an attorney, or I could focus my energy on preparing for my court date; I opted for the latter.

Court: April 18, 2012

Proceedings began with minor's counsel noting that Seth is dishonest and can't follow orders. Seth's new attorney tried to defend Seth's lies and was stopped by the commissioner. Mr. Hanson then realized that he was arguing against the commissioner and regressed, stating that Seth wasn't really lying, he was just "saying what the court wanted to hear." Mr. Hanson then said that if the court did wish to continue supervised visitations, they'd ask for this to be reevaluated in three months.

The commissioner came down fairly hard throughout the hearing and essentially said that Seth had lost all credibility in the courtroom. He acknowledged that the evidence suggested he lied about attending church and even referenced Seth's previous lie about where the children were residing on his visit.

The commissioner then reinstated Seth's visitation, unsupervised, from 10 a.m. to 4 p.m. Saturdays and Sundays on the first, third, and fifth weekend of each month. I couldn't believe what I was hearing. The commissioner said that if Seth was lying, he would order supervised visits. Seth was lying. Why was he putting my daughters back in his care? Why wasn't he following his own words?

I felt like I was in a never-ending nightmare. The reality was that Seth's lie in court about attending my church derailed our six-month review hearing. None of the important facts were considered. The entire hearing was based on whether or not Seth went to church. I felt like vomiting. This system resembled a circus and not a court of law.

After court, I remembered that 10 a.m. to 4 p.m. on Sundays won't work. We have church from 9 a.m. to 10:30 a.m. and, more than anything, my daughters needed stability. I called Seth's attorney, who then agreed to call Seth and ask to change the order slightly. We went back and forth over a total of four phone calls with Mr. Hanson mediating.

Mr. Hanson had the nerve to say to me, "Seth will select a church to attend, and he will begin taking the girls on Sunday, so let's keep the schedule as is." At that point, I unleashed on Mr. Hanson. "Seth has had the opportunity to take my daughters to church for the past six months at the church they've gone to for several years. I have full legal and physical custody, and he does not have permission to take our daughters to a new church. They need stability! They do not need to go to a new church so that he can pretend to be father of the year." Despite this bulldog attorney putting pressure on me, I didn't waver under his threat of leaving the order as-is.

"That's fine, Mr. Hanson. I am happy to take this back in front of the judge. Go for it," I said firmly. If Seth wanted to pay his attorney $500 per hour to take this back in front of the commissioner over a one-hour time shift, I figured, let's do it. At that point, what did I have to lose? I already felt a huge loss that day. Mr. Hanson called back minutes later and said, "My client conceded and is willing to change the order to accommodate your church schedule."

Piper's Award Ceremony

The first weekend of Seth's visitation being reinstated, I was reminded of one of the reasons that Seth turned out the way he did: his creepy, asshole father. Seth and I agreed to meet at a local park for a ceremony during which Piper was scheduled to receive an award. I was sitting in the very back row with the girls, Glenn, and my family members. Seth and Leonard walked up and greeted the children, who didn't react in the way they expected them to. The girls were standoffish when they saw Seth and Leonard and, given the fact that they knew they were going back to see them unsupervised, I didn't blame them at all.

Out of all the places to stand, Seth and Leonard took their places standing directly behind us. Leonard purposefully began speaking loudly enough for us to hear him. "This is the first time Piper hasn't acted excited to see us. Tina has her so brainwashed. This is ridiculous." At that point, I turned around and said, "We can all hear you, please stop." Leonard then looked at me and chuckled before saying, "Maybe I will just talk a bit LOUDER, TINA."

Glenn, being a calm and collected individual, is non-reactionary. As my mind was racing and my heart was beating out of my chest, Glenn turned his entire body to look at Seth and Leonard and said firmly, "Now, you have my attention," at which point they shut their mouths and stayed quiet for the rest of the ceremony. "Thank God for Glenn," was all I could think in that moment.

At the end of the ceremony, we were scheduled to turn the girls over to Seth. I knew the park would be a good distraction so that I could leave without the girls becoming distraught. That meant exchanging car seats in advance with Seth, which Glenn offered to do. He approached Seth and asked him to take a walk to the parking lot with him to get the car seats, and Seth obliged.

As they were walking, Seth attempted to make small talk with Glenn. "So, no hard feelings about anything," Seth said, with no response from Glenn. Seth continued on, "I'm sure you didn't realize that Tina and I were actually still married when you first started dating." His attempt to imply that I was manipulative or somehow misled Glenn was quickly shut down when Glenn replied, "No. I knew everything. We're going to exchange car seats; let's just do that." The conversation ended as abruptly as it began with Glenn making it clear that he refused to engage in small talk with him.

A 10K of Freedom

I decided to run a 10K race in spring 2012, and it wasn't just any 10K. This particular race had a lot of significance to me. It was 6.2 miles of tears (real ones) and sweat, but it also brought tremendous insight, healing, and growth.

During my marriage, I was critiqued at every turn. If I ordered fettuccine alfredo at a restaurant, I was met with a look of disgust. If I didn't exercise for a week, then I was lectured about having thrown six months of fitness down the drain by taking a break. If Seth noticed my post-pregnancy stomach bulge as I was bending over, he would bring home a book on how to obtain perfect abs. After several years of comments and lectures, my view of my body was incredibly distorted. I believed that I was fat. No matter what I did, I was never good enough for Seth.

Seth and I used to run 5Ks together, and it was the same story. It was competitive. At every race, Seth would be running beside me saying things like, "You aren't going to let her pass you—she's 40 pounds heavier than you are!" or "You aren't going to let her sprint ahead of you to the finish line—she's 15 years older!" At the finish line, I was always given "constructive criticism" about my posture, my pace, or what I could improve on. I hated running because running equaled failure.

When I signed up for this race, my post-Seth race, it became a mental, emotional, and physical challenge for me. I felt like I was finally running away from Seth's voice. I hadn't trained, yet there was some force pushing me to sign up. I remained non-committal until the morning of the race, and then decided that I wanted to run it. I needed to run it. I laced up my shoes and headed to the coast.

At the start of the race, I didn't have the normal pre-race jitters. There was no anxiety about my performance. I knew I wasn't going to be critiqued. I was out there to cross the finish line and, if someone heavier or older passed me, I would silently cheer for him or her. That person who was 40 pounds heavier could be on the tail end of a 400-pound weight loss. That person who was 15 years older than me could have been training for this race and, by God, deserved to pass me. I knew that when I crossed the finish line, there would be no one to tell me what I could've done differently.

For me, the race was symbolic of life. There were rough patches to cross, boulders to go around, a stream to run through, and even places where my feet sank into the sand and I felt immobile. There were people on the sidelines cheering us on, and there were some people who lent me a hand as I crossed the rocky parts.

There were others who were so consumed with their own battles that they didn't even think to assist those around them; I connected with those people, also. Sometimes, you must fasten your own oxygen mask before assisting others. Each person was on his or her own journey, yet we were all on a journey together to the finish line.

When I started the race, I had no idea how much I would personally grow from running 6.2 miles. It was a reminder of how far I had come and how much I had healed. The race was brutal and beautiful at the same time. I felt a sense of pride when thinking of my life three short years ago and how far I had come since then. I cried while running from mile 2 to mile 3 due to an equal combo of emotions and physical pain. I completed 6.2 miles in 1 hour, 17 minutes, and 8 seconds. It was one of the most powerful experiences of my life and brought with it tremendous healing.

The Today Show

I don't normally watch television, but I happened to stumble upon an interview on *The Today Show* in March 2012. Matt Lauer was interviewing actress and supermodel Christie Brinkley, and the topic of her divorce came up. Christie's ex-husband, Peter Cook, is a diagnosed malignant narcissist who continuously tried to gain media attention regarding their divorce and custody battle.

I watched as Matt Lauer, using his 1950s Neanderthal man-brain, re-victimized Ms. Brinkley by asking her, "Why can't you two just move on for the sake of the children?" My jaw dropped. I expect ignorance from the general public when it comes to narcissism, but Matt Lauer has a duty to be educated on topics before he opens his mouth and speaks. He continued to bully her and was relentless in his abusive ambush.

I watched with tears forming in my eyes because I knew how Christie Brinkley must have felt in that very moment. How do you explain to someone the sheer hell that you are living through at the hands of a narcissist? Her response to Matt Lauer and to the general public was four simple words, "Google 'divorcing a narcissist.'" Christie then went on to say four additional words that likely resonate with anyone who has been victimized by a person with narcissistic personality disorder: "I just want peace."

On that morning, I watched as my blog took off on the internet. People all over the world were beginning to read this little journal that I had started. I received an email from a woman all the way in Ireland who said, "You saved my life today," and went on to explain the desperation that she was feeling.

My email inbox began to blow up with messages from every corner of the world. I was connecting with women and men who understood what I was going through. The narcissists who had us believing that they were so unique and so special weren't so special after all. They were all the same. My story was not unique. It was not one mom's battle. It was thousands of parents' battles.

Shortly after the interview on *The Today Show*, Christie mentioned my blog as a resource for others going through a divorce with a narcissist. A few weeks later, Christie's personal assistant contacted me and said that Christie wanted to invite me to see her performance in the Broadway musical, "Chicago," at the historic Pantages Theater in Hollywood. Glenn and I arrived at the Pantages Theater to discover that our seats were front and center in the sixth row!

After the show ended, Glenn and I walked to the backstage area, and there were only two names on the list. Christie came out shortly after and was even more beautiful in person than she is on television. I stuck my hand out and said, "Hi! I'm Tina Swithin, and I write the blog, 'One Mom's Battle.'" Christie's eyes lit up, and she explained that she found my blog and immediately thought, "Someone gets it!" Christie then went on to say that my blog was a light in the darkness for her personally. She encouraged me to keep writing and keep telling my story, which helps others to heal.

The meeting with Christie left me with the realization that narcissism does not discriminate. It can affect the old and the young, the rich and the poor, and everyone in between. While Christie Brinkley and I are worlds apart in many ways, we also share a bond. We are two women deeply affected by narcissism and the court's inability to act appropriately when it comes to this disorder. It showed me that even with a diagnosed malignant narcissist (Peter Cook) and the financial means to hire the best legal counsel that money can buy, the battle is daunting no matter who you are.

The Near Drowning

For one of Seth's visitations in May 2012, Glenn and I dropped the girls off at Robert's house. Because of Seth's recent DUI, I was ordered by the court to make the 45-minute drive to the family compound, which made me feel sick to my stomach. It was horrible enough to have to turn the girls over to Seth but even more excruciating to drive them to the home that Leonard, Robert, and Seth shared. When we arrived back there that afternoon to pick the girls up, I noticed that Sarah's little face was beat red and blotchy from crying.

"What happened?" I asked Seth.

"Well, the girls were pushing boundaries in the pool and went underwater for a short period of time," Seth replied, seeming annoyed but flustered.

My immediate thought: remain calm and composed. Do not overreact. Listen to the entire story before you open your mouth.

Piper then chimed in and stated, "Sarah slipped off her noodle and went underwater. I tried to save her and hold her above the water, but then her head was higher than mine and I swallowed water, also."

"They were pushing boundaries; it was scary and they learned a lesson from it. They are both fine," Seth said, looking furious that Piper was speaking the truth but also trying to retain his composure with Glenn and I watching him.

We got Sarah and Piper into the car as a million thoughts were going through my head. I remained calm and didn't want to react until I knew more. We drove home and, over the next few hours, I heard the entire story. It was my worst nightmare unfolding in front of me.

Piper and Sarah had never had swimming lessons. They were in a pool without an adult in the water. They didn't have life jackets on. Sarah slipped off her swimming noodle and was trying to doggie paddle to the edge. She inhaled two gulps of water before Piper saw her struggling and jumped off her own noodle to save her. Piper explained that she was trying to hold her sister out of the water so that she could breathe but, in turn, she went under several times.

Piper said that she tried to get their dad's attention, but Seth was lying out sun tanning and wasn't paying attention. Upon realizing what was happening, he jumped into the pool and pulled them up. Sarah is adamant that she swallowed five huge gulps of water. "I counted them, Momma!" she said. Piper went on to say that she believed Seth was sleeping.

The girls brought up the incident throughout the night and several times the next morning. At bedtime, Piper asked if she could write about the experience in her journal. I am incredibly thankful to her teacher who advocated daily journaling, as I think this practice is invaluable. The next morning, Piper asked if she could share her journal with me on our drive to church. This is a snippet of what she wrote:

> "Today was a scary day for me and my sister. It happened at my dad's house. When me and my sister were playing in the pool and we didn't know how to swim and (my sister) fell off her floatie and almost drowned. I tried to save her then I fell off my floatie but was holding (sister) up higher than me. We drank chlorine water. I think either my dad was not watching, he was not paying attention or he was sleeping. But after about 12 seconds dad jumped in and got us out of the pool. After that dad took us inside and we had cinnamon raison bread, milk and chips and salsa."

My personal belief was that Seth was likely hungover from the night before and dozed off while the girls were in the pool. I will never understand how he could leave two little girls unattended in a swimming pool, especially when one of our children has a seizure disorder. Then again, I will never understand anything this man-child does. My greatest fear came out of the darkness: the question of whether my daughters' near-drowning experience was intentional. As quickly as the thought entered my mind, I pushed it back into the darkness, as I could not bear to think about the reality that this very well could have been purposeful.

I questioned whether it would take one of my daughters dying or being seriously injured for the court to finally protect the girls. One of my friends described the situation best when she said, "I think that we (as mothers) get punished for being too vigilant. Seth is too hell bent on having no restrictions and rules that he is ignorant of how inept he is as a father."

I relayed Saturday's pool incident to my daughters' therapist by phone on Saturday night, and she recommended that I contact Child Welfare Services immediately. I did as instructed; however, I was told that they couldn't take a report because my daughters were now safe. Are you fucking kidding me? I pressed harder, insisting that a report was taken, and I was told to call back on Monday morning. I was reminded how flawed our entire system is, regardless of the division that you happen to be working with. It should not be this difficult to protect a child.

I struggled with my emotions while writing an email to Seth's attorney and the girls' attorney, Mr. Anders. I relayed the near-drowning incident, and this is a snippet of what I wrote:

> "What will it take for someone to protect my daughters? I would love for one of you to tell me the answer to that because I am so angry with this system that continually puts my daughters' lives in jeopardy."

Seth called several days later, and Sarah answered the phone. She spoke to Seth on speakerphone while sitting at the dining room table. Glenn and I were in the kitchen talking and working on dinner preparations. We heard Seth ask Sarah what she wanted to do on the next visitation. Sarah replied that she wanted to have a play date with friends and Seth suggested swimming instead. She said, "I don't want to go swimming." Seth sounded flustered and laughed nervously. He pressed further and she said it again, "I don't want to go swimming." I was proud of her for using her voice. Seth changed the topic and then spoke to my oldest daughter shortly after.

Sure enough, I received a text message about an hour and a half later.

> Seth: Sarah swam happily in the pool all afternoon Sunday. Piper went in and swam her best yet. I clearly know you are brainwashing the girls because the first thing Sarah said to me today is, 'Mommy said I don't want to go swimming.' It's just so damaging what you are doing to our daughters.
>
> Tina: We were standing in the kitchen during your call and will testify that she never said that. Do not text me.

Asking Seth to stop texting me was my second or third request that week. I engaged him more than I should have with my response and kicked myself afterwards. I shouldn't have responded at all. Shortly after, I was cc'd on an email from Seth to his attorney and minor's counsel that depicted my youngest daughter swimming in the pool with floaties and Robert holding her. I felt rage at the thought of Robert being anywhere near my children.

I never want my daughters to feel like they are in the middle. I would never wish that on them or any child. I've learned to listen without probing, and I think they will respect me one day for my approach. There are two tools that I have come to lean on through this process: encouraging my daughters to journal their feelings and utilizing the services of a therapist.

I had been struggling with whether or not to have Piper speak directly to minor's counsel. She is very articulate about her wishes when it comes to her father, and I was leaning toward giving her a voice in this issue. It made me sad that her voice was needed, but I felt like I was left with few options at that point. Sadly, while I had faith in my daughter to speak the truth, I had little faith in minor's counsel. At the age of 7, Piper once again had taken on a very grown-up role and a responsibility she shouldn't have to bear: being her little sister's protector.

On Wednesday night, I took the girls to see their therapist. The girls bravely discussed the events that took place on Saturday afternoon at their dad's house. Piper explained that she was trying very hard to hold Sarah's head out of the water, but her own head kept going underwater. It was difficult to listen to her talk about the event in detail. I sat there while my little girl told her story but felt physically ill to have a full picture of the event that she was so vividly and bravely describing.

In that moment, I wished more than ever that I could afford an attorney. I would spend every penny that I had to hire someone to fight this battle for me. It had then crossed over to a territory that terrified me. I wanted to be my daughters' advocate while they are living—not because I lost them to a tragedy.

The next morning, I discussed the option of speaking to minor's counsel with Piper and at her level. I asked her, "Do you want to talk to Mr. Anders and let him know your feelings about everything?" "Yes, Mom. I do want to talk to him." Piper responded. I called Mr. Anders' office and set up a time for her to talk to him. I have taught her to use her voice since she was 2 years old, and she would get to do that.

Wearing a Cape

Able to leap between tall buildings in a single bound? Some days, I feel like I should have a cape. In the middle of the night, I finalized my paperwork for the *ex parte* hearing pertaining to the swimming pool incident. Sometimes I wonder if I should go to law school, and then I am reminded that I hate everything about this process and being a part of this system would destroy my soul.

I juggled school drop offs, copying documents for the court and for attorneys, and trying to keep my job. Everything had to be copied, filed, and served by 10 a.m., which was no small feat. I felt like a kid sliding into home plate as I made it in and out of the courthouse with three minutes to spare. I needed those three minutes to breathe because breathing had taken a backseat that morning.

I had come to know the process at the courthouse. I always held my breath, hoping and praying that I had the right number of copies and the correct forms. As the main clerk flipped through my stack of papers examining everything carefully, she confirmed that everything was perfect. I had my gold star and went on with my day.

I drove the thirty miles back home and received a call shortly after from the clerk, who stated that my fee waiver was no longer valid. She said that it expired when our permanent support order was made. For the hearing to be placed on the calendar, she needed me to bring in $105 by 3:30 p.m. She called back a half-hour later and said that I actually owed $275 for prior filings.

Basically, I couldn't fight to protect my children unless I went back to the court for the second time that day to pay $275. That was very difficult to do because Seth was $35,000 behind in child support payments by this point. Paying for the copies was difficult enough, but now I had to find the funds for the filing fees. I got back in my car, drove back to the courthouse, and paid the money they had demanded—cursing this broken system the entire way.

Our *Ex Parte* Hearing: May 30, 2012

I arrived at the courthouse at 8:15 a.m. for the *ex parte* hearing. For an emergency hearing, there is no opportunity to speak to the commissioner. The paperwork is reviewed behind closed doors, and a decision is made. The commissioner went through the cases on calendar and then notified me that his ruling was upstairs in the clerk's office. I sat reading the paperwork submitted by Seth's attorney and my daughters' attorney. My heart sank as I read it.

Here are a few snippets of what I was reading from minor's counsel:

- I do not consent to the requested order, but I consent to the following order, that the court NOT issue any *ex parte* orders regarding supervised visits at this time;
- A hearing be set at a later time to address the issues at hand; and
- Spoke to the children's therapist who *did* recommend supervised visits.

In the paperwork, Seth's father's declaration claimed that the girls were happily playing and their floatation devices slipped out from under them. He claimed that Seth jumped in right away and got the girls out. He went on to claim that the girls went in the very next day with zero fear or hesitation. The ironic part was that his own wife, Cleo, contradicted this statement in writing when she discussed talking to the girls on Skype and admitting that Sarah was "emphatic" about *not* going in the pool the next day.

I sent several text messages to friends and family as I waited in line at the courthouse, stating, "I don't feel good about this—minor's counsel is recommending unsupervised visits." I walked to the counter and watched as the clerk filled in the paperwork according to the commissioner's orders: Professionally supervised visits pending next hearing. One hour per week. New hearing set for June 20, 2012.

Thank you, God. I almost cheered right in the middle of the clerk's office. We were going to have almost a full month of peace. The girls were able to see their father, but they would be safe while doing so. To say that I was thankful is an understatement.

The court order stated that Seth could call every other night at 6 p.m. Sometimes, Seth called according to the court order and, other times, it was sporadic. Seth called on Wednesday night to talk to the girls, and they were at counseling. I answered the phone and could hear the angry tone in his voice as he asked to speak to the girls—anger stemming from the earlier judgment. "This isn't your night to call; you just called last night," I said to Seth. I let Seth know that the girls were not home, to which he mumbled, "You are a manipulative bitch," and then hung up.

I sent an email to Seth's attorney regarding the earlier judgment, and I notified him of the phone call. I asked the attorney to advise his client to cease the attacks. At 9 p.m. that night, Seth responded by email:

> Dear All,
>
> What Ms. Swithin states is again a lie. I said she is the manipulative person. I believe this is evidence to have Glenn under oath on the witness stand. I believe she must be punished by taking her custody away for lying under oath 12 times. Why is this woman being allowed to continuously lie in court with no fact checks? Yet, I the father of my daughters has not been allowed to see my daughters on holidays, birthdays and during summer. This system is broken when a vindictive proven perjurer can file 41 pages on a Tuesday at 9:35 am, and have my daughters taken away from me the next morning, while I work 220 miles away.
>
> -Seth

Lying under oath? Fact checks? I wanted to tell Seth to pour another drink and sleep it off. That would go against my "no engaging rule," so I refrained from responding to him.

Attorney Withdrawal

We hadn't heard from Seth all week, and I was a bit on edge knowing that he was escalated. Not only was he escalated, but also he perceived the recent turn of events as losing, so I feared that he was dangerous. After court dates where Seth had some type of victory, I slept a bit easier knowing that my fear factor was decreased. When he perceived a loss, I lost sleep.

I wasn't expecting anything important in the mail at the time, so I almost bypassed my weekly stop at the post office. In a stack of mail was a letter from Seth's attorney. I threw it on my front seat and continued on my way, assuming it was the declaration that I had already read in court. As I was waiting to pick up Sarah from school, I reached over and opened the envelope. I immediately saw the words, "Notice of Withdrawal of Attorney of Record." Seth's attorney had quit!

While I am not sure of the details surrounding his withdraw, I suspect that it had to do with the insanity of our case in general, bounced checks, or Seth's inability to follow orders. Regardless of the reason he quit, I'm sure that it was completely my fault in Seth's mind. I had a boost of confidence in terms of my court case, yet my fear factor rose with that recent development.

When Seth has someone to quell him, he appears somewhat normal. This could be his mom's voice in the back of his mind, his aunt's pre-written script, or an attorney to talk for him. The attorney kept him at bay and didn't allow Seth to dig himself any deeper. In true narcissistic fashion, Seth was on top of the world because, in his eyes, he was winning. To a narcissist, winning is as important as breathing air. It is essential to survival.

A New Chapter of My Life

Over the course of three years, Glenn restored my faith that there are amazing men in this world. When Glenn tells me that he loves me, I already feel it in my heart. When I wake up in the morning, I know that I am adored, and that is something that I have never felt before.

Despite the negatives in the previous years, I learned what it means to be in love with my best friend. I don't believe in accidents. I believe that Glenn was put in my life at the most opportune time, when I was able to appreciate him completely. In celebration of our three-year anniversary, Glenn invited me to have coffee with him at the coffee shop where we first met in 2009.

As I rounded the corner, I saw three things: a table with a white tablecloth, a dozen red roses, and a guitar. I instantly knew what was happening, but it felt completely surreal. Glenn picked up his guitar and played "Marry Me" by Train while adding personalized lyrics as he sang. There was nothing business-like about this proposal, and there were no red-flag moments—just pure, genuine love and joy.

Aside from the birth of my daughters, it was the happiest moment of my life. Glenn got down on one knee and asked me to marry him. Of course, I said, "YES!" I believe that the age-old saying is true; the right person will come along when you are least expecting it. To think that I would spend the rest of my life with this amazing man put a permanent smile on my face. A new chapter in my life began.

Our relationship has everything I've ever wanted: love, communication, friendship, respect, stability, and mutual adoration. In addition to being the only real man I have ever been in a relationship with, Glenn gives my daughters the male stability and the love that they deserve.

Master Manipulator in Action

Today, it seems like many moons ago when Seth and I were going through the court-ordered custody evaluation. At the time, we were instructed by the evaluator not to say, "I am going to miss you" to the girls when they were going with the other parent. She stated that it made the girls feel responsible for their parent's feelings. She suggested that we say things like, "I love you, and I hope you have a great time." To this day, I am careful in my choice of words whenever the girls leave for a visit, as I don't want them to feel torn in any way.

Unfortunately, as narcissists are master manipulators, they don't care about making a child feel torn. They thrive on manipulations. Seth had not made an effort to see the girls since the previous *ex parte* hearing in May. His supervised visits were supposed to be one time per week for one hour each visit, yet we hadn't seen him at all.

One evening in the beginning of June 2012, Seth called to tell the girls about his triathlon. He wanted to talk about himself and how far he swam, rode, and ran. Being that they were only ages 5 and 7, they just don't understand or care. Seth went on to explain that a 15-year-old girl participated in the triathlon and that, in a few years, they could sign up to race, also. He didn't care what they are interested in; he only cares about what he is interested in. Seth wants them to be his puppets just like I was for so many years.

He ended the call with the manipulation level cranked to high. "This was supposed to be Daddy's weekend to see you but … well … Daddy can't see you for a while, and that makes me sad. We would have gone swimming together and had a lot of fun. Daddy will be able to see you soon. I hope I will get to see you this summer." He was hoping to evoke some response from them, but he didn't get it, so he switched to using his mom's visit this summer as bait. "I hope that Noni will get to see you."

Without saying a word to them, I can already tell that the girls see through their dad. I am thankful to their therapist for helping them to understand that we can't control other people or their decisions. I am thankful that they are intuitive and know what is real and what is contrived. I am thankful that they have a voice. I am thankful that they don't move on cue when the puppet strings try to control them.

After Seth had spoken in great detail about this triathlon, an anonymous person emailed me after reading my blog in which I detailed Seth's phone call. She stated that Seth didn't do the triathlon at all. He was at the event lurking but did not compete. I scanned the race results, and Seth was not registered.

In June 2012, Seth called the girls and reminded them both that it was Father's Day. He then proceeded to play the victim card by explaining (again) that he was going to be in town and that it was so sad that he wouldn't be able to see them.

After mentioning that he couldn't see the girls multiple times, Seth said to Piper, "I want you to make me a Father's Day present and maybe figure out a way to give it to me." Piper looked unsure of what to say and didn't respond to him. Of course, he continued by saying, "I don't know how you can get it to me, but maybe you can figure out a way since I will be in town?" She stared at me with a confused look and shrugged her shoulders.

Seth then went on to say, "I am here with your uncles and your grandpa, and you should be with me today." I looked into Piper's eyes and saw how uncomfortable she was. After a few times of hearing Seth repeat his sob story, I took the phone and walked into another room to politely ask him to stop. Seth said, "BLAST OFF, TINA!" and began to yell at me. I hung up the phone and sent him the following text message:

> Seth- You are welcome to call back anytime this evening before 8 p.m. if you can refrain from discussing adult or court-related topics with the children.

Seth called back at 7:51 p.m. and kept telling the girls that he loved them "up to the sky" and that he is sad. Seth then told Sarah that he loved her and she said, "Ok." He responded by saying, "You have to say it—that you love daddy." By this point, she said it back to him. His voice was low and bizarre; he was extremely intoxicated. To hear Seth tell Sarah that she had to say, "I love you" was almost too much to bear. He wasn't doing a good job of earning their love.

Hiring an Attorney

I was living paycheck to paycheck and cringed when well-meaning people said, "You really need an attorney." Hiring an attorney was not an option for me. Call me crazy, but feeding my daughters scored a bit higher on the to-do list.

However, I received a small sum of money back from my taxes and made the decision to hire a limited-scope attorney specifically for the June hearing to discuss the near-drowning. I had handled everything on my own to date, but there was so much on the line that I couldn't risk making a single mistake in court that day. I spoke to an attorney that I met at the women's shelter in 2009, and we met for coffee. I then spent much of the weekend after meeting with her creating a timeline of events to bring her up to speed, which was overwhelming and brought on multiple panic attacks.

Anyone who knows me can attest to the fact that things always seem to fall into place for me. In hindsight, I feel that God has always directed my path, even when I was a non-believer. It's not that I've led a privileged life—quite the opposite. My childhood falls into the category of "things that no child should ever have to go through." I'm a fighter and a survivor with a positive attitude. I don't believe in self-pity, and I flat-out refuse to be a victim. I work very hard to find the lessons that are hidden inside of each experience. Sometimes, those lessons are as clear as day and, other times, they are hidden in a really thick muck.

I have a difficult time giving up control. I have been behind the wheel of this battle to protect my daughters since day one. Placing my trust in an attorney was more difficult than I could have ever imagined. I was so close to obtaining a permanent order for supervised visits and needed someone with legal knowledge to take the wheel.

I had faith that everything was unfolding as it was supposed to and that there was a plan in place that I didn't understand at the moment. I needed to have confidence that those horrible and humbling days at the women's shelter needed to happen to make me stronger. Maybe the encounter with the attorney from the women's shelter three years ago was meant to be. Maybe this attorney was placed in my path for a reason and, in court, it would all become clear.

Court: June 20, 2012

Most days, I truly wondered if the commissioner flipped a coin in chambers: "heads" means supervised visits and "tails" means unsupervised visits. A rhyme or reason to what was happening didn't appear to exist. The attorney who helped me in court on June 20, 2012 said that she reviewed our court file and that the decisions to date were "all over the place." She described it as a circus.

We were in court to discuss the girls nearly drowning. I felt like vomiting as the commissioner's words left his mouth. He stated that there was no solid proof that Seth was sleeping or hungover when the girls almost drowned. It was his word against mine. Anything that the girls said or wrote in their journal was hearsay. I was told that the girls should probably take swimming lessons.

We asked that the order be written to say that my youngest daughter should be in a life jacket at all times due to her seizure disorder. The commissioner declined that request and said that he isn't going to micromanage the children's lives with what time they eat dinner, go to bed, wear a life jacket, and so on. The commissioner then went on to say something along the lines of, "Seth isn't going to let anything happen to the children. He would have to live with himself if anything happened to the them."

With that statement from the commissioner, I mentally checked out of the courtroom. I couldn't believe what I was hearing. It further proved that the courts do not understand high-conflict divorces with narcissists or other personality disordered individuals. I don't care what the diagnosis is. The bottom line is that Seth doesn't care about the children. He cares about winning the case. Seth would easily be able to live with himself if something happened to the children because he lacks a conscience. If something happened to the girls, he would actually derive from a high from hurting me.

We all walked out of the courtroom and, within two seconds of stepping foot into the hallway, Seth started spewing about my blog and how it is ruining his family's reputation. He wasn't excited about getting to see his daughters without supervision; he was upset that his family secrets were being exposed. He wanted me to stop telling the truth.

He Takes the Cake

Prior to a weekend visitation near the end of June 2012, Seth asked me if he could keep the girls late on Sunday because they were having a family party. I declined his request because we already had plans that evening. Sure enough, Seth asked Piper to call me from the party and ask permission to stay longer, knowing that his request had already been denied. Piper said to me, "Dad said we can't have cake if we don't stay later." I reminded Piper that we had plans and that I would call and discuss it directly with her dad. Seth didn't answer his phone.

On the way to pick up the girls, I stopped and bought cake because I had a feeling that Seth would be cruel enough to really withhold cake from them. As I arrived at Seth's house to pick up the girls, I immediately noticed that Piper had been crying. She walked straight up to me and wrapped her arms around me before climbing into my car. Piper said that something had happened that she wanted to talk about. Because I carry a voice recorder, I flipped it on to ensure I didn't forget details about what she was about to say.

According to Piper, Seth was furious as they left the party. He immediately began telling the girls, "It's your mom's fault that we can't have fun." He continued, "It's your mom's fault that I only get to see you for a short amount of time." Piper said Seth continued saying mean things about me. Piper used her voice as she was learning to do in counseling and told Seth, "Dad, you are saying things that I don't need to hear."

Seth continued with his rant while Piper tried to send me a text message to ask for assistance. Seth then reached into the backseat and grabbed the phone out of her hands while he was driving on the freeway. He informed Piper that it was illegal to text while in a car. He told her that his rules forbade texting on his visitation time. The entire recollection by Piper made my blood boil. He is a 7-year-old, mentally deranged bully in a grown man's body.

The phone was an ongoing source of contention, which worried me. I knew that Seth and his family were attempting to build a case that the girls were not permitted to have a phone. Cleo casually mentioned by email that Piper often plays with the camera feature on the cell phone during the visitations, which distracts her from her time with Seth. I spoke to Piper about the proper use of the phone and that it is not a toy. I didn't want to give them any reason to take the phone from the girls.

The phone was court-ordered to stay in Piper's possession during the visit. Seth had recently violated the order multiple times by removing it from her when she had tried to contact me. As I dropped the girls off one morning, I said to Seth, "I've spoken to Piper about proper use of the cell phone, and she will not be using it as a camera or a toy during her visits. Her phone must remain in her possession at all times." Seth replied, "I will be getting that changed in court. You are only using the phone for GPS tracking, which will end." Seth then went on to say, "You are also tracking me on my iPhone with spyware, which is illegal and will also be stopped."

The Private Eyes are Watching You

Between my private investigators and Seth's younger brother, Carter, I knew quite a bit about Seth's life, which often helped me in my custody battle. I found two private investigators who were not only great at their jobs, they had hearts and were amazing human beings. While I did not have the financial means to hire an attorney permanently, I committed to utilizing the services of private investigators to help build my case. I worked out an arrangement in which I mailed them whatever I could afford and chipped away at my bill. I didn't care if I needed to keep sending checks until my eightieth birthday; their services proved to be invaluable to me, whether it was documenting Seth's alcohol intake or following Seth during his parenting time just for peace of mind that my children were safe when he escalated.

On a Friday morning in August of 2012, my family was scheduled to arrive in Palm Springs for a big family reunion, Seth began posting photos of himself on social media claiming to be in Palm Springs. This is the type of mind-fuck that Seth excels at. I was left wondering if he was truly in Palm Springs and whether he knew where we were going to be staying. Were we going to be sitting ducks if he decided to go on a rampage?

I knew that Carter had the ability to track him through their shared Cloud server, so I reached out to him in a panic, explaining the situation. I told him that all I needed was for him to confirm whether or not Seth was truly in Palm Springs. I didn't care where he was in the world, but if he was really going to be in Palm Springs, I had some security measures to put in place.

Carter tracked Seth's location to a hotel in Valencia, California, almost three hours away from Palm Springs. He also verified this information through a credit card that he shared with Seth and said that he had made alcoholic purchases from the bar in the hotel. I was relieved but also furious that I had climbed back onto Seth's rollercoaster of insanity. I had gone into a state of hyper-vigilance only to experience the crash of relief that I had been accustomed to throughout our marriage. The ups and downs of the battle were exhausting.

Now that I knew my family was safe, an idea popped into my head. I had been relentlessly attempting to serve Seth with court documents for weeks; in true Seth fashion, he was evading service. I sprung into action, finding a process server in Valencia and sending him the electronic court documents needed in order for him to serve Seth. The process server waited in the hallway of the hotel until Seth emerged to attend a work conference in the hotel and successfully served a fuming Seth.

For several months, I hired my private investigator to follow Seth on Friday nights in an attempt to prove how much alcohol he drank. What Seth did on his time was his business, but it became my business when he was noticeably hungover and driving my daughters on Saturday mornings. In court, I could describe his bloodshot eyes, hoarse voice, and hungover appearance, but it was my word against his until a private investigator could confirm how much alcohol he consumed the night before his scheduled parenting time. My private investigator mentioned that Seth often drove erratically, constantly checking his rearview mirror as if he believed someone was following him.

Other times, I utilized the private investigator during Seth's visitations just to have peace of mind that my daughters were safe and that he hadn't driven them off a cliff. While that may sound dramatic to someone who hasn't been in a custody battle with a sociopath, it was one of my greatest fears. I knew he was capable of hurting the girls simply just to spite me. Seth was now openly accusing me of tracking him on GPS with an iPhone because he couldn't figure out how I was constantly obtaining information on him. What he didn't realize was that his own brother was supplying me with the majority of information that I had obtained.

Contempt of Court

Seth's child support balance had grown to $37,000 in arrears. While claiming poverty, he was somehow able to maintain a luxury lifestyle, including a 24-hour concierge service at his condo, new cars, and a membership at an elite health club. His definition of poverty and mine are obviously very different.

After only receiving three child support payments in a one-year timespan, I decided to file contempt of court charges against Seth. While I had managed to handle my family court case in pro se for several years, contempt charges fall into the criminal realm, and there are many formalities involved that I wasn't prepared for. While I didn't really know what I was doing procedurally, my goal was to simply bring the issue to the court's attention.

Just days before the hearing, I received the following email from Seth:

> <u>Original Message:</u> Tina- I am willing to pay you $3,000 to dismiss the Contempt Hearing with prejudice. I can pay $1000 on 8/21/2012 if you take this off calendar today, $1000 on 9/1/2012 and $1000 on 9/16/2012. I have notified the company I work for now of the child support for direct payments to State Disbursement office, so those payments will also be coming to you. Collectively, this means your normal monthly payments would be in your hands by the end of September. I would rather pay past due support than pay an attorney these monies.
>
> The Contempt Hearing claiming I made commission but didn't pay you will not be proven. Since I lost my job on June 3rd, 2011, I was unemployed over 6 months in two intervals of time. On November 17, 2011, my company laid off their entire staff. I earned $0 in commission. Thus, I had only unemployment until Spring 2012. I made no commission and barely got by for the past 14 months. When employment was gained again by me, you were paid in March, as well as in April and May garnishment. No commission was earned as they are a start-up company with instrumentation that has a very long sales cycle.
>
> The last 2 weeks I was in training with my new job and I cannot afford to lose this job by being brought to court mid-week over and over. If you are unable to accept, I will have no choice but to use these payroll funds to retain an attorney to defend my rights today 8/21/12. I will not have a choice but to spend money on an attorney in such a hearing. Best regards, Seth

My "Narc Decoder" allowed me to sift through the manipulations and lies to get to the real message:

> <u>"Snap, fizzle, pop" and out comes the decoded email</u>: Dear Tina- I am going to attempt to bribe you with money, so please don't focus

on the fact that I've never once kept a promise involving paying child support. You can trust me this time. I promise.

Once I heard about the contempt hearing, I promptly called Child Support Services and gave them the information about my job in an effort to stop the court process. I figured that I should probably notify them that I am working before I have to stand in front of the commissioner and try to explain why I continue to live a luxury lifestyle and fail to pay support.

Bear with me while I lie about my jobs and the reasons that I am fired every three months. Basically, it's always someone's fault. I've never once lost a job by my own doing. Lastly, I am starting to worry about being held in contempt of court and am pleading with you in my own twisted and warped way. The biggest issue that I have with all of this is the orange jail jumpsuit. It would really clash with my ruddy, alcoholic complexion. Best regards, Seth

My local courthouse is pretty friendly to those who are pro se in family court; however, the contempt charges were an entirely new ballgame. I struggled with the courtroom formalities and requirements and, while the commissioner looked at me with a bit of pity in his eyes, his hands were tied, and he could not guide me. The entire hearing was over an hour in length, and I was unsuccessful in proving that Seth willfully failed to pay his support. I walked out with my tail between my legs, and the experience reconfirmed my commitment to keep my focus on custody and let Seth keep his blood money. I'd rather live on Top Ramen than walk down this broken path again because it isn't worth my energy.

Losing My Co-Pilot

Seth and I separated when the girls were just 2 and 4 years old. In my financial survival mode, I had my calendar marked for September of 2012 as a finish line in many ways. This was the month Sarah was set to begin kindergarten and Piper would be in second grade. Most months, I had barely stayed afloat with the preschool expenses for both girls. Sarah's kindergarten starting date felt so far away for so long, but it was finally upon us and it was bittersweet.

In 2010, I had to make the decision to scale back on the number of days that Sarah attended preschool for financial reasons. I felt blessed to have a career that allowed me the flexibility to work from home, but it was difficult for both Sarah and I. She wanted to run and play yet was forced to sit by my side in coffee shops as I juggled appointments, conference calls, and Excel spreadsheets. She played quietly with puzzles and Play-Doh, watched DVDs, and completed art projects. My Mom guilt was at an all-time high because I wanted so much more for her.

The reality of this battle set in during kindergarten orientation. I had so many mixed emotions as I processed the next chapter of our lives. I was angry with Seth because I had been so focused on this milestone—not because I wanted to push my child into kindergarten but because I was so financially strapped due to his ongoing financial abuse and control. I envied the moms who were able to enjoy their children's toddler years without trying to figure out if groceries took priority over preschool tuition. I cried while walking Sarah to the kindergarten orientation, and I cried during the principal's speech to the incoming kindergarteners. I cried as we left the school parking lot, telling her how excited I was for her to make her own memories.

On the first day of kindergarten, Glenn and I accompanied Sarah to her class. The tears started as soon as Sarah hung her backpack on the little hook with her name on it. Sarah had been my co-pilot, but she had a new job as of that day. My house was way too quiet, and I sat with tears streaming down my face as I tried to concentrate on work. In my financial desperation, I had prayed for this day to come for so long but, once it arrived, I wished that I could push the rewind button.

Most parents want to savor each and every moment of childhood, but when you are sharing custody with a Cluster B disordered individual, you also pray for your children to grow up for a variety of reasons. You want them to be old enough to have a voice in the system. You want them to be old enough to put up boundaries and to know what is healthy and what is not. In my case, it was these things plus financial survival.

Home Versus House

Since my custody battle began, I had learned to embrace simplicity. I could scan through emails over the ten years that Seth and I were together, and I find a common thread: begging Seth to downsize our life. I was tired of keeping up with the Joneses, the Smiths, and everyone else with the newest Mercedes or biggest house.

In August of 2012, Glenn and I found a beautiful little home and moved in together. While we had been living together for a full year, the girls and I had been in Glenn's home. This was a new start and *our* home. As we pulled the moving truck into the driveway, I was struck by the symbol of a dragonfly on the side of the moving truck. We arrived at the charming little home, and the stained-glass light in the living room had the image of a dragonfly. I don't believe in coincidences, but I do believe in God moments.

Remembering that dragonflies symbolized some type of change, I quickly looked up the meaning of dragonflies to discover that they are symbolic of change, self-realization, and the deeper meanings of life. The dragonfly's lifespan is only seven months, and they exemplify the virtue of living in the moment and living life to the fullest.

I felt ready to embrace the deeper meaning of life and to live in the moment. I felt ready to begin compartmentalizing this battle so that it wouldn't consume me. Changes can be scary and overwhelming at times, but I looked forward to my new home and my new life. Our home would be based on the important things in life: love, family, and happiness. For these things, I am eternally grateful.

Torment and Abuse in the Court System

To date, I have completely lost count of how many times we have been to court. In 2012, Seth had a total of 22 unsupervised visits with Piper and Sarah, yet the amount of damage inflicted during that time is exponentially greater. I have also lost track of the number of times I've cried myself to sleep because I am skilled at putting on a brave face for my daughters but, once they are asleep, my walls come down and the floodgates open. Sometimes, I feel as though the family court professionals live in an alternate reality and that we speak different languages. I struggle to comprehend what it will take for them to protect the girls. Will my daughters' lives be reduced to a press conference during which everyone apologizes to me, and then they go on with their lives?

For several days after Seth's parenting time, Sarah would continue to suffer from nightmares and night terrors. Night terrors are horrendous to watch. Her eyes would be open, she could communicate to some degree, but she was often distraught, combative and zombie-like. She would grind her teeth during her sleep to the point that I've considered getting her a mouth guard, and she would not allow me to leave her sight when at home with me.

Both of my daughters were potty trained during the day at the age of 2 and at night by the age of 4. Sarah completely regressed in potty training during both day and night. She has had countless periods of regression all centered on Seth's visitations. There have been multiple occasions where she's defecated in her pants during Seth's visits or on the Mondays or Tuesdays following Seth's visitation and urinary accidents had become almost a daily occurrence. There are no words to describe the pain in my heart as I have watched my daughters struggle.

My frustration built as much of my mountains of documentation seemed to be in vain. There's nothing more frustrating in this world than to watch my children suffer emotionally or physically and have no power to fix it, being at the mercy of the family court system. The courts have a threshold of what they deem as acceptable, but as mothers, as fathers, and as a society, our thresholds should be much higher. Much like a doctor becomes accustomed to the cycle of life, I believe our courts have become accustomed and calloused to abuse, neglect, and abandonment. In clinical terms, this is referred to as compassion fatigue.

Compassion fatigue is an issue that starts in the courtroom and trickles down to everyone who has a hand in the court system. This includes the very people who are supposed to protect our children, such as parenting evaluators, counselors and therapists, primary caregivers, *guardians ad litem* (GALs), and Child Welfare Services. As a society, we should demand a higher threshold when it comes to our children. Sadly, these issues come back to parental rights and the fact that parental rights seem to supersede the rights of a child to be healthy, happy and loved.

At the end of 2012, minor's counsel stated in a declaration, "Declarant is at a loss as to whether the mother, Tina Swithin, is overreacting to incidents of the father's poor judgment in his parenting of the children during his visitation."

If emotional abuse and torment are not considered "poor parenting," then yes, I am guilty of overreacting. If you do not consider leaving a child unattended in a car for 30 to 45 minutes "poor judgment" in parenting, then yes, I am guilty of overreacting. If you do not consider leaving two very young children unsupervised in a swimming pool "poor judgment" while parenting, then I am guilty of overreacting. If you do not consider telling a 4-year-old that you are going to lock her in a dark parking structure "poor judgment" in parenting, then I am guilty of overreacting.

The Bear

Another mother from the girls' school stopped me to relay something that she overheard while Piper and Sarah were at her house. Piper said, "My dad is mean. Last week, he was pretending to be a scary bear, and Sarah was crying."

I asked the girls about the incident after school, and they verified the story. According to them, they were driving when, out of nowhere, Seth got a mean look on his face and kept swiping his hand back at them while pretending to be a scary bear. He wouldn't stop even though they begged him to quit. This episode resulted in Sarah crying hysterically. Seth took their phone, and they were unable to call or text me for help.

This wasn't the first time I'd heard about the bear. It was Seth's way to instill fear in Sarah and he used it often. From what I had been told by the girls, he would distort his face, growl, and swipe his hands at Sarah until she was distraught. He seemed to target her specifically while homing in on her greatest fears and tormenting her with them. She was afraid of dogs, so he'd tell her that he would put her in the dog pen at his brother's house if she didn't comply with his orders. When she was fearful of the spider at his house, he threatened to make her sleep in the dark parking structure that he knew she was afraid of.

Narcissists are known to choose a "golden child" and, in our case, it has changed over the years. Originally, Sarah was the golden child until her seizures began. Seth immediately wanted to know who in *my* family had seizures. His child could not possibly have any type of disorder or medical issue with his perfect family genes. Almost overnight, I watched his focus shift to Piper as the chosen one, and Sarah took the brunt of his anger and attacks.

The Phone and Another Emergency Hearing

At the very end of 2012, I scheduled yet another *ex parte* hearing because Seth had been taking the phone from Piper during his visitation. I had picked the girls up several times when they were visibly shaken only to have Seth hand me their phone from the front seat of his car.

The court order stated that the phone was to be fully charged and in the girls' possession at all times. Seth admitted to the girls' attorney that he had taken the phone from them. He then put it in writing that the girls were no longer permitted to carry the phone with them during his visits. Seth said that they could use *his* phone if they needed to call me and cited the GPS feature as the reason why they weren't allowed to carry the phone. Last time I checked, he wasn't allowed to override the commissioner's orders but, in the mind of a narcissist, he truly believed he carried that power. Based on the fact that he couldn't follow court orders and admitted to taking their phone, I was asking for supervised visits to be reinstated.

I received a call from the girls' attorney. He said that Seth took the cell phone from the girls was due to my continuous interference with his parenting time. According to Seth, I was texting or calling constantly during the visits—yet another lie and one that was easy to disprove. I printed the phone records from the past 12 months and took the detailed records, along with the phone itself, to the attorney's office and dropped them off. I color-coded each entry for incoming and outgoing calls to make it easy for Mr. Anders and the court to review. I had been so careful about communicating with the girls during Seth's parenting time, and this was one topic that was black and white versus the gray area in which narcissists thrive.

Mr. Anders filed his response to the court: "The records provided by Tina are not consistent with Seth's recitation of the number of contacts between the children and their mother during visits." Mr. Anders' statement could be easily broken down and simplified: Seth was lying. Where was Mr. Anders' backbone? The reality was that Seth's claim of "constant interruptions" totaled less than four text messages or calls in a three-month period. One of those phone calls was at Seth's request to see if he could extend his visit against court orders. Mr. Anders went on to suggest that a new custody evaluation was necessary, and I was in complete agreement. Not consistent with Seth's recitation? Why don't we call it like it is, Mr. Anders? Seth is a liar.

Since our last custody evaluation in 2010, I had become much more educated on high-conflict custody battles and Cluster B personality disorders. In the 2010 evaluation, it was my word against his but, now, patterns of behavior had been established, and I had stacks of documentation and endless emails that would allow me to show what the problems were. In addition, there were two new alcohol offenses, two child welfare reports, and multiple police logs, as well as more lies than I could count. The girls were also older and able to speak the truth.

I arrived at the courthouse to discover that my *ex parte* request had been denied. The family court system again put the lives of two little girls back into the hands of a sociopath. I didn't need an $8,000 psychological evaluation to tell me whom I was dealing with. I dealt with a man who's out of his mind, and a court system that is ill equipped to handle high-conflict custody battles.

The court saw a man who *said* he wanted to be a parent, but the point that they were missing was that his actions did not align with his words. He did not want to be a parent; he wanted to hurt me. The reality was that compared to the deadbeat dads that the courts typically see, anyone who claims to want to be a part of their child's life is a welcomed relief to the court. What the court failed to understand was that Seth loves the girls the same way he loves his car: as possessions. To Seth, the girls were merely pawns that he could use in the game of hurting and controlling me. Seth had continuously failed in so many aspects of his life that he was determined to "win" the custody battle. His quest wasn't about love and genuine interest in the well-being of the girls. He proved that over and over again.

His objective was to prove to everyone that he is a good father and even a good person. He fought for 50/50 custody not because he wanted it but because it's a badge that he wanted to show off to those around him. The last piece of his public image to salvage in our community was his image as a father. But, I have continually refused to allow the well-being of my children to be compromised for Seth's ego show. My daughters exude kindness and strength beyond their years. I consistently refuse to sit back and watch their lives become ruined and their potential in life tarnished at the hands of a broken system and sick, disordered father.

Upon further review of Seth's responsive declaration, I read one of his most bizarre statements to date: "Supervised visitation is not a service for men holding down challenging careers." In other words, because he is superior to those around him, he is within his rights to do anything he wants to his children regardless of the damage that it causes. In Seth's mind, men of his status do not need supervised visits.

While my *ex parte* request was denied, the commissioner did schedule a new hearing for October 24, 2012 to formally address the issues that had been raised.

Weekend Visitation

Seth emailed me near the end of 2012 regarding his upcoming weekend visitation. I typed a simple response asking that he meet me in a public location versus his family compound. Because Seth is incapable of "yes" or "no" answers, he sent the following message instead:

<u>Original Message:</u> *Tina- Neither my father, Robert nor I have ever committed any act of harm towards any woman ever. We do not like you anymore this is true, but we are not going to do anything to any woman ever to hurt them. It's just delusional that you have such a fear.*

You are creating in your mind a storyline to fuel your little blog Tina. I don't care about your blog. It's funny to me at this point. You attack Mr. Anders when he doesn't want to meet with you. You attack the Commissioner. You attack the Superior Court for not believing your exaggerations. Where does all this hatred and vengeance come from Tina?

I just want a normal, healthy relationship with my daughters free of your micro-management of every minute that I am with my daughters. Your continuous attacks on my character and every member in my family need to stop.

You are seriously jeopardizing my job at this point. You've had me in court, middle of the week 220 miles from my job responsibilities 12+ times this year. Let alone the amount of time I must waste to respond to your hearings that you file with 2-3 days' notice. I should be 120% to plan making money and moving on in my career not devoting 3 days of every work week well responding to your opinions, lies and exaggerations, which you do in every declaration, more and more frequently.

If I lose this job, because court is always in the middle of the work week, I will be unable to get another job in this industry. I will be unemployed, and you will not get any money except a small portion of unemployment. You make money, why don't you just be happy and get on with your life. It is time you call it quits. This is about two innocent children. You have conducted a severe level of Parental Alienation Syndrome and the damage is apparent but will grow more severe as the children reach teenage years. Do you really want to be in court all the time when the girls are 3, 5, 10 years older Tina?!?

Sarah wetting her bed is on you Tina. She never wet her bed in 2011 when she was with me overnight. I'd wake her up to potty at 11:30 p.m. or so, and she'd be fine until the morning. Her having nightmares is on your conscience. You have caused this Tina.

These children need to know they have two loving parents. They need to have a relationship with me their father. They can call Glenn their step-dad but the pressure you put on them to accept him as their dad is causing them to have severe emotional strain and anxiety. They want me to be their dad Tina.

I am sorry I sold all the furniture back in 2009. But you had no income. The family needed any available money to fund your home and my living in two places for the sake of the girls. You'll remember you went bankrupt and did not work for 8 more months.

Since we have had the exchange at my house, I have had at least one person present as a witness, either Robert's wife or my dad. I have previously thought about having the exchange at the Police Department. The problem is this is scary setting potentially for the children. There is no reason for it. You think after you dragged me to court for three years over nonsense and exaggerations, I would risk yelling at you or harming you, it's just preposterous Tina. I am not going to do anything to hurt you. Nor would I say anything to you in the presence of the children you could use against me in court.

Go on in your life with Glenn. I am pleading with you to leave me alone. Years from now, the girls will be emotionally scarred and damaged by what you've done in this divorce. I think that they're perception of having an exchange at a Police Department, which is completely unnecessary, will weigh on them as uncomfortable and cause increased anxiety. When I was a kid Police made me nervous.

I would be willing to consider an exchange at the children museum. Or maybe at the downtown park in the square. How about that Tina? I am truly sorry you feel like I hurt you so badly by falling out of love with you back in 2007, but I did. I am sorry I felt compelled to sell all the furniture, but we were broke and you were unemployed and it was prior to my filing for divorce. I will compromise and agree to the children museum or the park. Will that work for you? Seth

When placed into the Narc Decoder, Seth's email actually reads:

<u>"Snap, fizzle, pop" and out comes the decoded email</u>: *Tina – I have not **yet** been convicted of harming a woman but I am starting to worry about the declarations from three different women who have come forward to testify that they live in fear about my actions and instability relating to stalking and threats. Somehow, my brother Robert has operated under the law enforcement radar for years. My father ... we all know about his label as the "pervert principal," but I promise that he's not going to grab your butt because he hates you at this point.*

I am obsessed with your blog, which is why I mention it to anyone who will listen and include references to it in each and every court document, even though the commissioner has made it clear that I need to stop whining about it.

I am incapable of a normal, healthy relationship of any kind and we both know that. I don't like court orders or following rules. By you telling the truth about my family, we are no longer able to hide our long-held family secrets and dysfunctions.

How dare you hold me accountable for my actions when I am with my daughters! They are my possessions, and I should be allowed to do anything I please sans authority or repercussions.

I am about to lose my job, again, because they are already starting to see through me. It's been about four months, and that is the life cycle of each job that I get. I need someone to blame for my loss of employment so that my parents will still believe that I am perfect.

I am trying to keep my stories straight. Did I sell the furniture or did I hide the furniture in storage while you were out of town? Which is the last version of the story that I told? I can't remember. I need to twist the bankruptcy story around so that I have no responsibility for the fact that I ran up almost $1.7 million, which included spending my parent's retirement money to support my need for a lavish lifestyle. I am going to blame you for the bankruptcy. Remember that time you were out of work for three months? I am going to add five months to the real number because it sounds better in my head.

Due to all my run-ins with law enforcement, police make me nervous and cause increased anxiety. Let's agree to meet away from them.

My ego is so big that I must believe that our break-up had nothing to do with the fact that you saw my true colors and fell out of love with me. I'm going to recreate the story in my own mind (and believe it!). I hope you don't catch on to the fact that the story changes every so often. Last week, the demise of our marriage was because you cheated on me with four different men in four months. This week it is because I fell out of love with you! Keep up with my stories, Tina! -Seth

I felt like saying, "Would you like some cream and sugar with your large cup of insanity?" but, instead, I sent a short, simple email: "Seth- I will see you at the Children's Museum on Saturday and Sunday at 11 a.m. I will plan to pick up the girls at the same location at 5 p.m. on both days."

The Apple Pie

After one of Seth's visitations in the final months of 2012, I picked the girls up to hear the words, "Mom! We made you an apple pie!" As we drove, Piper went on to explain that Seth drove 45 minutes south to a local barn to buy apples and bake a pie with them. They planned to present it to me the next day after Seth's Sunday visit. As much as I would love to believe that he has taken up baking with his daughters, I know him and I also know that there is a pending court date on the horizon. He needed additional photos to submit to the court, and there are no better photos than those of him baking an apple pie with the girls.

Truth be told, the thought of eating a pie made by Seth was enough to send me over the edge. My first thought involved sending it to a lab to be tested for poison! My second thought involved finding an apple pie from a local bakery so that I could swap the pies out when the girls weren't looking. I knew they would be crushed if I didn't eat the pie they baked, so I began driving to various bakers and called around town trying to find a replacement pie which, thankfully, I was successful in purchasing.

I knew Seth too well to trust anything that left his kitchen. Piper later said to me, "Mom, isn't it strange that Dad wanted to make you a pie?" I was careful with my response and said, "It was very unexpected, and I appreciate how hard that you worked to make it!" Even my daughters know him well enough that they found this to be abnormal behavior.

Just before midnight, I received a chilling series of text messages from Seth which included two photos of our daughters posing with the apple pie. I could see their forced smiles and noticeable discomfort on their faces.

The first text message read, "We made an apple pie. Their first pie ever!!! Bought some fresh apples at Avila Barn. I am better at BBQ than baking but now that its baked it looks pretty yummy!!! They want to give it to their Mom. So sweet of them."

I laid in bed frozen, questioning his motives.

The second text message followed minutes later, "Sorry, Tina. That wasn't meant for you. Why don't you just go on with your life with Glenn and stop obsessing on my life and what I do."

To my relief, Seth didn't send the pie home with the girls on Sunday, so all was well in the world other than the reality that I went on yet another Seth-induced rollercoaster ride.

Rebranding

With a background in marketing, I am very familiar with the term "rebranding." I am now familiar with the term as it pertains to a parent who is trying to fool people. The girls came home from their weekend visitation in December 2012 and exclaimed that Daddy was going to rent a little cottage for them to stay at on the weekends.

The timing was uncanny given the fact that I was going to press for a new parenting evaluation at our upcoming court date and Seth knew this. I had already been on this ride with Seth during our last parenting evaluation in 2010. He was obviously setting up another false front because there was a new evaluation looming.

Piper and Sarah went on to say that the cottage was actually in the downstairs area of Robert's home. I was then thoroughly confused, but I let them keep talking about this "cottage." Seth was manipulating them to be excited about the same place that they've been going for a year. He was rebranding it for the parenting evaluation. The length that Seth goes to in order to manipulate and lie terrifies me. The scarier part is that his family assists him in these charades.

The girls appeared distressed while mentioning that Seth was discussing new beds that they would be able to sleep in at his new cottage. He told them that they would begin staying overnight soon. The mere thought of my daughters spending the night in Robert's home was enough to send me into a tailspin. I didn't even like the girls being in his home during the daytime and, even in 100-degree weather, I forced them to wear leggings under their skirts during visits. My intuition was never wrong, and I did not trust Robert or Leonard around my daughters.

Court: October 23, 2012

I was not feeling inspirational before this hearing by any stretch of the imagination. We arrived at the courthouse, and I saw Leonard walking with an attorney. I instantly knew that they had retained counsel. Moments later, I was handed paperwork by Seth's new attorney, Mr. Slaromon.

Mr. Slaromon was not an attorney from our local *good ol' boys club*, and a quick Google search told me that he had driven three hours to be here. His ads on Craigslist told me that he was desperate for work. He looked like a slimy used-car salesman, and he didn't intimidate me at all. I knew that out-of-area attorneys didn't do well in our local courts, and I found it almost humorous the level of desperation Seth must have felt to actually hire this guy.

Mr. Slaromon casually mentioned to me that his goal was to help us work through our issues and begin to co-parent. I replied to Mr. Slaromon that the main problem lies in the fact that the courtroom version of Seth is not the version that I am forced to interact with. He then mentioned that he has read my blog and had the balls to state that it was "tragic." Yes, it is tragic that I have to resort to a blog to process and purge this insanity. It is tragic that Seth provides me with never-ending content for my blog. What my children have had to endure is tragic. What I have been subjected to is tragic. The family court system is tragic. It's all tragic. I was seeing red.

Our regular court hearings took place in a packed courtroom first thing in the morning, but I was pleased to discover that there was only one case in front of us. I sat reviewing the papers that Seth had submitted, with my jaw hanging open and my eyes wide in disbelief.

One of the items submitted was from Lamia. She wrote a declaration on letterhead from the nonprofit organization that she works for. Lamia recounted an alleged conversation between us from 2009. According to Lamia, my exact words were, "If Seth gets any custody of the children, I will destroy him." Anyone who knows me can verify that nothing like that has ever left my mouth. This was a blatant lie from a woman who works as an advocate for children in another branch of the court system. Not only that, but my guess was that the board of her nonprofit would be less than pleased to know that she was misusing their letterhead and her position with the organization.

Seth's new attorney began by suggesting that I was a litigious litigant, which was harshly shot down by the commissioner. So much for his goal of "helping us to work through our issues." He was going straight for my jugular, and the commissioner was not having it.

When given the opportunity to present my case, I found myself in defense mode. I tried to explain that I am hardly an overprotective mother. My children enjoy sleepovers with friends, play dates, and other such activities on a regular basis. Play dates with friends do not cause my daughters to have nightmares or potty training regression. Was I the only one who could see that there was something clearly wrong with this picture?

The commissioner ordered a full parenting evaluation, which was my overall goal. He reemphasized to Seth that the girls were to have their cell phone on and charged always. The commissioner also openly questioned why Seth was so concerned with the phone's GPS tracking ability.

While I was the one who pushed so hard for the evaluation, I hated that Piper and Sarah were going to have to endure yet another evaluation. I prayed that the evaluator understood Cluster B disorders and would act as my girls' voice and advocate.

The Beginning of the Evaluation

The relief of knowing that an evaluation was in progress was replaced by frustration with the system due to clerical errors and time delays. I had become someone numb and non-reactionary due to this broken system. I left court in October chomping at the bit for this investigation to begin, but weeks of waiting turned into months of waiting, and I was feeling increasingly desperate as I watched my children suffer at the hands of this madman and his family.

As it turned out, the commissioner forgot to file the needed paperwork with Family Court Services, so it took an additional court date to move things forward. The positive news was that the commissioner specifically ordered the head of the department, Edward Powers, to conduct the evaluation, and I had heard many positive things about Mr. Powers. My therapist had also heard great things about him, so I knew that I needed to release the anxiety and lean deeper into my faith.

In February of 2013, the evaluation finally began. That week, the girls came home from a visit and mentioned that Seth showed them photos of three different women online whom he claimed to be dating: Whitney, Sharon, and Kassie. He proceeded to tell the girls that he had to decide which one he was going to marry and wanted their input based on their photographs. He said that he was going to be engaged. I was flabbergasted that he would do this until reality set in: I was divorcing a sociopath—of course he would.

Prior to the evaluation, the commissioner gave us an opportunity to list the concerns we each wanted investigated. Where oh where to begin? Seth's concerns focused on the book I was writing (this one), my blog, and his firm belief that I was alienating the children through the publicity surrounding our case. In other words, his main concerns rested on the fact that I was publicly outing him, which is the worst thing you can do to a narcissist.

"Thank you, God!" is what I said while reading the final list of items that the commissioner ordered to be investigated. In looking at the list, I believe he sat with our case files and went all the way back to the beginning in 2009.

- Determine whether father's behavior is causing the children to experience fear or anxiety.
- Determine whether mother's behavior is causing the children to experience fear or anxiety.
- Determine whether mother's blog/website is causing difficulties for the children or is likely to cause the children to experience difficulty or dysfunction.
- Determine whether father's conduct, recently or historically, during visitation has posed a risk of harm to the children.
- Determine whether the children have been physically or emotionally abused while in their father's care.
- Determine whether the children have been physically or emotionally abused while in their mother's care.
- Obtain documentation of father's use or abuse of alcohol and investigate circumstances surrounding car accident in September of 2011.
- Interview witnesses as to father's anger issues, hostility, and rationality in daily living and his use or abuse of alcohol or drugs.
- Attempt to obtain "harassing" emails sent from father to ex-girlfriends.
- Investigate whether records from couple's former marriage counselor document injury related to oldest child.
- Interview former nannies who lived with the family to obtain information related to alcohol abuse and neglect.
- Interview father's former landlord as to father's stability, mental state, and whether and to what extent father "staged their mutual home" for the 2010 parenting evaluation.
- Investigate father's 2011 DUI and determine if this event happened on his visitation weekend.
- Investigate whether children have free access to their cell phone while in their father's care and if they've always had free access.

- Investigate what the reasons are, if any, that the children should not be allowed to be in the home of the father's older brother, Robert.

- What orders would be in the best interest of the children with respect to custody and visitation?

This was the break that we needed. This was more than just a standard custody evaluation; it homed in on case specific issues. Not only did we have a thorough set of items to be investigated, but also we had an investigator who was highly regarded by the court due to his expertise and integrity. This investigator was hand selected by the commissioner because he was the one person who could get to the bottom of these issues.

Once the order was in place and the evaluation was moving forward, Seth went into his manic phase by constantly reminding me that Mr. Powers would see through me in short order. He mentioned during a custody exchange that the "clock was ticking" and that my time was almost up. I refused to let him rock my confidence and reminded myself that Seth always acts overly confident when, in fact, he's riddled with insecurity. I had seen behind his mask, and I had to keep reminding myself of that.

Seth also went into overdrive readying his staged apartment in Robert's house for the evaluation. He began showing the girls bunk beds and daybeds that they could have once overnight visits were ordered. While I was doing a fairly good job of keeping myself in a positive mindset, seeing my children anxious over the thought of resuming overnights with Seth threatened to derail me. I repeatedly let them know that I did not think this was going to happen yet I struggled because I knew the realities of this broken court system. I could not let my mind wander too far down the "what if" path, so I did a lot of mental redirecting. My confidence was rooted in the truth and faith; both things that Seth lacked.

Involving the Police

After one Sunday visit in early January 2013, Piper got into my car and burst into tears. She proceeded to spill out the events of the day in between sobs. While she was helping Seth remove ornaments from the Christmas tree, he felt like she was being too rough and grabbed her arm and squeezed hard. She got scared and ran into the bathroom to escape him. Seth chased after her, banged on the door, and yelled, which only intensified her fear. She realized that she did not have her phone with her to call for help, so she finally opened the door and came out. By this point, Sarah was also crying.

Once out of the bathroom, Seth instructed Piper to sit on the couch, which she did. She saw an opportunity to grab her phone and, with it in hand, she bounded up the stairs toward Cleo's bedroom. With Seth right behind her, she got as far as the upstairs bathroom and proceeded to lock herself inside, but she was no match for Seth at the age of 8 years old. He forced the door open and was shaking so badly that she was petrified. He told her that if she told anyone, she would never see him again. He allowed her to go to Cleo's bedroom.

Desperate for Cleo to help her, Piper disclosed to her grandmother what had transpired. Cleo looked at her tear-soaked face and said in her best Mary Poppins voice, "It sounds like we need to come up with some ways that you don't make your dad angry!" Piper knew in that moment that Cleo was as ill as Seth and lost all hope in her grandmother's intervention. Cleo and Seth took the girls into the dining room area and instructed Piper to make a list of all the fun things they did together that weekend. Piper declined to do what was asked of her, so Seth promised her one of her favorite things if she complied: a dance party. Piper finally conceded and wrote down everything that she was instructed to write. "Mom, he lied. We didn't even get to have a dance party," she told me through tears.

I looked at her wrist and could see a faint redness where she had been grabbed, so I immediately drove the girls to the police station. A very kind officer met with us, who spoke to the girls privately and went forward with a report. I was told that he would be reporting the incident to CPS in additional to submitting the report to the district attorney's office for review. While I had little faith left in the system, I knew that, at a minimum, it would be a neutral third-party documentation, which would carry more weight than my own words did.

At the following visit, the girls were terrified at the thought of going with Seth. Fearful of repercussions for telling the police about the assault, Piper said she was not going. I explained to her that I was forced to follow court orders but that I would be happy to contact the police to meet us at the exchange location and that she could use her voice to relay her concerns.

With our meeting location being a Starbucks, I contacted the local police department for a "keep the peace." I had been advised to follow the court order and take the girls to the exchange but to call the police to document their refusal to go with their father. I was so thankful to see two female officers arrive, but that gratitude was short-lived.

I stepped away from my car to speak privately to Officer Kelly Nettles, who listened to my concerns. Corporal Michele Chambers approached and ordered me to stand next to her patrol car while the two officers interviewed my daughters. I was instructed not to even look at my daughters. At a petite 5' 2", I am not a confrontational person, and I have a tremendous amount of respect for law enforcement. I was pleasant and complied with every request from Corporal Chambers, but she was visibly angry. I was trembling as she came back toward me, looking like she was prepared to throw me up against her car and cuff me. Meanwhile, Seth was pacing back and forth while videotaping me and calling me a "parental alienator." While my intentions for calling the police were honorable and just, I regretted my decision tremendously and was terrified that she was going to arrest me. It was one of the worst 30 minutes of my life.

After a while, Officer Nettles came back over and explained that she could tell he was a "Type A personality" and that some people consider hitting a parenting style. I was speechless. She then went on to say that the girls would stay with me this time but that they had agreed to go with him the next day. She assured me that she would be at our drop-off location the next day at 11 a.m. to oversee the transfer. She then instructed me to go home and "be happy" about the transfer and to be encouraging about their visit with their father. I looked right at her and said, "Do you have advice on how to be encouraging and positive if forced to send your children into an unsafe environment?" Her exact reply was, "You had children together, and he is their father."

Despite my feelings toward Seth, I *was* positive and encouraging about visits. Sometimes it took everything in me to do so, but I did it regardless. I had worked very hard in therapy to compartmentalize my own anxiety about Seth so that I didn't transfer it to my children. When my daughters ask me to protect them from someone who is dangerous, how does one act positive and encouraging? As I started my car and pulled out of the parking lot, Piper began to cry and said, "Mom, I said I would go tomorrow, but I don't want to. I am scared of him."

Sarah, at 6 years old, was very shy. By that point, she had been in therapy for four years due to the ongoing abuse and trauma from her father. On this day, she finally found her voice. While in the back of the car, she looked at Officer Nettles and shared her recent experience when her father threatened to lock her in a dark parking structure and make her sleep there overnight. Officer Nettles looked into my brave little girl's eyes and said, "Oh, he was probably kidding. My parents used to say things like that to get me to eat my vegetables." To think that my daughter was discounted and dismissed by an officer who was sworn to protect her made me ill. Officer Nettles did not show up to facilitate the exchange the following day as promised, and the girls reluctantly went on their Sunday visit.

We had court dates set in April 2013 to review the findings, and I prayed that Mr. Powers would not rush through the evaluation but, instead, ask for a continuance. The two-day trial was scheduled three days after the day that Glenn and I were to be married. My heart sank when I saw the trial dates come through from the court because not only had my entire relationship with Glenn revolved around my custody battle but, now, so would our wedding. I struggled to find balance between starting my next chapter and this critical phase of protecting my children.

An Angel in My Life

I woke up early one morning in March to an email from a physician in California by the name of Deanna. She had stayed up overnight reading my book (this one). As it turns out, it helped her to make sense of her courtship, marriage, and divorce; because of that, she felt pulled to help me in my own battle.

Deanna's email went into my spam folder, which I rarely check. I happened to check my spam folder that morning, ironically. She wanted to know what she could do to help me. I was accustomed to people contacting me and asking for help. No one had ever offered to help *me*. I didn't even know how to respond, but the honest answer was that I didn't know how anyone could help me at this point. In addition, I had a difficult time admitting that I needed help or accepting help. This is a lifelong struggle for me.

Deanna didn't let me off the hook that easily. She pressed to know if I was still representing myself or if I had been able to afford an attorney. The truth was that I was still representing myself, but I felt so beaten down by that point that I had no idea how I would pull myself together for the trial in April 2013. I was overwhelmed with my case, my health, my job, and being a full-time single mom. Up until that point, I had managed to get through hearings but trials required complex preparation and legal knowledge, not to mention that this was a pivotal juncture that I could not afford to mess up.

Before I knew it, Deanna had sprung into action in an effort to locate an attorney who would take my case. She reached out to a friend of hers who was a district attorney in a neighboring county and received a recommendation for an attorney who would help me. Not only did she find an attorney, but also she paid for the attorney to represent me at the upcoming trial. While I had represented myself for over four years, I felt like everything was riding on this evaluation and the pending trial, which was accompanied by a level of anxiety that I had never experienced before.

There are two things that had become solid over the course of my custody battle: my backbone and my faith. Where I once lacked boundaries and the ability to stand up for myself, I grew stronger each year and surprised myself with the inner strength that I grew to possess. I credit God for the angel in my life, Deanna; the custody evaluator; and the fact that I finally had an attorney when I needed one the most. I struggled to find the words to properly thank Deanna. To be able to turn the technical aspects of this burden over to God and to a capable attorney was the light that I needed to continue putting one foot in front of the other.

My Wedding

When it came to my upcoming wedding, Glenn did what only Glenn would do: he took over the wedding planning. I chose the wedding colors, and he coordinated everything else from the catering to the candy bar. I found a dress and voiced my opinions on things as needed, but the rest was all on Glenn to orchestrate.

When asked to provide the date of our wedding to Seth, I gave him the wrong date. Our wedding was April 6, 2013, but I told him that it was April 7th. My worst fear was that my wedding would end in bloodshed and that we would be reduced to a feature news story detailing all the signs that had been present along the way. I knew how obsessed Seth was with my relationship with Glenn, and it was my goal to keep all the details, including the location, private; yet I knew he was pumping the girls for details at every opportunity.

What I discovered after the fact was that Glenn also shared the same concerns and, while he was fulfilling my wishes for goldfish to adorn the table tops of the reception, he was also devising a safety plan for the day. In Glenn's plan, the majority of the groomsmen as well as my father were to be armed with guns and lots of ammunition in an effort to protect the wedding party as well as the wedding attendees. This obviously took the term "wedding planning" to a whole new level.

The Evaluation

By the time the evaluation was underway, I had become a master at documentation. With that said, I knew there was a fine line between being organized and being accused of executing a vendetta against my ex-husband. My documentation system involved a binder for each year of my battle, trial binders, and an online documentation system. I also kept a binder that I referred to as the "nutshell version," which allowed me to stay focused and present an elevator-pitch version of my story at the drop of a hat to anyone who would listen. My goal was to present my case concisely and truthfully without overwhelming the evaluator.

Prior to my first meeting with the custody evaluator in spring 2013, I prepared a new 1.5" binder based on the items that the court ordered Mr. Powers to investigate. I knew that when my nerves are in overdrive, I have a tendency to ramble and get off track, so I wanted to avoid that at all costs. I had tabs for each item that he was investigating with my corresponding evidence and documentation. "Think forensically without self-diagnosing him," were the wise words that a dear friend shared with me.

I arrived to the appointment 20 minutes early and did three things before I left my car. I took the following steps: I said a prayer for the truth to prevail, I took deep breaths, and I made sure that I was emotionally centered. I walked into that first meeting repeating the quote, "Speak the truth, even if your voice shakes." Honesty is not just the best policy when it comes to speaking to the evaluator; it is the *only* policy. One false statement, no matter how small it may seem, ensures that you lose all credibility in short order. I allowed that mentality to be my foundation.

One of the allegations that Seth made had to do with my dysfunctional, abuse-filled upbringing. I let the evaluator know that I was an open book and that I would be completely transparent. While I would not deny that my childhood would make any psychologist cringe, my childhood made me who I am today. I recognized the dysfunction from an early age, and I had worked hard over the years to better myself. I made it my life mission to break every cycle that was familiar to me. Those words were my truth.

Our first meeting lasted just over two hours, and we covered a great deal of information and background. From there, I had an additional meeting scheduled with Mr. Powers. Home visits were scheduled for my house and Seth's staged home, and Mr. Powers planned to meet with Piper and Sarah alone. It felt overwhelming, but I had committed to remaining hopeful.

The fact that Seth didn't even live in the county yet his family came together to assist him in creating a fake residence was infuriating to me. I provided Mr. Powers with my documentation about Seth staging a home for the first evaluation in 2010 including his hand-written change of address notification, which was dated just 10 days after the completion of the 2010 evaluation. This topic seemed to pique his interest. I shared my concerns and facts related to the current residence and my fears about Robert, Leonard, and Cleo. Mr. Powers typed feverishly as I spoke and seemed to capture my every word on his computer.

One of the topics that Mr. Powers had been tasked with investigating had to do with accusations that I was alienating my daughters with my books and blogs. Mr. Powers' concerns seemed to diminish as I explained the great lengths that I had gone to in an effort to protect my daughters. The girls knew that I had written a book but didn't even know the title. I was able to show how proactive I had been in keeping them from my advocacy, my blog, and my books. In fact, I had gone so far as to install parental controls on our home computers, which blocked my writings and books from even showing up on search engines.

When it came time for my home visit in late April 2013, I stood firm in my truth; I didn't need to prepare, as I had always been transparent about whom I was as a parent. Mr. Powers came into our home late one afternoon, did a walk-through noting general details along the way, and then sat at our kitchen table and conversed with Glenn and I as the girls went about their business playing in the backyard and zipping around on scooters. Conversation flowed normally and wasn't forced. He spent some time talking to the girls about their daily routine, likes and dislikes, and school. I felt that his visit went smoothly.

During Seth's parenting time on the following Saturday, the girls came home and said that Mr. Powers had visited them at the home Seth shared with Leonard, Cleo, and Robert's family. They seemed perplexed by Seth's odd behavior. According to the girls, he had purchased wooden birdhouses for them to paint, but he wouldn't allow them to start the craft until Mr. Powers was pulling into the driveway. He had also bribed them for their good behavior and cooperation with gum and candy. "Isn't it strange that Dad bought us crafts?" Piper asked. The thought of Seth doing crafts with the girls was laughable at best. Things like this left me feeling desperate yet hopeful that the evaluator would see through Seth's façade.

During the months before our final trial date, I began to pray like I had never prayed before. I prayed in the car, in the shower, in bed, and even got down on my knees. I visualized the outcome that I wanted, and then I prayed more. I took things a step further and wrote out the outcome that I wanted. That piece of paper kept me focused and centered when doubt crept in.

I knew in my heart that the only thing that would keep my daughters safe was professionally supervised visits. Everyone had told me that it was a long shot, but I refused to allow others' words to enter my mind. Supervised visits were the only acceptable answer in this case. I reflected back on the beginning of my case, when I truly believed that Seth was capable of co-parenting and putting the girls first. How far we had fallen from my naïve pipe dreams. It was hard to grasp the direction that things had gone. The mask that Seth wore for so many years covered a level of evil that I didn't know existed.

Weeks turned into months, and my frustrations with the system were mounting. Originally expected to be completed by early April, the evaluation pushed past April, past May, past June, and into July. Every time I put the girls into Seth's car, I feared that I would never see them again. I memorized their words, their faces, and what they were wearing, and I allowed their hugs to make an impression on my soul in case my worst fears crossed into reality. The girls were reporting that Seth was acting odd—talking to himself, snapping at them more than normal, and pacing back and forth. Once again, I began hiring a private investigator to follow Seth during visits so that I had peace of mind that my daughters were safe.

Self-Sabotaging the Evaluation

The new trial date had been set for July 10, 2013, and as I was anxiously awaiting the results of the evaluation when something happened that would change the outcome of our case in a way that I never anticipated. As the girls climbed into my car after a visit with Seth, my oldest daughter said something that I will never forget: "Mom, Dad was drinking alcohol today. He was drinking beer at lunch. He lied and said it was soda, but I heard the waitress say, 'Here is your beer.'"

A quick check of the girls' phone GPS confirmed that they had been at a local Irish pub. Seth had taken the girls into a bar for lunch, and his parents were also present and drinking. These were either the stupidest people on the planet or the most arrogant. To make matters worse, after drinking several beers, he put the girls in the car and drove them to our exchange location.

I was in disbelief over what I was hearing. Alcohol had played such a large role in our marriage and throughout our custody battle. The court order was incredibly clear: Seth was not allowed to drink alcohol for six hours preceding the visits, and there was to be absolutely no alcohol around the girls during his visits.

Leonard had recently submitted a declaration stating that he was aware of the alcohol clause and that he monitored Seth for compliance. Apparently, in a narcissistic family, monitoring for alcohol compliance means defying court orders and drinking together. Leonard's exact words just months before were as follows:

> "I thank the court for restricting Seth's alcohol consumption completely for six hours prior to arrival and abstention during the visits. I can attest to his honoring that restriction and know that I check on that carefully."

The fact that Seth took the girls into a bar and drank alcohol with his parents while our custody evaluation was underway blew my mind and showed me that, once again, they were above court orders. I had made comments along the way that nothing Seth did could shock me anymore, but I was wrong. The realization that this man had a genius IQ further boggled my mind. I couldn't believe that he had just handed over the final piece that I needed to protect my daughters.

I knew the clock was ticking, so I immediately emailed the custody evaluator and scheduled an appointment for him to interview my daughters. I downloaded the GPS record of my daughter's phone, which substantiated her claims that they were in a bar. I then called the private investigator who had been following Seth on and off for weeks and hired him to go to the bar and talk to the manager about obtaining surveillance video of Seth drinking, along with the receipt for Seth's purchases.

If there's one thing I've learned in this battle, it is to have concrete, black-and-white evidence. The narcissist prefers gray matter because it gives them wiggle room to lie and manipulate, but it doesn't fly in court. I was *not* going to risk the court saying that my daughters' account of the incident was hearsay. I wanted the commissioner to watch Seth drinking beer in a bar with my daughters. I wanted the commissioner to see Seth's parents drinking at the bar—the same parents who promised that they would ensure that Seth obeyed court orders at all times. Seth's father had recently written a declaration claiming to be aware of the alcohol clause and vowing to ensure

Seth's compliance. I wanted the commissioner to watch them all blatantly defying court orders. I wanted the commissioner to see Seth's narcissism firsthand.

The private investigator, another angel in my life, was able to make contact with the general manager (GM) of the Irish Pub where Seth had been drinking. The GM knew Seth well and immediately expressed his dislike for him. John, the private investigator, was able to view the surveillance video and verify that Seth was shown drinking. However, we needed to secure approval from the owner of the pub before we could take the video with us. Once again, I sprung into action and called everyone that I knew to try to connect with the restaurant owner. In the meantime, my new attorney was preparing a subpoena to attempt to obtain the video in time for court, which was just two days away.

The fact that my entire head of hair didn't go gray this particular week still amazes me. I was operating in fight-or-flight mode and would have probably benefited from a Xanax or five. While I was officially in overdrive, I was still waiting to hear if the custody evaluation would even be done in time for court.

On Tuesday, July 9, 2013, just 24 hours before court, my attorney called. I immediately pulled my car over to the side of the road and took the call that would change everything. I listened intently as she read me the most important pieces of the report. I was in shock. The investigator got it. He saw through Seth. There were 43 pages in the report, which completely validated every sleepless night, every claim of abuse that was inflicted on my daughters, and every concern that I had ever expressed.

I hung up the phone and began to sob. I called every one of my friends and family members until my phone battery was completely drained. I would have climbed up on the nearest rooftop and started shouting had I been able to find a ladder. The investigator was strongly recommending permanent, professionally supervised visits along with a myriad of other stipulations, which I knew that Seth would never agree to. I also knew that the commissioner finally had everything that he needed to protect my children. The report could not have been any better had I personally dictated all 43 pages.

Court: July 10, 2013

Glenn and I arrived in court on the morning of July 10, 2013, and we immediately saw Seth, his attorney, and his parents. We had fully prepared ourselves for Seth's attorney to ask for a continuance claiming that he hadn't had ample time to review the custody evaluation. In other words, he needed to buy a full set of shovels to try to dig Seth out of this one. Each party was legally entitled to have the report in hand a full ten days before trial, so my attorney was fully prepared to ask for supervised visits pending the final trial dates. The thought of another delay was devastating because I couldn't imagine waiting any longer, given the report that I held in my hands.

I noticed that there was another person pacing in the courtroom and, based on his demeanor, I could tell that he was not there willingly. The gentleman was the GM of the Irish Pub and in his hand was the surveillance video that my attorney had successfully subpoenaed. The attorneys all agreed to meet privately in chambers. From that moment on, the next hour felt like a complete whirlwind.

After about 30 minutes, the attorneys and the commissioner reentered the courtroom. I quickly noticed that Seth and his father were not present. My attorney relayed that when Seth's attorney, Mr. Slaromon, asked for a continuance, the commissioner snapped back that while he was entitled to a continuance, nothing he could say in trial would sway him from the orders he was about to hand down. With that, Mr. Slaromon stepped outside to talk to Seth and returned to explain that they were prepared to accept the entire laundry list of recommendations; the most significant was permanent, professionally supervised visits.

Seth's attorney was waiving the white flag and, at that point, I was told that Seth had retreated to the steps outside the courthouse and resembled the Tasmanian Devil. According to witnesses, he was huffing, puffing, and yelling that he was going to start videotaping my every move. While that would prove to be a fairly uneventful documentary entitled, "A day in the life of a working mom," I wished him well with his endeavor.

While they had relented to supervised visits, Seth's attorney was requesting that Cleo be allowed to supervise. No. No. No. I quickly told my attorney that I was adamantly opposed to this. Seth's mom had been in the bar and was drinking with him! She knew they were in violation of the court order, and she participated in violating the order. I couldn't believe they had the gall to even ask this of me or the court.

When the commissioner spoke, he firmly stated that Seth's mother and father had been a part of this case from the beginning, and they were fully aware of the court orders. He stated that he would absolutely NOT approve Seth's mother to monitor the visits. He was scanning the recommendations from the evaluator and began to make each one part of the order. As he got to the second recommendation, he said, "Strike that. I am not going to order any of these because we all know Seth isn't going to follow them anyway." He then said words that I will never forget: "The following orders are *final* custody orders. Professionally supervised visits—first, third, and fifth weekends per month."

The commissioner went on to dictate his orders and stated, *"Evidence has been presented in support of a request that the contact of 'Seth' be supervised based upon allegations of physical abuse, alcohol abuse, use of threats, and tendency to be dishonest. The court intends for this to be a final custody order."*

It took everything in me not to scream. It was over. My battle was over! My daughters were safe! I left the courtroom in a complete daze. I didn't cry. I was elated, but I didn't cry. I had always expected that a moment like this would bring a flood of tears so vast that a dam would need to be constructed in the town square. Days later, I was still in a fog. The only way I could explain it to people was that there was a "block"—I felt that my emotions were blocked and nothing was sinking in. I couldn't seem to grasp the concept that my children were finally safe and that we would have peace. I didn't even know what peace felt like anymore.

After the final judgment, I spent several days in a state of shock. It was the exact verdict that I had hoped and prayed for, but I wasn't prepared. I had prepared myself that court would be delayed for another month. Everything happened so fast, and I wasn't even a part of it. The attorneys handled everything, and I felt like I was caught in a tornado of commotion—spinning so fast, and then, it was over. We had just been granted an order of *peace*.

Part 4: No Calm After the Storm

Seth's excuse for drinking alcohol with the girls, according to the evaluator, was that *it was all a test*. He claimed that he was setting us up. He said he was testing the girls to see if they would report the information back to me. Ironically, his mother had already admitted to the evaluator that they were drinking because had she not, Seth's answer would have been different. His answer would have probably been complete and utter denial. It would have been a doctored video, a doctored receipt, and the girls would have been labeled as liars.

The new court order specified that the girls could see Seth for two hours on Saturday and two hours on Sunday for the first, third, and fifth weekend of each month. There were two different options listed for professional supervisors so, within days, I made contact with both agencies and was told that Seth needed to initiate visits and, once that happened, they would contact me.

I explained our new reality to the girls, who were both relieved. The new order did not mention phone calls, so I was prepared to allow them but keep firm boundaries as I always had. After the final custody order, Seth continued to call on a weekly basis. His phone calls ranged between manic and bizarre to slurring and intoxicated. Thankfully, there was a previous court order in place, which allowed me to record calls. As time progressed, the girls began turning his calls down with increased frequency.

After three months of not seeing Seth, the girls' therapist recommended that I reach out to him to ask his intentions for the visits. If he was not planning to exercise visits, it was her goal to discuss this with the girls. Leaving them hanging was not healthy. I emailed Seth as instructed and received a bizarre but expected rant.

From that point on, every three months, I made it a point to reach out to Seth to inquire about his intentions. His replies ranged from completely ignoring me to drunken diatribes about how his mentality needed to be that of a soldier who was away at war and unable to see his family. I continued to share his replies with Piper and Sarah's therapist and, after a while, therapy ended because the girls were thriving in their new lives.

In the spring of 2014, Piper and Sarah had mentioned to Seth that we got a new puppy: a black, female Standard Poodle named Pixie. Weeks later, Seth called one night and sounded manic and intoxicated. "GUESS WHAT I AM

DOING RIGHT NOW, GIRLS?!" Seth asked. The girls looked at me, confused by his tone. "What?" they asked.

"Daddy is getting a new puppy tonight! It's a black Standard Poodle puppy, and it's a girl!!!"

The girls were both speechless, looking to me for assistance. They went on to tell him for a second time about their new puppy. He pretended to be hearing this for the first time, "What? Are you kidding me? YOU have a black Standard Poodle puppy?" he asked. "Yes," they replied.

I instantly panicked. This man was absolutely insane. From that point on, it made me nervous to let our new puppy outside unattended as I had no idea what his intentions were and, while I had become accustomed to his bizarre antics, this one seemed psychotic on a variety of levels. Around that time, the girls began to refuse all calls from Seth.

One afternoon in June 2014, I was alerted to a Facebook message on the One Mom's Battle page from a woman named Sharon. She had previously dated Seth and was reaching out for assistance. This was the fifth woman who had reached out to me for help since the demise of my marriage. According to all five women, Seth told them that I was a sociopath who was so obsessed with him that I ran a blog about him. Had I not heard the same story from all five women, I would have doubted that Seth would really continue to tell people about my blog as their declarations continued to show up in my court filings.

Sharon's message said:

> Tina - I know your ex-husband. I went on a date with him and it ended in a police report after he tried to attack me while really drunk in a hotel. The hotel called police and they threatened to arrest him if he stepped foot back inside the hotel. He stole all my money so I could not travel home. I left him in Florida. He is mentally unstable. He stole my debit card as well as a $500 camera because he was looking for blackmail. He has stalked me and everyone I know. I was scared for my life. I've moved and changed my phone number. How did you deal with him? The police report was in Jacksonville, Florida in February of 2013 after I competed in a marathon. I thought he had moved on but I just found out he has contacted every single friend I know this year. I live in fear of him. He snapped with a rage in his eyes I have only seen in animals. I've wanted to reach out to

you but he bugged my computer after he broke into it. I think he still logs into my Facebook so please delete this after you read it. You are my hero. Two dates and he turned my life upside down. He is blackmailing me with pictures and a conversation an ex-boyfriend sent me. He tried to turn my own family against me. Please help! – Sharon

I immediately contacted Sharon for additional details. The hotel room incident that she referenced took place during our child custody evaluation, when one would think that Seth would be on his best behavior. She provided additional details that would help my case, and I quickly reached out to the police in Jacksonville, Florida to obtain the report that she alluded to.

Within moments of speaking to a police dispatcher, I was holding the police report in my hands. According to the report, Seth accessed Sharon's laptop and phone while she was running a marathon, and then proceeded to get intoxicated in the hotel lobby. He went so far as to change the passwords on her electronic devices. When he returned to the room, he then attempted to grab her cell phone out of her hands, and a struggle ensued. He forcibly grabbed her by her wrist, and she began screaming for assistance. Sharon's screaming resulted in two neighboring hotel guests calling both 911 and hotel security. Seth was advised by hotel security that he needed to leave the property, which he did prior to police arriving.

Thankfully, there were no current court proceedings between Seth and I and, by that point, it had been eleven months since we had seen Seth. The girls had not even spoken to him by phone since April 2013, three months prior. While I wasn't naïve enough to think we had seen the last of Seth, it had been a nice break for the girls. I filed Sharon's message and the police report away in my documentation for whenever Seth reemerged from the underbelly of narcissistic society.

My 40th birthday party was planned for September 24, 2014, and I had friends and family coming from out of town. Two weeks prior, I received a call from a professional supervisor named Sasha whom Seth had contacted. Seth had requested the first visit in over a year was to begin on September 24, 2014: the day of my birthday and my party.

I told the supervisor that while I was happy to get the ball rolling, Seth had been absent for 15 months; to arrive and demand to begin visits on my birthday was highly suspect. She reminded me that there was a court order. I reminded her that he had been absent for over a year and had caused significant trauma to my daughters, which was why there was an order for professionally supervised visits in the first place. I knew this dance, as I had done it so many times before with family court professionals. The dance involved maintaining boundaries without bruising the ego of an individual who held a great deal of power over my case. It was a frightening dance to participate in.

I scheduled an appointment with the girls' new therapist, Megan, because I wanted her guidance in breaking the news to the girls. Every time I attempted to tell them that he was back, I lost my nerve. When I looked into their eyes, I saw two little girls who were thriving and at peace. I did not have the heart to rob them of those things. Seth stealing my joy failed in comparison; I was an adult who made a conscious decision to allow him into my life. These little girls didn't ask for a sociopath to be their father, and I vowed to do everything in my power to continue fighting for them.

We arrived at Megan's office, and I couldn't even stay focused. It was the worst feeling in the world to walk my daughters in knowing the news that was about to be delivered. I felt nauseous. Ten minutes later, we found ourselves sitting on the all-too-familiar couch, delivering the news. At the mention of Seth reentering our lives, 7-year-old Sarah lost her bladder and had her first "accident" in a year and a half, right there in Megan's office. While it is one thing to read about children urinating in their pants as a result of early childhood trauma, it is another thing to actually watch it happen to your child. My heart shattered as we ended our session early and retreated to our car. The girls were sullen and barely spoke on our drive home.

When I first sensed pushback from the supervisor, I set up an appointment with minor's counsel to discuss the current issue: Seth's return. Our attorney, Mr. Anders, sat back in his chair, listened to what I had to say and agreed that visits should begin slowly. I proposed one hour versus the current court order that allowed for two hours for each visit, and Mr. Anders agreed. I wanted to propose zero visits, but I also knew the reality of the system and knew to tread lightly.

The first visit was scheduled for October 4, 2014, and we met with the supervisor, Sasha, the week prior to allow her to become acquainted with the girls. In the days leading up to the appointment, Piper was showing signs of increased anxiety and missed school due to stomach pains, which was unlike her. This was the little girl who begged to go to school with a fever. By the time we met with Sasha, I watched Piper curl up on her couch writhing with stomach pain. Sarah clung to me for several days after our meeting with Sasha and refused to leave my side.

I watched as a year and a half of healing and progress was vanishing right before my eyes. On the day of Seth's first visit, Piper told me that she wished he'd disappear forever. I wanted so badly to tell her that I also wished he'd disappear forever but, instead, I gave her a long hug. I hated what he was doing to us.

We arrived at Sasha's office and parked curbside as instructed. Sasha came out to get the girls, while Seth waited in her office. Glenn and I returned after an hour and heard Piper and Sarah's portrayal of the visit. According to the girls, Seth brought photographs of them and photographs of his family members. He pulled out his laptop and began to quiz the girls about who their teachers were, who their friends were, and so on. Sasha redirected him, and he relented and put his computer away. He then proceeded to let them know that his disappearance for 15 months was not his fault, and she told him that this was inappropriate and, again, redirected him. I have babysat toddlers that didn't need redirected this many times in 60 minutes.

The girls were distraught for days after the visit. Piper complained of stomach pain, Sarah was regressing in a variety of areas, and against the girls' therapist's recommendation, Sasha was proposing that we combine Saturday's hour and Sunday's hour into one day *and* add an extra hour to make a three-hour visit. I was in shock and desperate for someone to intervene. On multiple occasions, I tried to explain to Sasha that I had worked very hard to establish boundaries with someone who had no regard for boundaries. One of my major boundaries was the court order and, by her taking it upon herself to change it, she left me in a very uncomfortable position.

With little faith in minor's counsel to help me, I filed a request for order with the court to ask that visits be decreased to only one hour per weekend on the first, third, and fifth weekends of the month with a step-up plan put in place after six months. If Seth could consistently follow this schedule, then we could consider an increase to two-hour visits after six months. I doubted that Seth would comply but, with a supervisor in place, it would give me third-party documentation for court.

I knew that I was rolling the dice and that I risked making the commissioner angry. The current order was a final custody order and, considering the fact that parents with heroin needles hanging out of their arms have more access to their children than Seth does, I knew that going back in front of the court was a significant risk. Once again, I needed to lay my head on a pillow knowing that I had done everything in my power to protect my children. I had to protect my daughters.

My gears were set to "stress overload" and weeks later, I found myself sitting in my neurologist's office to review my annual MRI and blood work. My neurologist casually mentioned that he felt my diagnosis of multiple sclerosis wasn't accurate and in fact, my autoimmune disease had always puzzled him. He suspected that I had a rare disease called, Neuromyelitis Optica.

My head began to spin and panic set in because this was not the first time a neurologist had mentioned their suspicions of this debilitating, and sometimes fatal, autoimmune disease. I had researched it heavily over the years and it terrified me. Thankfully, the I.V. treatment I had been on since 2004 was a recommended treatment. I made the mental decision to let go of the diagnosis that my doctor was busily typing into his computer. There were four days per month that I was forced to focus on my disease due to the I.V. treatment and aftermath but there were approximately twenty-six days that I could focus on my love for life, my family and protecting my children. I refused to accept this label and made the decision to lean into my faith and turn the diagnosis over to God.

Back in Court

I arrived at the courthouse on October 28, 2014, just over one month since being hit by Hurricane Seth's reappearance into our lives. I saw Seth's attorney and Mr. Anders standing in the court hallway. I hated the fact that the three of us were forced to breathe the same air. They both repulsed me, each for different reasons—Mr. Slaromon because he represented the man who harmed my children and did so for the almighty dollar, and Mr. Anders because he was a poor excuse for minor's counsel and had been hit-and-miss in his half-hearted advocacy for my children. Glenn and I entered the courtroom behind them.

> IN THE SUPERIOR COURT OF THE STATE OF CALIFORNIA COUNTY OF SAN LUIS OBISPO BEFORE THE HONORABLE JOHN J. OLSON, COMMISSIONER
>
> SETH COLLINS, PETITIONER, VS. TINA SWITHIN, RESPONDENT

SAN LUIS OBISPO, CALIFORNIA TUESDAY, OCTOBER 28, 2014 8:56 A.M. * * *

The Court: Let me call case FL-09-0333, Seth Collins and Tina Swithin. We are here on Mr. Collins' – I'm sorry, I guess we are here on Ms. Swithin's requests for orders.

Mr. Anders: Yes.

Mr. Slaromon: Vinnie Slaramon on behalf of Seth Collins, who is not present.

The Court: Ms. Swithin in present. Mr. Anders is present on behalf of the children. Mr. Collins doesn't visit for a year and a half, and now he's demanding visits. Is that the scenario?

Mr. Slaromon: I don't think that's exactly how it happened, your honor. What I think happened is that he started his visits after a long absence, and it was a suggestion of Ms. Sasha Smith to increase the time to two hours – and then I read the response and the other responses, and I am guessing they are suggesting that he have an hour fixed, supervised, and that you could increase up to two hours based on the children and how they are doing in the sessions.

The Court: Where does he live?

Mr. Slaromon: San Diego

The Court: Mr. Anders, what's your position?

Mr. Anders: Well, I got some new information today. I filed a responsive declaration, and it is my understanding Mr. Collins has not visited in 16-months. He had some limited telephone calls, and his relationship with the children, I think there is what would be characterized by a growing rift based upon his non-contact, and I believe he's had two visits…

Ms. Swithin: One.

Mr. Anders: One visit supervised by Sasha Smith. In my responsive declaration when I made a proposal to the court about cautious reimplementation of visits, I recommended that based upon my discussions with Megan Golden, who is the children's therapist, Mr. Collins may contact her and meet with her in order for him to gain some insight into making progress with his relationship. He never contacted the children's therapist. I spoke to the therapist, and she indicated to me that she's been seeing them once a week for almost a year.

The Court: Can you remind me – how old are the girls?

Mr. Anders: Piper is none and Sarah is seven. Mr. Golden had a 45-minute meeting with each child, and she said that Sarah used the bathroom beforehand, but when they started talking about the visits, she became anxious and distressed and tried to make it to the bathroom, but she ended up wetting her pants on the way to the bathroom, and Sarah exhibited some anxious and fearful behavior at the time that she was departing the bathroom. This was all centered around the conversations they were having about how they were going to see their dad, how they felt about it, how the telephone calls were going. I asked her what she recommended – and, based upon last night, she thinks that before any efforts are made to resume the visits between the girls, Mr. Collins needs to meet with her, and there needs to be…

The Court: Meet with her to do what?

Mr. Anders: So he understands the needs of the children.

The Court: He hasn't understood the needs of the children in four years.

Mr. Anders: I agree with that. I think that's true. The fact is he disappears for 16-months, and now his reappearing is causing stress in the children's lives the way – I guess the way in which he's re-entering their lives. She said he should be limited to calls and sending them letters, and she's not comfortable transitioning into visits, even supervised, until the children have a resumption of their relationship with their father. If you read the reply declaration of Ms. Swithin and look at the emails and texts that are back and forth, I think Ms. Swithin has made a pretty substantial and significant effort to connect with him to try and persuade him to see the kids, and, on many occasions, he doesn't respond in an appropriate fashion and continues to blame her and mischaracterizes the circumstances and doesn't take any responsibility.

The Court: I guess that's why I'm sort of wondering why we are going to force the kids into relationship with a guy who has demonstrated repeatedly He's not capable of putting the kids' interests ahead of his own. Everything is on his timetable. He's flat-out lied to the court about various facts. We all remember the history here. He appears to be a sociopath. Why are we forcing them? Children who wet their pants at the mere discussion of the possibility of seeing Mr. Collins, why are we forcing them to do that? It is pretty drastic to say maybe the kids never see this guy again, but, you know, he's the person who chose to be gone for the last 16 months. Maybe I should ask Mr. Slaromon.

Mr. Slaromon: I just think in every family law situation, there are fathers and mothers that have problems much worse than what Mr. Collins does, and his have been characterized as just a lot of, as the court pointed out, actions that were unacceptable. That's why He's in the position He's in.

The Court: Not really. He's in the position he's in because he did a lot of things that ended up with him being limited to supervise visits. But he's the person who's chosen not to see his kids for 16 months.

Mr. Slaromon: That's why he asked me to come and why we filed the response because he just wanted some opportunity to be able to reunify with them under some structure. And, I think terminating his parental visitation isn't appropriate if we can come up with a way we can gradually get back into the kids' lives. That's our goal.

The Court: How do you propose doing that?

Mr. Slaromon: Well, I thought that starting with supervised visitation and seeing how it goes would be a good first step, intertwined with the therapeutic approach that Mr. Anders was saying. I think Mr. Collins does need to engage slowly and show good conduct over a period of time and maybe set a review hearing and then have, you know, one visit every week for an hour, and let's see how he does. And I understand that the kids—according to Ms. Smith, She said that the kids said that they want to see Him and that She thinks it would be good for them, so maybe we should have her come in and talk about, you know…

The Court: What's their own therapist's opinion about the kids seeing him? The kids see their own therapist, and Ms. Smith is the supervision therapist.

Ms. Slaromon: Yes, she's the supervision therapist.

Mr. Anders: She's only met with them for one hour, and that's in 16 months.

The Court: What do you think ought to happen, Ms. Swithin?

Ms. Swithin: The past 15 months have been the most peaceful for my children. They have returned to having a childhood with zero stress. They are thriving 100% in every aspect of their lives. Mr. Collins' phone calls to them involve instructing me that I need to talk to them about child support and how he has put a roof over their head—the calls are inappropriate. In some of his phone calls to them, he's clearly intoxicated, calling from bars, and the girls have refused to talk to him since April because of how bizarre his phone calls are. They are in control of their phone at all times. In the one single hour that he has come back into their lives, he has turned our world upside down. My oldest daughter, who has a near-perfect attendance record through fourth grade, has missed school due to anxiety surrounding the visits. My youngest daughter has now started wetting her pants again at 7 1/2 years old, after not having a single accident for 15 months. During his one-hour visit, he brought in a laptop computer and grilled them on questions that were inappropriate. He told them that the lack of visits was not his fault. Ms. Smith had to stop him and tell him that the topic was inappropriate. This may be hearsay, but Mr. Anders can probably verify this. This has been traumatizing for them. Just one hour and my daughter's nightmares have restarted. We are back where we were 15 months ago, and I don't think his presence in their life is helping them at all--or is in their best interest. Now there is also the issue of the recent police report which I included in my declaration. Mr. Collins attacked his fifth victim, and that incident occurred during the time of our 3111 evaluation when Mr. Collins would seem to be on his best behavior. I agree with you that his tendencies lean towards that of a sociopath. He terrifies me and he terrifies the children. I would ask that the court completely remove his visits. I don't think visits are in their best interest.

The Court: Mr. Anders, anything else?

Mr. Anders: Just—no. I think talk is cheap, but I think his conduct speaks louder than words. Mr. Collins' conduct demonstrates that it is all about him, and he doesn't appreciate the needs of the children, and for him to, I guess, reenter the children's lives in the manner in which he has, causes more disruption. Certainly, I encourage and advocate that children need both parents but, that being said, I think that both parents have to have an appropriate role in the children's lives, and stepping out for 16-months and then reappearing … and I do corroborate that I spoke to Sasha Smith…he started the visit by attempting to say that none of this was his fault, why he hasn't been visiting. I think this misleads the children and causes the children more distress than focusing on having a relationship with the children. What I told the court is what Ms. Golden recommends, and whatever the parenting plan or proposal the court proposes or orders, I think it ought to be very slow, and I think it ought to be aimed at protecting the children from Mr. Collins' unstable behavior. I guess I'm concerned. Also, I tried to call Mr. Collins' ex-girlfriend; her phone number is in the police report. I tried to identify myself, and I called her a couple times and tried to get a call back so I could corroborate what's written in the police report. I find alarming what is in that police report. There's been similar behavior with other women that's been reported throughout this case over about five years, and it is just odd that this has happened on multiple occasions with Mr. Collins, and I think he has some sort of problem.

The Court: I don't think it's odd. I think you could go wander around to any criminal department in this building and see similar kinds of patterns of behavior.

Mr. Anders: The other issue is he's written to the mother and really minimized his use of alcohol—he never abused alcohol. Everything that he says, he minimizes it and says that he never uses alcohol in any different pattern than any professional or parent. I just don't think the record supports that. I think with his criminal cases against him and his alcohol-related offenses, it's just all around a bad circumstance.

The Court: Okay. So, I'm going to give Mr. Slaromon the last word but, before I get to him, the dilemma for the court is, on the one hand, there's a policy that kids need both parents. On the other hand, there are certain parents who don't belong around their children. Where is he?

Mr. Anders: Well, I think the court's got to balance competing interests.

The Court: Actually, rather than phrasing it as "where is he," the question should be, where do these kids belong?

Mr. Anders: I think the court's got to balance the kids' stability against any further instability or harm that there is by the circumstance of continuing what's currently going on. I mean, has he inflicted physical force on the children? Not recently.

The Court: But that's not the be-all and end-all.

Mr. Anders: I understand that. These children are experiencing emotional distress as a result of what is going on in the last two or three months, and I think the court ought to restrict his contact with the children until he is able to demonstrate…

The Court: I guess that's my question because, to date, he has checked out. He has really put his kids in a horrible position. I think, probably, Mr. Slaromon might even agree with that. The question really is, well—and based on all of that, I'm not convinced he should be seeing his kids even one hour supervised at this point. What does he have to do to demonstrate that he's not a danger now to his kids? And now it is going to be very difficult for him because I've concluded that he's a liar. I don't believe what he says. It has gone on for years. He's got this issue with his various girlfriends, all of whom seem to end up in some sort of police contact. He has fabricated claims about getting beat up in San Francisco when, actually, he put his car into a light pole on the Embarcadero. What could he do to convince you or convince me he is not just a sociopath and shouldn't be around his kids? Is there anything he could do?

Mr. Anders: Not much. The only suggestion that I know of is to start off with a series of letters and have the opportunity to have contact with them that way, but my thinking is if the court makes an order like that, he won't follow it and check out. It is a very, very tough issue. I think he's received plenty of opportunities from this court, probably six or seven opportunities to have a normal relationship with his children, and he's rejected them or acted in a fashion that is inconsistent with appropriate parenting decisions.

Ms. Swithin: In regard to the letters, I want the court to know that I would only feel comfortable with those going through the children's therapist because his phone calls are completely inappropriate. My husband can attest to that. He's in the courtroom now. He has heard them on speakerphone. I don't trust anything that he would put in writing wouldn't further damage the girls.

The Court: Mr. Slaromon?

Mr. Slaromon: I'm hearing a lot of the things we have heard over and over again throughout the course of the case, and the conflict is resultant. Mr. Collins seems to do the obvious things wrong, but I think a lot of the early conflict comes from the relationship between Ms. Swithin and Mr. Collins. I have heard lots of complaints about her using her divorce as fodder for her profession and a book. Now, she's written a second book. She's very into publicizing this.

The Court: I haven't read her book. I know she has one. I know she has a book. I don't have any interest in reading it, but Mr. Collins provides a lot of material.

Ms. Slaromon: I just think that if we close the door to it, there's no opportunity. If we give him some opportunity, but letter writing is the thing that you think is the best solution, I don't necessarily think that's the best solution. I think he needs to have some contact with the therapist that also sees the kids, and maybe he could have his open separate therapy for x-amount of sessions, make him do some real engaging therapy with their therapist and she can monitor what he's saying and what he's doing, and then come back in three months and have the therapist say "He's a sociopath," or "He's not a sociopath." He has chosen over the last 15 months to ostrich it, stick his head in the sand, and not do the visitations because he was ordered supervised. I told him myself to do his visits, do them from the beginning, and do them good, and he didn't. I asked him to do that. I mean, I think that I just would like to see the court try to fashion a plan that can give him a window, an opportunity that can either close again and fail, or succeed, which might be in the best interest of the kids in the future.

The Court: All visitations between Mr. Collins and the children is suspended. Mr. Collins may communicate with the children in writing through Megan Golden. All telephone contact between Mr. Collins and the children is terminated at this time. If Ms. Swithin does receive any telephone calls to the children despite this order, which wouldn't surprise me, she can record them are there any other orders you think we need?

Mr. Anders: No.

The Court: Okay. Mr. Anders will prepare the order.

Mr. Slaromon: Thank you.

Ms. Swithin: Thank you, your Honor.

The Court: Thank you.

(AT 9:18 A.M. PROCEEDS WERE CONCLUDED.)

I had walked into court that day with a speech prepared. My goal was to create a step-up plan for visits because the reality was, I knew Seth wouldn't jump through the necessary hoops. My planned speech was my attempt to protect the girls while working within the parameters of the broken family court system.

Seth's reentrance into our lives was prompted by guilt from his mom's recent summer visit but also his need to ruin my birthday celebration. He needed to appease his mom and hurt me which was a double victory in his eyes. I knew he didn't really care about seeing the girls which was evident by his behavior during his first supervised visit with them.

When the commissioner questioned why we were forcing the girls to have any visits at all with Seth, I quickly readjusted my sails and prepared a new speech. Had I walked into court suggesting that Seth's parenting time was permanently suspended, I believe I would have met resistance but when the commissioner himself began to walk down this path, I quickly joined him. Minor's council had proven to lack a backbone for several years and was known to waffle and I feel he was even caught off guard by the commissioner's proposal. The starts aligned that day and the commissioner finally saw through the madness that was our case. He finally did the right thing; he acted in the best interest of my daughters.

Leaving the courtroom was surreal. It felt like a dream. Seth was gone from our lives and I felt at peace knowing that he'd never follow through with writing letters to the girls, and my prediction proved accurate. That day, we were given peace and long-awaited justice. My daughters were given the best gift ever, the gift of their childhoods.

Cleo's Goodbye Party

Despite my personal feelings for Cleo, I had always allowed her to see the girls. With that said, I would never permit her to be alone with them despite her ongoing requests to take them shopping or on other adventures. When she would visit for summer vacation or during the holidays, Glenn and I would accompany her to dinners or to get frozen yogurt, and I vowed to continue doing this for as long as the girls expressed interest in seeing her.

It took everything in me to sit at those restaurant tables while entertaining her efforts at small talk, but I did it because I never wanted my children to question why I blocked her from their lives. If they chose to see her, I would support their wishes. On one visit during the Christmas holiday, the girls were mortified when Cleo came waltzing in with a small fake Christmas tree to adorn our table while reenacting Christmas morning. The girls were embarrassed, and I was nauseous.

Once visits with Seth ended, the girls made it very clear that they no longer wanted to see her. I assume that they finally felt safe to cut off all contact with the family when they knew Seth had no power over them. While discussing whether or not they wanted to see Cleo, Piper said, "Mom, she didn't even protect us when I told her that he hurt me!" That was all I needed to hear to send Cleo on her way. Bon voyage, Cleo.

1,897 Days

My battle began on August 18, 2009 and "finished" on October 28, 2014, which is a total of 1,897 days (almost six years), but who's counting? I am. This battle robbed my children of a large part of their childhoods. Instead of savoring every precious moment, I, as a mother, wanted to do the unthinkable; I wanted to push fast-forward on Piper and Sarah's childhood. I wanted them to be old enough to have a voice, but in my prayers for them to grow quickly, I missed out on so much. I was in survival mode trying to protect them, trying to educate a broken system, trying to work full time, trying to act as my own attorney, and trying to keep groceries in our refrigerator and a roof over our heads. Despite all of this, I am one of the "lucky" ones.

When my battle ended, I wanted an apology from everyone who had a hand in "protecting" my daughters. They all failed miserably. My own conscience urges me to *right my wrongs*—to send apology letters or to have a heartfelt, face-to-face meeting when my actions have caused harm or distress. There was never an apology from my first evaluator, from any of the CPS workers, from Seth's attorneys, from minor's counsel, or from the various police officers who traumatized us, not to mention from the commissioner.

It took almost six years for my family court commissioner to understand who Seth was and to see the damage that was being done to my children. In many of the cases that come across my desk as a family court advocate, it's too late. Precious lives are reduced to press conferences and scripted apologies.

Every week, I hear of the atrocities happening in the family court system. Most only hear about the ones in their communities, but my eyes are wide open and I cast my net far and wide. One child lost at the hands of this broken system is too many. According to the Center for Judicial Excellence (2018), we have lost a total of 631 children who were murdered by a parent with allegations of abuse in separations or custody situations from 2012 through 2018. Many women leave abusive situations to protect their children only to discover that the very system that was designed to protect their children is failing their children at every turn.

The Lemonade Sisters are Born

Since the inception of One Mom's Battle in 2011, I had felt pulled to create a retreat specifically for those enduring high-conflict custody battles with Cluster B personality disordered individuals. A retreat with Lundy Bancroft in the spring of 2015 inspired me to take a leap of faith and host my own retreat, which I affectionately coined, "The Lemonade Power Retreat." If there is anyone who knows how to make lemonade with life's lemons, it's those of us who have survived narcissistic abuse.

Truth be told, I had no idea what I was doing when I scheduled my first retreat in November of 2015. My fear of public speaking scored up there with my fear of clowns, moths, and skydiving. What I *did* know was that I had a strong desire to connect people and to give them hope. I also wanted to give them the tools that they needed to navigate their own custody battle. As the retreat date drew near, I became more and more anxious. I even recruited my little sister to attend for moral support. I had a plan in place but, apparently, the quote about "If you want to make God laugh, tell him your plans" rang true on this particular weekend.

One by one, they arrived at the retreat center in San Luis Obispo County, many with a look of desperation on their faces. Some cried as we embraced, letting me know that my story had inspired them to keep fighting. The first night was a casual "meet and greet" of sorts and, the following morning, we came together in a circle to get down to business.

My intention was to allow everyone to introduce themselves and share a bit about their story. What I didn't realize was that for most of these women, it was the first time they had ever shared their story. To sit in a circle, surrounded by other brave warriors while feeling validated and heard was worth its weight in gold. There was laughter, there were tears, and there was an unspoken bond that had formed each time someone purged the details of the isolated hell they had been living. If it's possible to "feel" healing, I was feeling it and watching it before my very eyes.

On the way home from the retreat, I didn't even have words to describe the weekend to my husband. I was thankful that my sister had been there to witness the magical bonding and healing that had occurred, and she said that she was forever touched by the stories and the tenacity of this group. Individually, they were fierce, but together, they were a force to be reckoned with. They came in as strangers and left as sisters. They left as The Lemonade Sisters.

The Lemonade Sisters have become my closest friends and the family that I have always yearned for. Growing up, I was raised by my dad and, aside from my Aunt Bev who lived 2,000 miles away, I really didn't have positive female role models in my life. My closest friends have always been male, and I allowed myself to believe that all women were "drama" and that I didn't *need* female friendships. If I really scrub this down to be truly authentic, I was abandoned at a young age by my mother due to her mental illness and addiction issues. Distancing myself from female friendships was somewhat of a protection mechanism for me.

While I spent forty years distancing myself from female friendships, I secretly envied my friends who have had lifelong friendships, sorority sisters, and those bonds that seem unconditional and unbreakable. Enter the Lemonade Sisters. They took my lifelong beliefs (protection mechanisms) and put them in a blender; they proved 40 years' worth of thoughts and beliefs to be self-serving and flat-out wrong.

I often tell people that the survivors of narcissistic abuse are a special group and, after the Lemonade Power Retreat weekend, I understand the depth of that statement more than ever before. Narcissists target people who are kind, loving, empathetic, and honest. They target people who have all the traits that they lack. They break these people down until they are a shell of who they once were and then, as survivors, they rebuild with a foundation of love, kindness, and truth. They rebuild stronger than ever before, but they maintain the qualities that made them some of the most amazing human beings you'll ever meet. As Lemonade Sisters, we are bonded by trials and tribulations and war stories that few will ever truly understand. We are bonded by laughter, tears, love, and heartache.

These are my people. The Lemonade Sisters are my sorority. God knew exactly what I needed, even though I couldn't see if myself. This is where trust and faith come into play. Ironically, I had been praying for something that I had only admitted to my husband; I prayed for girlfriends. Since my first retreat in 2015, I host a Lemonade Power Retreat each year and, with each new retreat, the sisterhood grows with Lemonade Sisters from all parts of the country. They hold reunion events, cruises, camping trips, and more. I am grateful every day for their gift of love and friendship. These women know how to make lemonade with life's lemons.

The Arrest

Aside from the one-hour supervised visit in the fall of 2014, it had been three years since the girls had contact with Seth or his family. Three years of peace and normalcy. Three years of doing typical childhood things. Seth had never once sent a letter to the girls through their therapist, even though he was able to do that through the court order. A narcissist's ego cannot handle loss, and the final court order caused him to pack his bags of dysfunction and go on his merry way. With each year that passes, I leaned just a little bit deeper into the peace that we had come to know in our lives.

On June 23, 2016, my ex-brother-in-law, Robert Collins, was arrested. As of May 2018, he remains in jail awaiting trial, as he is charged with thirty-two counts of sexual abuse with at least forty victims, most of them very young children. Fourteen of the charges he is facing carry life sentences, including: oral copulation or penetration of a child under 10 years old; lewd acts with a child; and using a concealed camera to record people.

At the completion of Robert's criminal trial (anticipated to take place fall of 2018), I will detail our journey through this nightmare on my blog but, until then, I need to practice caution as to not jeopardize criminal proceedings. What I will say is that his arrest has devastated me on a multitude of levels. I have tremendous anger toward Cleo, Seth, and the family court professionals who ignored my pleas and continued to place my children in harm's way. Prior to Robert's arrest, I had already dedicated my life to family court advocacy, but the atrocities that have been exposed within this sick family only further fuel my desire to make changes in this system.

Part 5: Open Letter to Family Court Judges

Dear Family Court Judge,

You may be on your way to work when suddenly your thoughts shift to your afternoon calendar. By this point in your career, you are probably struggling with compassion fatigue and are tired of listening to people argue back and forth like human ping-pong balls. You probably feel that familiar twinge of annoyance at the thought of the high-conflict couple that is once again on calendar today. You have likely bought into the notion that it takes two to tango in family court. You secretly wonder why these two adults can't put their wild accusations and differences aside and do what's best for their children?

Maybe those wild accusations are not fabricated. Maybe one of the parents standing in front of you isn't lying and typically avoids conflict like the plague. Do you chalk these accusations up to a high-conflict couple and order a 50/50 custody split because that is what seems "fair?" Do you dismiss the concerns contained in the countless declarations on your desk? Do you subscribe to the belief that, "She chose to marry this person so he can't be that bad?" Are you truly acting in the best interest of the child or are you trying to be fair to the two adults standing in front of you? Our judicial officers are supposed to rule in the best interest of the child but that guiding principle of family court has become distorted and lost over the years. As someone who regularly sits in courtrooms across America, I can tell you that what is happening in the family court system is *not* in the best interest of the children.

Ana Estevez pled with the family court system in Southern California to protect her young son, a five-year old affectionately known as, "Piqui." In 2017, his heartbroken mother, Ana Estevez, watched as her son's tiny casket was carried through Holy Family Catholic Church in Pasadena, California. Little Piqui lost his life at the hands of his father, the very man who should have been the one to protect him. Just eight hours north in Santa Rosa, California, another mother sits in mourning, drinking tea while wrapped in her young daughter's blanket. In June of 2017, her ex-husband took his own life after killing their two children, a 6-year-old girl and an 18-month-old boy. This mother had also pled with family court professionals to help her protect her young children.

Please begin by educating yourself on Cluster B personality disorders (antisocial, narcissistic and borderline personality disorders). Everyone in the family court system who has a hand in deciding the fate of a child should recognize the correlation between Cluster B personality disorders and high-conflict divorce. Having narcissistic personality disorder (or any Cluster B disorder) does not simply mean that one has an inflated ego, it means that this individual thrives on conflict. It also means that this person poses a significant danger to the healthy parent and the children. He or she will appear as Dr. Jeykell in the courtroom and will resume their true identity of Mr. Hyde outside of the courtroom doors. This individual sees the children as a weapon to continue to control and abuse the healthy parent. The ultimate way to inflict pain on the healthy parent is to hurt, or worse, murder the children.

The Cluster B disordered parent is incapable of love and sees the children as possessions. This individual may appear perfectly normal and often, they are so skilled at impression management that they can even mislead and charm mental health professionals. The Cluster B disordered individual claims to love their children yet their actions are not in alignment with their words. I beg you to pay attention to actions and not words.

Those with Cluster B personality disorders are often pathological liars which allows them to lie under oath and in court documents with ease. Lying to the court further fuels the disordered individual because they take great pride in manipulating systems and people. While perjury does not seem to carry a lot of weight in family court, it should be taken more seriously than it is. Perjury is a crime in every court of law and I plead with you to take swift action if someone is caught lying in your courtroom. Someone caught lying under oath should be a glaring red flag to family court professionals.

Another glaring red flag for family court professionals is that the high-conflict parent will purposefully become delinquent in child support to exercise financial control over the other parent. In 2011, my family court commissioner stated, "I can't make him be a good dad, but I can ensure that he supports his children." That statement initially left me hopeful, but the reality is that no one in the system can guarantee anything when it comes to personality disordered individuals.

Judges and family court professionals are often fooled when a high-conflict individual proclaims that they want to be an active participant in their child's life. The narcissist's portrayed interest in being a part of the child's life is the furthest thing from the truth. I refer to this as the courtroom mask—the narcissist is wearing a mask in the courtroom or when the eyes of a court professional are upon them. Outside of the court setting, the mask falls, and the narcissist's true colors show. This is where it is critical to pay attention to courtroom statements versus actions.

I have seen countless psychological evaluations come across my desk with results that are positive for antisocial personality disorder or narcissistic personality disorder yet the court orders a 50/50 parenting split regardless. In many cases, the mental health professionals site, "high narcissistic or antisocial traits" yet they don't make a firm diagnosis due to legal liability and ramifications. The lack of education on Cluster B personality disorders is alarming. The judicial system does not understand the magnitude or severity of this diagnosis but for the sake of our children, it is critical that you and other family law professionals begin to educate yourselves.

When you are making a decision that impacts the life of a child (present or future), it is important to err on the side of caution if a parent shows impaired empathy, disregard for boundaries, and/or poor impulse control with their children or former spouse. It is my hope that you will recognize the individuals (male or female) who may appear to be a loving, devoted parent through their testimony or declarations yet their actions prove otherwise. I ask that you protect the children who are counting on you to uphold their rights to be safe, secure, and happy. These rights should supersede parental rights.

There is an overwhelming belief that two parents are better than one and, in most cases,, I believe this to be true. The exception should be when one parent has been diagnosed or is suspected to have a Cluster B personality disorder. This person is not capable of placing the child's needs above their own needs. This parent lacks the ability to love, respect boundaries, have empathy and is incapable of doing what is best for the child. Unlike your average divorce, a divorce with this type of individual will not end until the children have reached adulthood. Sadly, many of these cases end in murder as the ones described above. In fact, Only in these cases do the courts pay attention but by this point, it is too late. Please remember that in a high-conflict divorce, it does *not* take two to tango.

I appreciate your time and am available to answer any questions that you may have. Feel free to contact me at tina@onemomsbattle.com. It is my goal to work with the family court system (not against) to educate and raise awareness of this pervasive issue. – Tina

Part 6: To the Warriors on the Battlefield

Dear Mom (or Dad) Fighting to Protect Your Children:

This is likely the most daunting journey you will ever face – never give up. I have seen the direst circumstances take a 180 degree turn. You never know what is around the next corner. No matter how defeated you feel in this moment, I believe in you and you will get through this. Most importantly, your children need you to continue to place one foot in front of the other so grab your oxygen mask and let's discuss how you can navigate this battle.

I believe that the key to my success had multiple facets. I learned my local court system like the back of my hand by sitting in courtrooms for hours at a time, speaking to attorneys in the hallways, going to the law library and utilizing a variety of community resources. By sitting in the courtroom and listening to cases that were not my own, I was able to desensitize myself to the system. I quickly learned that there was no place for my emotions in the courtroom. I also learned the importance of thinking strategically.

In the beginning, I read everything I could find on Cluster B personality disorders- knowing your opponent is critical to being successful in this battle. With that said, there is a fine line between educating yourself and letting the information consume you. Listen to your gut when walking this line. Once you have a clear handle on Cluster B education, close the books and the web browsers and start putting your knowledge to work.

Be prepared for the waters to get downright muddy. Projection is one of the narcissists' best weapons and they will project their shortcomings onto you. If he (or she) has an alcohol problem, prepare yourself to be painted as an alcoholic. Respond to false allegations calmly with credible, factual information but don't get caught up defending every minor allegation as tempting as it may be. This is the time to choose your battles wisely.

You need to continuously remind yourself that you are dealing with a narcissist. If needed, write yourself a post-it note that says, "Reminder: I am dealing with a narcissist" and stick it to the front of your binder or notepad. Many battles in history were lost simply due to the element of surprise. Do not let history repeat itself on your watch. Do not expect a narcissist to follow the law, rules or protocol of any kind. Expect lies, vicious attacks, bizarre behavior, and the unexpected. Practice offense and defense and keep your playbook ready.

Get your documentation system in order by devoting a set amount of time to it each week. Take the emotions out of it by thinking of it as a part-time job or a special project. MyFamilyCourt.com is a wonderful resource for organizing your documentation and getting a system in place. Create a timeline of events going back to major incidents in your marriage and continuing through present. Your timeline is a work in progress and you will continue to add to it as time goes on. Having a clear picture of your case will help you articulate the issues better when meeting with your attorney or other family court professionals.

Instead of trying to convince the court that you are divorcing a narcissist, antisocial or borderline personality disordered individual, think forensically and show patterns of behavior that are prevalent in your case. In my case, the main categories were alcoholism, abuse, harassment, disregard for the court orders, and disregard for the parenting schedule. Additional categories came into play during evaluations such as Seth's need for control and his lack of empathy. Every case is different with many variables so be very clear about what the main issues are in your case.

Another important area to focus on is communication. My book, "*The Narc Decoder: Understanding the Language of the Narcissist*," delves into communication strategies, real life emails and gives suggested responses. It helps you to develop your own "cookie cutter" responses so you can disengage with the narcissist and in turn, he/she will begin looking elsewhere to find their narcissistic feed. In the book, you will learn to communicate in a court-approved fashion which is imperative during child custody battles.

Most importantly, stand firm in your truth. If the narcissist says the sky is red but you know it is blue, there is no need for you to engage or to be triggered as you know your truth; the sky is blue. Period. When I am firm and clear in my truth, I am less likely to be sucked into the narcissist's rollercoaster. His (or her) jabs have much less of a sting when I am honoring my truth.

Build your foundation from rock—the rock that comes from knowing your truth. Prepare a "truth" and "lies" list and absorb the truths to your core (mind, body, and spirit). If through this process, you find some truths that hurt then put them on your list of "things to work on" and re-write the truth with a positive spin. Here is a personal example that I will share with you:

> Truth: I do not have a college degree.
>
> Self-work: learn to value my education and knowledge gained from outside of the confines of a classroom- college degree versus life

experiences, reading, seminars, mistakes, observations and the wisdom shared by others. Look into a college "Life Experience" credit program; enroll in an online class.

Re-written truth: I do not have a college degree at this time. I currently have knowledge, skills, and life experiences that are far more valuable than the information gained from a 4-year program. The world is full of educated idiots and I am not one of them.

After you've re-written your truth into a "positive," find a quote or manta to remind yourself of your truth. Mine is, "We are students of words: we are shut up in schools, and colleges, and recitation rooms, for ten or fifteen years, and come out at last with a bag of wind, a memory of words, and do not know a thing." - Ralph Waldo Emerson

Please know that you are not alone and there are a variety of resources available to you through my websites: www.OneMomsBattle.com or www.TinaSwithin.com. I offer retreats, private coaching, private online forums and more. I also offer packets to help educate your judge or family court professionals through our #educateyourjudge program.

You've got this – I believe in you! – Tina

Love and Gratitude

To God: I am often guilty of questioning God about the cards that I've been dealt. Having faith requires a great deal of trust, and I am a work in progress. I am beginning to understand that things do happen for a reason. I am beginning to see that my trials have had a purpose. I will continue to, "Let go and let God."

To Piper and Sarah: My life began when you were born. I am in awe that God believed in me enough to be your mom.

To Aunt Bev: You have been the strong, loving voice that I've had in my corner since the day I was born. Thank you. I love you!

To Glenn: Thank you for being my best friend and my "rock." Thank you for loving me and for standing by my side through the storms. I love you.

To Dad: Thank you for being both my mom and my dad. Thank you for always believing in me.

To Renee and Eric: You two (and your families) bring such joy to my life, and I am honored to call you my sister and brother.

To the Lemonade Sisters: You have changed my life and brought sunshine to my cloudy days. Thank you for your love, support and friendship.

To Christie Brinkley: Thank you for bringing narcissistic personality disorder into the spotlight with such strength and grace. I am forever grateful for your support over the years and for the platform you've given me, which allowed me to shed light on a dark subject matter.

To Kelly Rutherford: My heart breaks for what you have endured at the hands of this broken system. I am thankful that I was able to be by your side for a small part of this journey, and I look forward to celebrating your children's homecoming one day.

To my OMB Warriors: Thank you for inspiring me daily. There is power in numbers and I am grateful for our little village of warriors.

References

American Psychiatric Association. (2013). *Diagnostic and Statistical Manual of Mental Disorders* (5th ed.).

Washington, DC: Author.

Center for Judicial Excellence. (2018, April 05). Retrieved April 23, 2018, from http://www.centerforjudicialexcellence.org/

Lovefraud Reader. (2012, February 10). The Gray Rock method of dealing with psychopaths. Retrieved April 23, 2018, from https://lovefraud.com/the-gray-rock-method-of-dealing-with-psychopaths/

American Journal of Preventive Medicine (1998, Volume 14, pages 245–258).

https://www.ajpmonline.org/article/S0749-3797(98)00017-8/abstract

myfamilycourt.com